BRITISH MILITARY PLANNING FOR THE DEFENCE OF GERMANY, 1945–50

STUDIES IN MILITARY AND STRATEGIC HISTORY
General Editor: Michael Dockrill, Reader in War Studies, King's College, London

British Military Planning for the Defence of Germany 1945–50

Paul Cornish
Research Fellow
International Security Programme
Royal Institute of International Affairs
London

in association with
KING'S COLLEGE, LONDON

First published in Great Britain 1996 by
MACMILLAN PRESS LTD
Houndmills, Basingstoke, Hampshire RG21 6XS
and London
Companies and representatives
throughout the world

A catalogue record for this book is available
from the British Library.

ISBN 0–333–63995–2

First published in the United States of America 1996 by
ST. MARTIN'S PRESS, INC.,
Scholarly and Reference Division,
175 Fifth Avenue,
New York, N.Y. 10010

ISBN 0–312–12960–2

Library of Congress Cataloging-in-Publication Data
Cornish, Paul.
British military planning for the defence of Germany, 1945–50 /
Paul Cornish.
p. cm. — (Studies in military and strategic history)
Includes bibliographical references and index.
ISBN 0–312–12960–2 (cloth)
1. Great Britain—Armed Forces— Germany (West). 2. Military
planning—Great Britain. I. Title. II. Series.
UA649.32.G3C67 1996
943.087'5—dc20 95–37739
CIP

10 9 8 7 6 5 4 3 2 1
05 04 03 02 01 00 99 98 97 96

Printed in Great Britain by
Ipswich Book Co Ltd, Ipswich, Suffolk

For my parents

Contents

Acknowledgements

I am indebted to several people for the time, advice and encouragement they have given at various stages of this project, including Dr Anne Deighton, Dr Saki Dockrill, Mr Eric Grove, Dr Hugh Macdonald, Dr David Reynolds, Professor Hew Strachan, Dr Philip Towle and Professor John Young. Any errors of fact or judgement are, of course, entirely mine. I am grateful for the assistance provided by archivists and librarians at the National Army Museum, the Imperial War Museum, Churchill College Cambridge, Cambridge University Library, the Foreign and Commonwealth Office Library, and the Public Record Office, Kew. Crown copyright material in the PRO is reproduced by permission of the Controller of Her Majesty's Stationery Office. Production of the final manuscript could not have been achieved without the help of Nick Redman and my brothers, Anthony Cornish and Martin Cornish. Special thanks are due to Fiona Cornish, my wife.

A Note on Sources

This book makes use of the usual mix of secondary works, published papers and documents, and unpublished government documents held in the Public Record Office. In the course of researching this book, a number of previously retained government papers were released on the author's request to the PRO, in accordance with the June 1992 'open government' initiative. Papers relating to the work of the Joint Intelligence Committee were not released, but a selection of some thirty Chiefs of Staff and Joint Planning Staff papers were made accessible and are listed separately in the bibliography.

Glossary

ACC	Allied Control Council
AOC-in-C	Air Officer Commander-in-Chief
BAFO	British Air Forces of Occupation
BAOR	British Army of the Rhine
BTO	Brussels Treaty Organisation
CAS	Chief of the Air Staff
CCG (BE)	Control Commission, Germany (British Element)
CFM	Council of Foreign Ministers (5 Power)
C(I)GS	Chief of the (Imperial) General Staff
C-in-C	Commander-in-Chief
CNS(FSL)	Chief of the Naval Staff (First Sea Lord)
COS	Chiefs of Staff Committee
DMO	Director of Military Operations
DRPC	Defence Research Policy Committee
ERP	European Recovery Plan/Programme
FARELF	Far East Land Forces
FDP	Future Defence Policy (DO (47) 44)
FGA	Fighter Ground Attack
FO	Foreign Office
GOC-in-C	General Officer Commander-in-Chief
HMG	His Majesty's Government
HQ	Headquarters
IDC	Imperial Defence College
ISR	Imperial Strategic Reserve
JCS	Joint Chiefs of Staff (US)
JIC	Joint Intelligence Committee
JPS	Joint Planning Staff
JSM	Joint Staff Mission (Washington Embassy)
LOC	Line(s) of Communication
MCFP	Military Committee of the Five Powers
MELF	Middle East Land Forces
MoD	Ministry of Defence
MoS	Ministry of Supply
MSA	Main Supply Area
MTDP	Medium Term Defence Plan (NATO)
NATO	North Atlantic Treaty Organisation
NS	National Service

OEEC	Organisation for European Economic Co-operation
PHP	Post-Hostilities Planning Sub-Committee
PHPS	Post-Hostilities Planning Staff
PUS	Permanent Under-Secretary
SHAEF	Supreme Headquarters Allied Powers Europe
SLOC	Sea Lines of Communication
TA	Territorial Army
(2)TAF	(Second) Tactical Air Force (successor to BAFO)
VCAS	Vice Chief of the Air Staff
VCIGS	Vice Chief of the Imperial General Staff
VCNS	Vice Chief of the Naval Staff
WU(C-in-C)	Western Union (Commanders-in-Chief Committee)
WUCOS	Western Union Chiefs of Staff Committee
WUDO	Western Union Defence Organisation

Introduction

> 'We should be mad to entangle ourselves in a continental strife on land. Our medium is the ocean way.'
>
> Esher[1]

The Paris Agreements of October 1954 saw Britain's 'formal acceptance of a large-scale, peacetime military presence on the Continent'.[2] Four army divisions and one tactical air force were committed to NATO's conventional defence of West Germany and Europe. For almost forty years, until the end of the Cold War, the peacetime deployment in Germany, and the prospect of conventional war on the Central Front, dominated operational and tactical thinking and equipment procurement, in both the British Army and the Royal Air Force (RAF). Britain's 1954 commitment figures prominently in writing on the development of the West's strategy during the Cold War, as a means both to counter-balance German rearmament and to allay French fears, and to ensure that NATO became the West's main defence institution. The 1954 commitment also has some celebrity in the history of British strategy. The commitment was untypically bold and unequivocal, earning its description as 'the one really substantial, firm contractual commitment in Britain's postwar defence experience'.[3] The 1954 decision also represents, for some, a departure from a largely naval strategic tradition in Britain, a tradition which meant detachment from the Continent in peacetime and reluctance to become involved in wars there. Yet British strategy has never been a clear choice between discrete options – 'naval' versus 'continental'. The British Empire consisted of colonies and outposts which had to be protected by the army. But these territorial possessions were served, connected and exploited by long communications and trading routes watched over by the Royal Navy. The acquisition and protection of Empire was thus a 'grand strategy' in which both army and navy had an essential part. Similarly, Britain has also always been a European power, or at least one perched on the edge of that Continent, and has always been involved in Continental affairs, reluctantly or otherwise. British history is replete with examples of invasion by and of Continental powers, of assisting one power against another, and of resisting hegemonic ambitions. Rather than choosing between 'naval' and 'continental' options, Britain's commitments and geographical position have usually demanded a hybrid strategy, with the real point of argument being the relative strength of the naval, land and, latterly, air forces. In 1911 the British strategist Sir Julian Corbett offered one solution in the form of his 'maritime strategy':

> naval strategy is not a thing by itself... its problems can seldom or never be solved on naval considerations alone... it is only a part of maritime strategy – the higher learning which teaches us that for a maritime State to make successful war and to realise her special strength, army and navy must be used and thought of as instruments no less intimately connected than are the three arms ashore.[4]

In Corbett's view, naval and land forces were merely elements of a maritime strategy, Britain's natural posture which allowed it to be both an imperial, naval/land power and, when necessary, a power capable of intervention on the Continent: 'The paramount concern, then, of maritime strategy is to determine the mutual relations of your army and navy in a plan of war'.[5] Corbett died in 1922. Had he managed to struggle on to his 100th birthday, he would just have witnessed the 1954 agreement. What might have surprised him about the agreement was not that Britain was preparing for military operations on the Continent, but that it had been agreed to station ground and air forces in Germany in peacetime, assuming of course that he would have understood Cold War Europe as being 'at peace'. In these terms, the agreement would have seemed too much of a departure from the hybrid, maritime strategy that had emphasised operational flexibility. On the other hand, persuaded by the fact that the Cold War in Europe had become heavily militarised and that there was certainly conflict if not actual fighting, Corbett might have accepted that Britain's involvement in the conflict was prudent and reasonable. But Corbett might also have sensed that the whole edifice of the maritime strategy was being undermined by the influence of Sir Halford Mackinder, the geopolitician/strategist. Mackinder, who died in 1947, had argued that the 'Columbian epoch' of sea power was coming to an end and that the locus of power was shifting to industrialised, populous powers which were capable of dominating the Eurasian land mass. Four years before his death he identified the Soviet Union as the main problem in this regard, and became convinced that 'the greatest danger for the democratic states was that the dominant land power in the Heartland [the Soviet Union] would become strong in the maritime arena and challenge the sea powers *at sea*'.[6]

The first step in understanding where the 1954 commitment fits in to

British strategic history is to ask how and why it came about. Thought by many to portend a Soviet invasion of Western Europe, North Korea's attack on the South in June 1950 had an effect on the Western Alliance which can only be described as electric.In Britain, the period of conscripted military service was increased to two years, additional forces were promised for deployment to West Germany and the rearmament budget increased exponentially. By the end of 1950, the United States had also promised to commit substantial ground forces to the defence of Western Europe, in exchange for a readiness among its European allies to shoulder a fairer share of the increasing defence burden. The US reiterated its demand for West German rearmament, a prospect about which France in particular was uneasy. In September NATO adopted the 'forward strategy' for the defence of Western Europe as far to the East as possible. In December the NATO Council finally agreed, in principle, to German rearmament but accepted that the formula contained in France's Pleven Plan, launched two months previously, for German rearmament within a European Army, should be attempted first. NATO's Supreme Headquarters Allied Powers Europe (SHAPE) was established in February 1951 under command of Eisenhower, the Supreme Allied Commander Europe (SACEUR). Pleven's European Army, and its proposed successor, the European Defence Community (EDC), both came to nothing, as did NATO's over-ambitious Lisbon force goals of February 1952. In October 1954 the Western Alliance finally settled for limited rearmament of sovereign West Germany in NATO, via the expedient of membership of the regenerated Western Union, now to be known as the Western European Union. As part of the package, Britain's commitment of ground and air forces was meant to sweeten the pill of German rearmament.

The Cold War did not, of course, begin with the Korean War, but was intensified by it. By the end of the 1940s, economic, diplomatic and military relations between East and West in Europe had deteriorated dramatically. In a perverse way, North Korea's invasion – not entirely unexpected in intelligence circles – was welcomed as final proof of Soviet/Communist perfidy and of the righteousness of the West's defensive preparations. In Britain, and throughout the fledgling NATO, there were already signs of a shift towards increased defence and procurement spending, of a willingness to countenance West German rearmament, and of a keener appreciation of the Soviet threat to Europe.

With the Cold War originating in the mid and late 1940s, if not earlier, some historians have felt that the roots of the 1954 commitment might also go back beyond June 1950, to the first five post-war years. By one account, Britain's experience of aerial attack from Europe during the war ended forever the 'insular security' it had enjoyed.[7] Furthermore, with thousands of troops stationed in Germany on post-war occupation duties, Britain was both militarily involved and vulnerable, leading several historians to the conclusion that in 1945, or very soon thereafter, Britain had at most accepted a continental strategy or, at least, had become 'willing to be tied to the continent'.[8]

Yet the trend in military thinking immediately after the war was very much anti-continental and even navalist.[9] The military, of all services, and others were extremely wary of becoming entangled again in European conflict. And it is possible to exaggerate the military significance of the occupation commitment: occupation was more accurately a matter of civil affairs and police operations than military strategy. The troops so involved would have been hard put to defend anything, although their mere presence in Germany did come to be regarded as an ideological defence against Soviet Communism. If this is the case, how is it possible to explain the transition from strategic isolationism and a weak occupation commitment to the firm decision taken in 1954? The simple answer might be that isolationism and interest in the ideas of Alfred Thayer Mahan, the naval strategist, were but a short-lived reaction to the war and that, as Europe descended into Cold War, the more convincing seemed Mackinder's analysis that power was rooted in an economically robust and productive landmass, which could not be balanced by maritime powers looking to the protection of ships or trade routes and the command of the oceans and intervening only reluctantly and temporarily on land. With strategic detachment from the Continent appearing increasingly unsustainable, a shift towards interventionism then took place, in several stages: the moment in February 1948 when Ernest Bevin, the British Foreign Secretary, was won over to the idea of defence on the Continent; the decision, made in spring of the same year, to fight on the Continent 'with what we have'; and finally, the decision in March 1950 to reinforce the troops in Germany in the event of war.

With, on one hand, the view that the British military were willing to be drawn to the Continent very soon after 1945 and, on the other, the argument that there was a swing to isolationism and navalism which only gradually gave way to continentalism, there is clearly room to debate the way in which the foundations for the 1954 commitment were laid. The object of this book is to decide which, if either, of these views is most accurate and to chart precisely the tone, direction and intensity of any continentalism or Europeanism in post-war British military thinking.

If a commitment is thought to have been made more or less immediately, as a consequence of Britain's involvement in the war, then it is important to have a clear idea of the size, structure and capability of the occupation forces. If, in contrast, the process is to be described as a temporary shift to isolationism and navalism followed by a gradual acceptance of a Continental involvement, then it is important to understand what was meant in the various decisions to join battle and to reinforce troops in Germany; what was the quality of the reinforcing troops, the timetable by which they were to be deployed, and how much air and other support were they to have? What part, if any, did the occupation forces play in the transition from navalism to continentalism? By reconstructing the way in which the military chiefs and their planning staffs thought and wrote about the defence of Germany and Western Europe between May 1945 and June 1950, it will be shown that there were in fact few indications of a willingness to accept a permanent, peacetime military involvement on the Continent, of the sort that was to be agreed in 1954. Rather, a succession of half-hearted reassurances and token promises masked – not always successfully – the determination to minimise peacetime entanglements altogether. Neither was Mahanian navalism a serious possibility, however; the British military gradually became convinced that British and Western European security were indivisible and that an expeditionary strategy of some sort would be needed in time of war. But if this was Corbett's maritime option, it had been adulterated significantly. Struck by the value, in defence and deterrence, of long-range bomber aircraft, the British military advocated intervention in the form of a strategic air attack. The result was a complex, self-contradictory juxtaposition of concern for the peacetime, political cohesion of Western Europe, with a preference for a maritime/air strategy in time of war. It was not until the Korean War that the British military escaped, or were dragged, from the conceptual labyrinth into which they had descended.

With Britain's relations with post-war Europe receiving ever more attention in the literature, it has become clear that Britain was deeply engaged, politically and economically, in European reconstruction after the war. The image of a confident, victorious Britain, using its imperial strength and its 'special' relationship with the United States to dismiss involvement in Europe has long been seen as a myth.But what is suggested here is that, until at least June 1950, military thinking about German and European defence was very much the application of old principles through new technology, however powerful the sense that British and West European security were becoming indivisible. In other words, the 'military Europeanism' of the 1954 commitment has little foundation in any political and economic Europeanism seen during the reconstruction of post-war Europe before 1950.[10]

This book has two secondary functions. The military's caution in committing ground forces to Europe was carefully and clearly reasoned. One function of this book is, therefore, to counter the tendency, evident in so much writing on British policy-making in the early Cold War, to overlook or caricature the military contribution to policy-making. Too often, use is made of blimpish stereotypes, with the military held to be competent only in their immediate area of knowledge, and limited to offering advice based on worst-case analysis, seemingly the 'classical approach to security politics'.[11] Finally, this book also joins the developing fashion for drawing analogies between the reconstruction of Western Europe after World War II, and the reconstruction of Europe after the Cold War. With calls for democratisation, the deepening of political and economic ties, large-scale investment and for retrenchment in defence spending, the parallels are indeed compelling. As far as this book is concerned, British defence spending in the context of uncertainty about the future of European security structures offers the clearest parallel of all. At the time of writing, in late 1994, the British defence policy-making establishment seems no closer to resolving the circular debate between the definition of overseas commitments, treasury spending forecasts and defence planning, than it was in 1945-50. Having substituted one or two names and figures, a newspaper article appearing in September 1994 under the title 'Rifkind tries to hold line on £22bn defence budget' might well have been written shortly after 1945.[12]

Chapters one and two covering, respectively, threat perceptions and the pressure for retrenchment in defence spending, set out the broad parameters for post-war thinking about the defence of Germany and Western Europe. Chapter three examines the 'ten year, no-war rule', a singular feature on the post-war policy landscape which combined both threat and budgetary considerations. Chapters four to six set out the development of military thinking and planning from the end of the war in Europe in May 1945, to the beginning of the Korean War in June 1950.

1 Threat Perceptions, 1945-50

'Why, you may take the most gallant sailor, the most intrepid airman, or the most audacious soldier, put them at a table together – what do you get? The sum total of their fears!'

Churchill[1]

A military threat perception has at least two components; an assessment of a potential adversary's *capabilities* along with a prediction of his likely *intentions*. A clear division of labour is often thought to exist in the development of the assessment, with capabilities a matter for military staffs, while intentions are thought to be more the stuff of sophisticated political and diplomatic analysis:

> In estimating the security threats the military man looks at the capabilities of other states rather than at their intentions. Intentions are political in nature, inherently fickle and changeable, and virtually impossible to evaluate and predict. The military man is professionally capable of estimating the fighting strength of another state. But judging its policies is a matter of politics outside his competence.[2]

There are other aspects to the perception of a threat, such as a state's financial health; a wealthy state may be more sensitive to the threats to its security or interests, because it will be in a position to do something about such threats.[3] Another component is the sense that possessions, interests or 'values' are, or could be, vulnerable to the perceived enemy.[4] Threat perceptions may not begin with a *tabula rasa*, but may be based on a prior assumption of enmity, and therefore serve as self-fulfilling prophecies. It is important to determine whether a perceived threat is 'real', or simply the product of a massive, irrational sense of insecurity, and whether the processes of threat perception have allowed one part of the bureaucracy to influence – or, indeed, even to create – an 'enemy image' in order to strengthen its position within government. The *feindpolitik* conspiracy theory has generated great interest in a phenomenon known as 'worst-case analysis'. Huntington considered that, as a professional threat assessor, it was the duty of 'the military man' to *stress* the dangers to military security and that he should be expected to err on the side of caution and overstate the threat; 'consequently, at times he will see threats to the security of the state where actually no threats exist'.[5] 'The dangers of worst-case planning'[6] are that, unless restrained, the military man's predilection for such practices may have the effect of precipitating conflicts where they might otherwise have been avoided. Alternatively, some argue that, in certain circumstances, worst-case analysis may be both the safest and most reasonable course, whatever the risks involved.[7]

Much of the writing on British threat perceptions immediately after the war tends to play down the role of the military, to concentrate upon the political work of the Foreign Office and diplomats abroad, and to define the process in terms of the timing and manner in which the Foreign Office moved from a conciliatory to a more confrontational position *vis à vis* the Soviet Union. To some extent this bias is to be expected; the Foreign Office was the department of government responsible for recommending and carrying out policy, not the Chiefs of Staff (COS) and their staffs. It may also be that the relative lack of access to relevant military papers has tended to push historians in the direction of the Foreign Office archives.

Whatever the explanation, it is widely agreed that Britain's threat perceptions developed along the following lines. As early as autumn 1944, the COS had formed the impression that the Soviet Union would present the next serious threat, but the Foreign Office rejected this view as confrontational and insensitive to the possibility of continuing in alliance with the war-time ally. Then, at some point in the unfolding Cold War the British perception of the Soviet threat swung noticeably towards the COS position. Or rather, political assessments of intentions *coincided*[8] with military assessments of capabilities. Historians differ as to when this confluence took place, with suggestions ranging from early 1946 to January 1948.[9]

British perceptions of the Soviet threat in the early Cold War, and the role of the British military therein, are coming under ever closer scrutiny, in spite of limited access to JIC papers. Opinions vary as to the character, origins and significance of these perceptions. Thus, while Dockrill has argued that, during the late 1940s, 'Britain did not perceive an imminent military threat from the Soviet Union',[10] Grove and Till have suggested, rather cryptically, that from soon after the end of the war the Red Army '*seemed*... to pose a *real* threat to the security of Western Europe' [emphasis added].[11] Schwartz has also pointed out that whatever the quality of the military threat perception, there was still the danger of Soviet/communist subversion with which to contend.[12]

The perception of a threat is integral to foreign and strategic policy-making, and within government more than one method could be employed resulting in different, if not conflicting, assessments. It is also clear that although the threat analysis carried out by the British military has come under closer scrutiny recently, there is still room for debate. With this in mind, this chapter traces the development of British military threat perceptions in the late 1940s. In what ways did British military threat assessments influence their thinking about Germany and Europe? How much 'threat manipulation' was there? Were the threat perceptions upon which the military based their thinking the product of 'worst-case analysis'? Is it reasonable to characterise the military contribution to the wider strategic and foreign policy decision-making process in terms of *feindpolitik*? There were two possible adversaries with which the COS concerned themselves; Germany and the Soviet Union. For the period under discussion here, a German threat to British interests could have manifested itself in one of the following ways: the Nazi threat – the problem, up to May 1945, of defeating Germany's armies and then, in the weeks and months following Germany's surrender, of dealing with any 'pockets of resistance'; the threat of internal disorder, prompted by the collapse of government and harsh economic conditions; and, finally, the threat of German reconstitution and resurgence at some point in the future. The Soviet threat was also perceived to be multi-faceted: aggression against the Continental land powers (better described as the 'military threat'); 'Cold War' threats of subversion, destabilisation and an expanding sphere of influence (the 'political' or 'ideological threat'); and the danger of 'war by miscalculation', whereby in the short term the second threat would develop unintentionally into the first. Finally, of course, there was also the 'nightmare vision' in which both possible enemies would come together – or be driven together inadvertently – and threaten the West in a reborn "Rapallo pact."

FROM WORLD WAR TO COLD WAR AND CONTAINMENT: 1945-47

In the final months of the war the main, short-term danger was that of a less than complete victory for the Allies. It was feared that the war might end 'untidily', with pockets of resistance remaining and ignoring the call to surrender.[13] Generally speaking, however, problems of this nature were thought to be temporary and easily manageable with the military resources available. Although in these months COS thinking was understandably dominated by the need to defeat the enemy they had known since 1939, they did anticipate post-war threats against British interests.

The principal concern, identified since autumn 1944, was the Soviet Union but the COS were also, even before Germany's defeat, alive to the danger of German resurgence.

By January 1945 the COS had few illusions about the Soviet Union's intentions in Germany and elsewhere. The minutes of the 11th Meeting of 10 January 1945 contain numerous references to the 'Soviet threat' and the 'hostile intentions' of the USSR.[14] Reference was also made at the same meeting to the danger of a resurgent Germany forming an alliance with the Soviet Union. As the year progressed, perceptions of Soviet intentions, and the language used by the COS, hardened somewhat. By October, the COS were arguing that military commitments for the period 1946-50 should be examined in the light of *the possibility of having to meet Russian aggression.*[15] For the COS and their staffs, the Soviet Union had by now become, unequivocally, the main threat to Europe and Germany, and therefore to the British forces on occupation duties. However compelling this perception, three other considerations served to dampen its effect on military planning. First, it was known that the Soviet Union would require a good deal of time to recover from the war before becoming more than a hypothetical threat. Second, the use and possession of atomic bombs by the USA was fast becoming an umbrella under which the British felt they could shelter. And finally, it was considered that Germany was less likely to be the scene of conflict with the Soviet Union than the Middle East. Not only was the Soviet Union considered vulnerable in this area, with the oil-fields of Soviet Central Asia, but British possessions, resources and lines of communication were themselves seen to be most in need of protection. If 'deterrence' was to be found in Europe, 'mutual vulnerability' was to be found in the Middle East.

The papers for 1946 suggest that, where Germany was concerned, the threat was increasingly being seen as a matter of internal disorder, or of disaffection breeding Communism, rather than a direct military, or even political, challenge. In mid-February the COS discussed the implications of likely cuts in the manpower and funding of the forces. One possible implication was 'a potentially dangerous weakness in Germany'.[16] If the fragile law and order structure imposed on occupied Germany were to break down, there might then be an unwelcome requirement for a disproportionate and costly commitment of troops. As time wore on the realisation also dawned that disaffection resulting from appalling economic conditions in Germany could give rise to a more serious security problem, whereby Germany would become a 'breeding ground' for Communist doctrine exported from the Soviet Union or, perhaps, some sort of German nationalist revival. Otherwise, during 1946 the COS had come to accept that Germany by itself was no longer a concrete, active threat to British interests.

The Soviet Union was not viewed with similar equanimity. Comments made throughout the year, concerning a variety of British overseas interests, show that the Soviet Union did indeed have the unrivalled lead in the COS demonology. Already accepted as essential for the protection of British interests in the immediate area, and for the security of Sea Lines of Communication (SLOC) through the Mediterranean, British bases in the Middle East also came to be seen as a means to launch a strategic bombing attack on the Soviet Union.[17] The possibility that the Soviet Union might try to turn the tables and threaten British interests in the area was discussed in May 1946, when it was noted that 'There were certain signs of increased Russian interest in the area though this had not yet taken any definite form.'[18] The possibility of Soviet aggression in Europe could not be dismissed entirely, however. Well before the Soviet atomic bomb test in August 1949, Montgomery demanded that the scenario for an Army staff exercise being planned for May 1947 in Camberley include the use or threatened use of atomic bombs in Europe by 'an enemy'.[19] Before too long, the COS were speaking frankly of the possibility of 'war between the USSR and the Western Democracies'.[20] By the end of the year, the Soviet Union had been elevated in the minds of the COS and the defence minister, A.V. Alexander to, more than a merely a general threat, the 'one enemy which was likely to attack us in the foreseeable future'. This assumption, proposed and discussed by Alexander, was not one which the COS saw any need to contest.[21]

The position at the end of 1946 was that the Soviet Union was perceived by the British military to be the most, or indeed the only, serious threat to Britain and her interests, both in the Middle East and, to a lesser extent, in Europe. This position had been reached slowly and cautiously. For the gradual change of emphasis from Germany to the Soviet Union to have taken place, two judgements were required, both of which took time to develop. First, the COS and their planning staffs had to be confident that there could be no chance of German *revanchism* and that the German problem was either one merely of maintaining law and order in the British zone of occupation, or simply symptomatic of the wider problem of creeping Communism which would have to be addressed elsewhere. Second, the COS had to come to the conclusion that the Soviet Union was engaged in policies which could lead to war with Britain either intentionally or, more likely, through miscalculation. In April 1946, Alanbrooke, coming towards the end of his long appointment as Chief of the Imperial General Staff (CIGS), summed up this important realignment of perceptions.

Germany, Alanbrooke felt, should not be considered a threat 'unless she was forced into co- operation with the Russians. Our major policy should then be to build her up sufficiently to obviate becoming a liability to ourselves, yet independent of Russian threats ... Our long-term policy must take full account of the fact that Russia is a more dangerous potential enemy than Germany.'[22]

Comments made in the early part of 1947 confirm that a shift in attitudes was taking place. Although the military planners were still alive to the possibility of a German threat in some form, this contingency was being taken less and less seriously. On 28th February the JPS advised the COS that 'Our long-term policy with regard to Germany must take full account of the fact that Russia is a much more dangerous potential enemy than Germany; it cannot be shaped solely from the point of view of preventing a revivial [*sic*] of a threat from Germany.' A clearer exposition of the JPS view could not be wished for but, to muddy the waters somewhat, the JPS then went on to cover all possibilities and warn that 'We have to consider both the danger of Germany becoming a Russian satellite and the independent resurgence of German strength.' German resurgence and the threat of a German-Soviet pact do appear by this stage, however, to have been something of an afterthought.[23] Frequent mentions were made of the more likely, and familiar, German threat; that of a breakdown in the internal security of the British zone. As in the past, however, this problem was addressed largely as a police matter, and was not the stuff of strategic planning.

On 23 April 1947, while discussing the progress of the Future Defence Policy (FDP) report, the Directors of Plans made clear their view that the Soviet Union should be named as the main potential threat. Whatever political reasons there may have been for discussing threats anonymously, the planning of Britain's future strategy would make far more sense if it could be geared to a known enemy, force structures, tactics and so on. Yet an overt declaration of enmity with the Soviet Union was still politically unpalatable. An anti-Soviet strategy could, however, be disguised since 'The main strategic arguments ... would be unaltered if either Russia or a resurgent Germany was regarded as the potential enemy.[24] This idea was reflected in paragraph 8 of the FDP report which was produced the following month, indicating that military thinking *vis à vis* the German threat – such as it was – was to 'double hat' the inchoate anti-Soviet strategy:

> Should a resurgent Germany again become a menace, it would be possible to adjust our Defence Policy, if we have meanwhile prepared against a presently greater threat.[25]

The FDP report spoke in clear terms of 'the possibility of war with Russia', of 'standing up to Russia', of 'Russian expansion' and so on,[26] all sentiments reflected in the COS papers. On New Year's day, 1947, Slim, then commandant of the Imperial Defence College (JDC), presented the COS with the JDC's IDC general policy review. The COS expressed 'general agreement' with the review which identified Russia as the 'only potential aggressor', the 'only possible enemy', and cautioned in particular against any policy of appeasement.[27] The minutes of the 34th and 57th meetings, held before the production of the FDP, show that the COS were clear as to the most likely threat to Britain and its interests. While the COS were not overcome by an anti-Soviet frenzy by the end of the year, nothing in the papers suggests that their perception of the threat softened in any way. This is, however, to overlook the most important aspect of COS thinking: the development of a characteristically British, and *military*, version of containment, probably the clearest example of the way in which threat perceptions had a direct bearing on COS thinking about Germany.

CONTAINMENT

Turning back to the discussion of the IDC review on 1 January, contrasts appear between the emergent COS view of the Soviet problem and the doctrine of containment, then taking hold in the US. The contents of the COS papers prompt a number of questions. Was a policy or set of ideas taking shape which might reasonably be called the 'British version' of containment? If so, was it intended to be economic and political (as in the US conception), or was there a military component, or some combination of all three? If British containment had a military component, why was there no rush to garrison and defend Germany? What was to be the role of Germany in this 'policy'? What was meant by the term 'bulwark'?

In February 1946, Kennan had sent his 'long telegram' from Moscow. Describing the Kremlin as 'neurotic', Kennan spoke of Soviet 'insecurity' and presented totalitarian Russian rulers and Marxist 'dogma' as being inextricably linked together and the real villains of the piece:

> The "long telegram" had the great influence that it did because it provided a way to fuse concerns about totalitarianism and communism in dealing with the Soviet Union... no actions the United States or its Western Allies could take would alleviate Stalin's suspicion; the best one could do was to look to one's own defenses.

The 'totalitarian-ideological' model was perfected the following year in Kennan's 'Mr X' article in *Foreign Affairs*, in which he explained 'the Russians' failure to cooperate with their former allies in building a lasting peace', 'absolved the United States of responsibility for the breakdown of wartime cooperation', and 'made any future relaxation of tensions dependent upon changes of heart in Moscow, not Washington.'[28] Containment was in the first place to be a political and economic, rather than military, policy.[29]

Something of this 'totalitarian-ideological' model appears in the IDC review. Russia's 'forward policy' (i.e., expansionism) was cited as the possible cause of an accidental war, against which Britain should guard. Describing the problem in Kennan-ite style, the IDC decreed that 'Russia *by reason of her policy, Government and mentality* can be taken as the only potential aggressor' [emphasis added]. The IDC saw few limits to Russian ambition. Russia's intentions were thought to be hard to discern but the IDC felt that they would be driven by fear of the West and that this would lead to Russia building up its war potential and establishing a defensive glacis. Fulfilling Mackinder's prophecy, Russia would build up its enormous natural resources to become a super-powerful state and would develop its political and geographical position, *without fighting*, 'to such a point that when she is ready to gain world hegemony, she can demand what she likes'.[30] These comments, however, appear to have more in common with Gaddis' description of the post-revisionist 'imperial model' than with the 'totalitarian-ideological' model. The 'imperial model' accepts, first, that the Soviet Union felt insecure and acted cautiously. But it is also held that Moscow did indeed set out to collect colonies; a policy which filled the US and Western Europe with alarm. The Soviet method was, just as the IDC suggested, the insidious one of seeking 'to fill power vacuums where this could be done without encountering resistance'.[31] Containment, by this post-revisionist interpretation, may have been provocative but was certainly reasonable, and it would seem that this was precisely the view held by the IDC and, through their concurrence, by the COS.

What is clear is that the British military were developing their own understanding of containment, and that their version also had a distinctly military component. The IDC review showed that 'defence by the shield', against a Russian attack on Britain, 'would not be effective' and so the answer was, in effect, an early version of massive retaliation. The Soviet Union was to be resisted in the following way:

Real defence in the atomic age must lie in making an aggressor realise

> that while he may wreck the nation he attacks, he will at once be subjected himself to such a counter blow that, whatever success he gains in his initial attack, will be purchased too dearly. Our main defence should be a counter blow the moment we are attacked, and the knowledge that it exists.[32]

The counter-offensive force was to be some 50 squadrons of 25 aircraft each. Military containment of the Soviet threat was to be achieved, therefore, by deterrence through air power rather than by some territorial strategy, still less one involving Germany.

How might the emergence of this British version of containment be explained? With the rapidly dwindling dollar loan, was it that Britain simply could not afford the notion of economic containment? Or were the COS were just deluding themselves and over-estimating Britain's military capabilities? Describing a paper by Bevin dated 3 May 1946 as 'in many respects... the primary source of Britain's containment policy for Europe',[33] Deighton suggests that the British version of containment 'reflected the ideology, assumptions, and world-view of the Foreign Office, *supported by the Chiefs of Staff*' [emphasis added].[34] The FO was 'backed' by the COS in its determination to structure and pursue a 'policy to contain Soviet power'.[35] Out of this FO-COS partnership, a self-confident and rather spendthrift version of containment developed: 'The containment of this [Soviet] expansionism would lie at the heart of British analyses, despite the financial cost.'[36] Official papers indicate, however, not only that the COS version of containment developed somewhat independently of FO influence or approbation, but also that 'the financial cost' was something of which the COS were sharply aware during these years.

Another explanation of the origins of containment in Britain has it that both the FO and the COS came to see Germany as the 'front-line' against the Soviet Union in Europe. Bevin's paper of 3 May 1946 has been described as a major shift in Britain's foreign policy in Germany and Europe, a shift which occurred in the spring and summer of 1946:

> This change of direction [Bi-zonal negotiations] in Anglo-American policy ... constituted a serious departure from the Potsdam agreements. It was now both possible and intended that the future Western German State would be formed as an anticommunist and anti-Soviet bulwark.[37]

Once again, however, the official papers show that from a military point of view, neither the nature and direction of the Soviet threat, nor the value of Western Germany as a 'bulwark' against that threat, had become as clear as is implied above. The COS were well aware, throughout 1946, that the Soviet Union represented a 'more dangerous potential enemy than Germany',[38] but the deduction was that Britain should shore up its defences in the *Middle East*, not Germany. Germany was still, largely, an internal security problem and was not to involve a major, strategic commitment of forces.[39] Even Montgomery, who might be expected to have grasped any opportunity to prove the Army's indispensability, found himself agreeing, in mid-summer 1946, that the occupation force should be reduced to just over four divisions; all that would be needed to meet basic occupation tasks.[40]

Yet, by the beginning of the following year, the COS seem to have outstripped their American counterparts in developing a doctrine of *military* containment. If the origins of this policy do not lie in FO leadership (Deighton) or in a 'bulwark' idea (Badstübner/Steininger), then where do they lie? The answer seems to be in the new thinking about atomic deterrence, referred to earlier, and in the FDP paper. Although Germany was not one of the 'three pillars' of this new policy (defence of the UK base, defence of SLOC and defence of the Middle East), it was incorporated into it simply because what was important was to resist *territorial* expansion of the Soviet Union; one aim of the new British strategy was to 'ensure that Germany does not become a Russian Satellite'.[41] This aim was to be achieved by military containment in the form of deterrence; 'territorial containment' without a 'territorial strategy'. This new policy was in turn a function both of the influence on perceptions of developing military technology, and straightforward inter-service rivalry.

The COS often discussed matters of technology and weapons characteristics, reflecting a fascination and concern with the new weapons which an enemy might launch against Britain. Sir Henry Tizard, chairman of the DRPC, was often present. In their discussion of the IDC review on 1 January 1947, the COS were presented with three possible forms of attack: air attack; advance over land to within rocket strike range; and attack by submarines on the SLOC. The first, air attack, would be by rocket or manned aircraft, with atomic, chemical or biological weapons. The COS were warned of the damage which might result from such an attack, with some 60 per cent of the 'white manpower' and industrial strength of the Commonwealth concentrated in Britain. The deduction was that the battle should be fought as far away (east) as possible. This in turn meant attacking the Soviet Union from the Middle East and destroying their supplies of oil. It also meant preventing enemy bases being established in Europe from which an attack could be launched.[42] Finally, Britain's perceived vulnerability demanded that air defences be brought up to standard. The second danger, that of attack over land to within rocket strike range, was simply an extension of the first, and prompted similar conclusions, suggesting that any COS interest in fighting in and for West European countries may at this stage have been less altruistic than operational. The threat of a submarine attack on SLOC was a legacy of the submarine warfare conducted by Germany in the Atlantic. The COS assumed that US assistance would be provided in a future battle and that the Atlantic SLOC would therefore have to be protected. They also recognised the vulnerability of the Commonwealth SLOC to Soviet interdiction. The COS were thus well aware of Britain's vulnerability to air and rocket attack. Yet they were sanguine about the inability (for ten years to come) of Britain's air defences to come up to the mark. This can be explained both by faith in the deterrent effect of the West's atomic advantage and the threat of a massive response, and by the conviction that the Soviet Union would not be in a position to go to war before the end of 1956.

If the threat to Britain was from the air, and if air power provided the best defence, there were clear implications for Britain's armed services, particularly the Army. It was not envisaged that the Army would provide any sort of land defence against the Soviets in Europe. No commitment to the defence of Germany was considered at this stage – no continental strategy – even though the COS saw the need to ensure that Germany would not become a launch pad or airfield for the Russians; a paradox which sums up perfectly the tensions within Britain's evolving strategy for Europe. In late February 1947 the COS were made aware of the JPS view that manpower difficulties would require a run-down in the British Army of the Rhine (BAOR) to approximately 30,000-40,000 by early 1949 and that occupation forces would eventually be dispensed with altogether.[43] That the Army was being forced to look elsewhere to justify its existence is suggested by the minutes of two meetings held in December 1947.[44] Here, the Army fought to secure for itself a larger slice of the defence estimates cake by stressing (with JIC support) the possibility of air and sea invasion of the UK. Only the Army could deal with such a threat, but the Navy and RAF Chiefs played down the danger.

Up to late 1947, British strategy certainly took account of affairs on, and threats to, the Continent, but to infer from this that Britain had a 'continental strategy' is to simplify a complex and contingent set of ideas and rivalries. Containment of the Soviet Union, a commitment of land forces to Germany and Europe, and the build-up of Germany as a 'bulwark', were not at this stage elements of a unified strategy, however much these ideas might appear to be connected. The only certainty, on which all services could agree, was the deterrent effect of the threat of a large-scale response with air power using atomic weapons. Out of this consensus developed the idea of 'passive' rather than 'active' containment, whereby territorial defence could be achieved by military means (air power) yet without a territorial strategy involving operationally capable ground forces, at least as far as North-West Europe and Germany were concerned. For containment to be more physical than conceptual would require the Army's place in overall British strategy to be on a par with or higher than that of the Navy or RAF. Against the weight of contemporary strategic orthodoxy, it is not surprising that the Army pinned its colours to the strongest post it could find; the 'bulwark' idea was not that post. If the Army was to survive at all, it would have to define threats, such as the invasion of Britain, which only it could meet; threat manipulation or *feindpolitik* thus became a feature of inter-service rivalry over budgetary allocations.

FROM COLD WAR TO KOREAN WAR AND REARMAMENT: 1948-50

If the British military view of the Soviet threat to Europe was somewhat complacent, there was nevertheless growing interest in Soviet military capabilities, atomic and conventional. Thus, early in February 1948 Tizard stressed to the COS the importance of being informed of the moment at which the Soviet Union conducted its first atomic test. This, he suggested, 'would be a most favourable moment' for 'the Americans to insist on a showdown'; a clash with the Soviet Union was inevitable within the next 15 years.[45] Days later, Montgomery provided detailed information on the size and character of the Soviet threat, information based most probably on JIC research. Montgomery described a Soviet build-up to a three-pronged attack into northern and central Germany, naming key towns and regions. The Soviets would use 21 divisions which would take between 6 and 15 days to arrive on the Rhine. By D+28 days, the Soviets could have 73 divisions on the Rhine.[46] A paper presented by Tedder referred to a 'conservative assessment' made by the Intelligence Staff that considerably more than 5,000 Russian aircraft would be made available in support of their 'field campaign'.[47]

Yet there was little sense of alarm. The British military were capable of thinking beyond and around mere military capabilities, and of producing rather subtle analysis, as the following reference to a JIC assessment indicates:

> though the Soviet leaders are unlikely to consider it to be [to] their

> advantage to go to war before the end of 1956, Russia may be expected to continue her present policy of piecemeal expansion up to the limit which she thinks she can go without provoking war. She will endeavour to surround herself with Communist-controlled States, thereby greatly improving her strategic position.
>
> The real danger of war lies in the possibility that Russia might, through mis-appreciation of Anglo-United States policy, take a step which would inevitably lead to war.[48]

Thus, in spite of their awareness of Soviet military capabilities in Europe, and of the possibility of an accidental war, the British military did not as yet feel any need to take dramatic decisions or indeed to change their basic planning assumptions. A planning date of 1956/7 gave a decent interval for preparation, while a conflict which broke out in the short term would, by its very nature, be a surprise and therefore impossible to plan for. In any case, if the Soviets were to launch their massive forces at Western Europe before 1956/7, there would be little the West's divisions could do about it.

The growing ambivalence over Britain's military role in Germany can be discerned from an exchange of letters between Bevin, Alexander and Robertson. Writing late in April, Bevin told Alexander of his concern that the Soviets, although keen to avoid outright hostilities, would nevertheless attempt to ruin the European Recovery Programme by subversion, civil disturbances and so on, and would try 'to force the withdrawal of the allied forces from Germany and Austria, since those forces represent the real bar to the further progress of Communism westward'. In Bevin's view, the job of the forces in Germany and Austria was to 'fight', not an open conflict with the Soviets, which he dismissed as unlikely, but a political or ideological conflict involving civil disobedience, sabotage and 'local diversionary attacks' rather than tanks and organised force.[49] Alexander's response was to ask whether the forces in Germany could meet the threat as defined by Bevin. Copies of Bevin's letter were also sent for comment to Robertson in Germany and to the British Military Governor in Vienna. Robertson's comments were forwarded to the COS in late June 1948.[50] Agreeing with Bevin, Robertson anticipated the Soviets applying 'progressive' pressure to bring about the collapse of the ERP. This might involve infiltration of the trade unions and the police forces by way of 'softening up'. The object would be to undermine German confidence in the occupation regimes and in the German institutions which had so far been established. There would then be sabotage, aimed at the police, industry and at the 'mobility of the Armed Forces'. Bands of German guerrillas, sponsored by the Soviets, might make incursions into the western zones, with the aim of making the occupying powers' position untenable. Like Bevin, he did not believe that the Soviets would attack, but if it ever seemed that a Soviet attack was likely, 'it would be necessary to reconsider the use of Germany as a training ground for national service men, and the replacement of the present recruits by seasoned troops.' Templer had some sympathy with Robertson.[51] However, while he agreed that the Allies should resist being 'pushed out of Berlin' since this would lose 'the faith of the workers', the plea for 'seasoned troops' was inappropriate since 'there were no seasoned troops available'.

Thus, although the COS were increasingly aware that the Soviets were capable of launching a massive attack westwards, they nevertheless continued to respond in a cautious way, in a way which fell short of active military containment of the Soviet Union through deployments to Germany. Part of the explanation for this state of affairs may be the uncertainty within British military circles as to the scale and direction of any Soviet attack. In November 1948 the COS discussed two more JIC papers.[52] Edelsten did not accept that the Russians were capable of mounting simultaneous campaigns in the Middle East and Western Europe, and conducting a bombing campaign against the UK.[53] Tedder disagreed. He believed the Russians could do all that had been mentioned, and more. In his understanding, they would feel compelled to make a 'maximum initial effort' in order to take full advantage of their numerical superiority. Slim concurred. The Russians would not go for consecutive campaigns, if they did, they would be inviting the Western Allies to defeat them in detail. The COS heard that the Directors of Intelligence estimated that the Soviets could have 174 divisions at 70 per cent strength then, with all at 100 per cent strength after twelve months. It was a 'practical probability' that all these divisions could be mobilised in five days.[54] The COS approved JIC (48) 100 as a background for further planning and study.[55] Early in 1949 the JCS accepted JIC (48) 100 'without comment' and the paper was distributed to the Canadian Chiefs of Staff, the British Commanders-in-Chief in the Middle and Far East, and the Commander-in-Chief/Military Governor in the British zone of Germany.[56] Some days later another JIC assessment of the 'possibility of war before a certain date' was discussed. Although the JIC paper[57] is retained within the Cabinet Office, the minute of the discussion was released in October 1992. The COS agreed that the JIC report should be amended as follows:

> The Soviet land forces, with their close support aircraft are at present sufficiently strong to achieve extensive initial success against any likely combination of opposing land forces. They have also, at present, relative superiority in the performance of their armoured fighting vehicles and of certain other weapons; if war is delayed the maintenance of this superiority will involve them in a re-equipment programme to the detriment of other industrial projects...The Soviet leaders may consider, therefore that in view of the defensive preparations of the Western Powers, this superiority is dwindling and should be exploited without delay.[58]

One more clue to the content of JIC (48) 100 emerges from discussion of the threat of invasion of the UK.[59] Slim argued for a new JIC/JPS study of the problem. Sanders, however, felt that this might not be necessary since, in JIC (48) 100 (Final), the JIC had 'already estimated that the Russians would aim to over-run Western Europe and to direct an intensive air and sea offensive against the British Isles with the object of preventing the use of the United Kingdom as a base by the United States forces. The scale and timing of a Russian invasion would depend to a large extent on the scale of air interdiction which we were able to impose.'

Another possible explanation for the curiously calm attitude of the military concerns the estimates being made of Soviet air defence capabilities. The first full intelligence assessment for 1949 appeared at the end of January. The COS discussed a JPS paper, the first part of which dealt with 'the threat to world security'.[60] The Soviet Union was to be regarded as a 'potentially hostile power', with the aim of imposing communism all over the world. This they would achieve through their patience and tenacity in a long-term 'revolutionary struggle' or, should the conditions appear suitable, they may 'assist this process by war'. War was not likely to be an option until the economic strength of the Soviet Union had improved sufficiently (probably at the end of the second, post-war five year plan). Having said that, economic strength could not be the sole determinant: if the Soviets felt that through war they could, at a given moment, achieve their goals rapidly, then they would possibly resort to it. This was by now a familiar theme, as was the possibility of a war by miscalculation or in order to maximise current advantages before re-equipment and modernisation was needed.[61] But a more reliable indicator of Soviet intentions was clearly needed if plans were to be made. Although the Soviets could start a land war 'at any time', before 1956/60, any early numerical advantages would be offset by the incompletion of the Soviet industrial plan. What was even more likely to hold the Soviets back, however, was the

Western preponderance in the strategic air balance. It was thought that the Allies had the advantage in strategic bombing technology and techniques, and that Soviet air defences were inadequate. To embark upon a land campaign, with at best only a temporary numerical advantage on the ground and while the air power 'umbrella' above was so heavily perforated, would have entailed immense tactical and strategic risks, and would have subjected the Soviet Union to a ferocious strategic air response. The JPS had therefore not only produced a clear rationale for the Western preoccupation with air power but had also established a key intelligence indicator: the 'efficacy' of Soviet air strength.

A discussion in mid-April of the logistic aspects of Plan SPEEDWAY, the emergency withdrawal plan, provides the next glimpse of the progress of threat assessments. The JPS listed Russian military aims as the destruction or neutralisation of Allied forces on the European and Asian mainlands, the seizure or neutralisation of the UK, the seizure of the Middle East and its oil resources, the seizure or neutralisation of all Allied air offensive bases, and, finally, the disruption of Allied SLOC by submarine interdiction, mining and air operations.[62] Discounting the effect of any Allied response to a Soviet attack, and therefore proceeding deliberately from a 'worst-case' stand-point, the JPS were keen to define 'the maximum success they [the Soviets] are physically capable of achieving'. They estimated that France and the Low Countries could be overrun within two months and that appropriate Channel and North Sea ports might only be available to the Allies for the first two weeks of a war. There was a threat of strategic bombing, but the report argued that, given the relative inexperience of the Russians in this form of warfare, this latent threat would only materialise if the Soviets were able to establish themselves in Western Europe, i.e., within closer range of the UK.

During the first half of 1950, before the outbreak of the Korean War, the familiar problem of inaccessibility to JIC papers presents itself.[63] Nevertheless, as for earlier years, a clear enough reconstruction can be achieved. One theme, manifest in the first meetings of the year, was that of possible German rearmament, a subject which the COS had first addressed towards the end of 1949. This notion gave brief life to fears which had been peripheral for some time; the dangers of German revanchism and, worse still, of a new 'Rapallo' agreement between Germany and the Soviet Union.

On 10 January the COS received a request from the Foreign Office for advice on the defence of Germany.[64] Early in December 1949 Adenauer had raised the subject of planning for the defence of Germany with the Allied High Commissioners, among them Robertson, who had duly reported to the FO's German Section. Adenauer referred to the creation of an East German army – thinly disguised as a *gendarmerie* – and expressed his concern at rumours that the Western Allies had plans to withdraw to the Rhine in the event of war, thus leaving most of the North German plain exposed to the invading forces. For these reasons Adenauer had, early in December, made a number of statements to the press floating the idea of German rearmament. Robertson, sensing that the matter would not rest, and having some sympathy for Adenauer's position, sought advice on the matter. The Foreign Office duly requested the COS view of the military aspects of the problem.[65] The JPS report was produced and discussed in March.[66] The planners and the COS showed some sympathy for Adenauer's plight and a good deal more interest than the Foreign Office in the possibility of rearming Germany in order to boost the Western Alliance's defences in Europe. Part of this interest was no doubt a result of the awareness in British and American circles (several months before the outbreak of the Korean War) that, in the event of war in Europe, the Western powers would still, in all probability, be unable to offer any meaningful resistance. Cautious as ever, the COS instructed the JPS in the following terms:

> A study should be made of the various forms of partial German re-armament – for example of allowing the Germans an Army without any tanks. The implications of a fuller measure of re-armament should also be considered. In this connection it was pointed out that we must not lose sight of *the serious longer-term threat that might arise to Western Europe and the United Kingdom from a re-armed Germany, particularly from a re-armed Germany which had aligned herself on the side of the Russians.* [Emphasis added]

The JPS produced their paper on 21 April, for discussion by the COS on 2 May.[67] Slessor felt that the JPS had not satisfied the terms of reference laid down in March and called for a 'broader and more fundamental study', looking beyond 1954. The COS agreed and instructed the JPS to rewrite their paper, stressing once again their basic fear 'that the whole of Germany might become united under the influence of Russia ... The Russians today could offer the Germans today many attractions.' However residual this fear, and however much the COS saw opportunities in German rearmament and reunification, it is of interest to note that comments of this sort were still being made as late as summer 1950. The JPS paper is, however, more useful for the light it throws upon the development of thinking about the Soviet Union.

In mid-March, while discussing 'the arguments in favour of promising United Kingdom land reinforcements for the defence of Western Europe in the event of war',[68] two milestones emerge in British military thinking: the first concerning Britain's view of European security and the second of the strategic importance of the Middle East. The JPS had come to the firm conclusion that successful defence of the United Kingdom would not be possible in the event of a Soviet invasion and occupation of Western Europe: 'We conclude that the defence of the United Kingdom and Western Europe must be considered together. The foundation of the defence of Western Europe in war is a strong France.'[69] There was nothing novel in this observation; British military thinking, both before and after the advent of the bomber and the rocket, had tended to see North-West Europe as something of a buffer-zone or glacis. What makes this comment so interesting is that the JPS were now willing to declare their sense of Britain's dependence (no longer merely interest) on the security of Western Europe. The JPS paper therefore represents an important development in British military thinking about European defence although, as will be shown, the British military were still some way from a priority commitment of ground forces to that task.

Two days later, the nature of Britain's dependence on a well-defended Europe came up once again. On this occasion, the subject under discussion was the military command structure for the defence of the UK in the event of war.[70] This paper refers to two JIC studies which would otherwise be unavailable for scrutiny, and is most revealing of the views of the planning and intelligence staffs regarding the Soviet threat. The JPS referred first to JIC (48) 35 (O) (Final) [date not given], noting the JIC's claim that the Soviet Union 'will aim at eliminating the UK as an allied base'. This would be achieved by aerial bombardment, a contingency which was assessed in both the short and the long term. In the former, it was feared that the Soviet Union might overrun the whole of Western Europe up to the Channel and Atlantic coasts, allowing them to launch missile and aircraft attacks against the United Kingdom with relative ease. In the longer term, with stiffened European defences preventing the Soviet Union from getting quite so close to Channel, Soviet forces could nevertheless put themselves into a position from which they could launch bombers carrying free-fall atom, biological and chemical bombs, as well as guided ballistic missiles against the UK. The simple lesson, in both cases, was that the air defence of the UK, along with offensive air operations against the Soviet bases, would be vital if Britain were to survive. If these operations were not successful then a 'critical condition' could arise by about D+6 months where London was so severely damaged that it would be unable to function as a command and control centre. One other possible result of Britain's inability to resist a Soviet air assault was also postulated: an invasion of the UK. This problem was being treated separately by the JIC.[71] JPS references to this latter paper show that the JIC had identified the key elements of a successful Soviet invasion of the UK: air superiority; control of narrow sea-ways (the Channel); and an adequate sea and air lift capacity. But the JPS and, it would seem, the JIC were sceptical that all these conditions could be met. Certainly, the JPS had elsewhere discounted the possibility of a Soviet invasion in the short term.[72] It would appear, therefore, that in early spring 1950, one year after the signature of the Washington Treaty, some six months after the creation of the West German state and at a time when the British were, supposedly, underlining their 'commitment' to the defence of the Continent by promising to despatch reinforcements there in the event of war, senior military staffs were still articulating their perception of the threat, and Britain's response, in a carefully circumscribed manner. Germany, the Netherlands, Belgium and France were not to be defended out of some sense of fraternal good-will, but because their security was necessary for Britain's defence. Britain's 'commitment' to the defence of Europe was still very much a hollow one, best seen as an attempt to establish – by persuasion rather than force – a defensive glacis against aggression from the East.[73] Britain's main defence and deterrent effort was still to be in the form of air power.

The second milestone to emerge from the COS mid-March discussion[74] concerned Britain's impression of the Soviet threat to the Middle East. The Directors of Plans argued that the paper, JP (50) 22 (Final), should contain some reference to 'the fact that it was now appreciated that the full threat in the Middle East would not develop until about six months after the war had begun'; the COS accepted this recommendation. A fundamental change of view was taking place in respect of the priority accorded to the Middle East in British defence planning, and this should be examined in some detail. The COS returned to the subject four days later. A confidential annex records discussion of Plan GALLOPER, the combined Anglo-American plan in the event of war in the short term, up to July 1951,[75] itself an adaptation of the previous short-term British plan (SPEEDWAY). The JPS referred to the 'radical change in the assessment of the threat to the Middle East',[76] and gave JIC (49) 80 (Final) as the source of this reassessment:

> Probable Soviet operations at the outbreak of war are estimated by the [JIC] to be:-

> (a) Simultaneously
> (i) A campaign against Western Europe including Italy.
> (ii) An aerial bombardment against the British Isles.
> (iii) Campaigns against the Middle East, including Greece and Turkey.
> (iv) Campaigns with limited objectives in the Far East.
> (v) Attacks with limited objectives against Canada and the United States, including Alaska and the Aleutians.
> (vi) A sea and air offensive against Allied sea communications.
> (vii) Subversive activities and sabotage against Allied interests in all parts of the world.
>
> (b) As soon as possible, after the occupation of the Channel Port areas, a full-scale sea and air offensive against the British Isles.
>
> (c) As soon as practicable, campaigns against Scandinavia and possibly against the Iberian Peninsula.
>
> The [JIC] consider that the Soviet Union would have sufficient armed forces and resources *to undertake all the campaigns listed above and still retain an adequate reserve.* [Emphasis added][77]

Further reference to this JIC paper was made a few days later. While discussing the distribution of Plan GALLOPER, and in particular the most appropriate way of explaining to the Commander-in-Chief, Middle East, that his expected allocation of air forces would probably not now be made, the COS indicated that the overall plan for the defence of the Middle East should be reviewed for a number of reasons. Foremost among these were 'The radical change in the assessment of the threat to the Middle East' and 'The inability of the United States to contribute armies or air forces to the Middle East in the first three months.'

Two reasons might be offered for this diminishing emphasis on the Middle East in British defence and foreign policy. First, the assumption that Middle Eastern oil was a strategic necessity was now being questioned by military staffs in Britain. That Plan GALLOPER could contain a comment to the effect that 'the recapture of the Middle East oilfields, *should* this oil prove essential for the continuation of the Allied war effort, *may* be considered a *possible* operation' for the Allies in the period D+6 months to D+12 months [emphasis added],[78] suggests that Middle East oil was no longer the vital asset it had been in late 1947, when it had been argued that 'The importance to us of present and potential oil supplies in the Middle East is greater than ever. In the foreseeable future, unless measures are taken to change the situation, our dependence on Middle East oil seems likely to increase rather than decrease.'[79]

But a more convincing explanation for the change of heart regarding the Middle East was, quite simply, that the Americans had adopted a new strategy, the 'Center Strategy' discussed in chapter six below. By spring 1950 Britain's strategic planners were subject to ever increasing pressure to keep in line with American thinking. The same applied to the JIC; JIC (49) 80 (Final) – the main source of the change of assessment in Britain of the threat to the Middle East and to Britain generally – was, after all, a joint American, British and Canadian effort and references to the JIC paper often appear in conjunction with 'ABCI 15', probably the joint, parent paper from which national threat assessments were drawn. The reluctance or inability of the Americans to commit troops to the defence of the Middle East, combined with (or, more likely, leading to) the British planners' own assessment that the threat to the Middle East would not materialise for six months, meant that a more relaxed view of the strategic importance of the Middle East could develop.

The JPS were far less sanguine about this fundamental change in strategic thinking than the JIC appeared to be. In late April the COS returned to the discussion of the priority to be accorded to the Middle East in defence planning.[80] The JPS had recommended that the Middle East should remain a priority commitment when allocating air assets, arguing that 'Any substantial reduction in the meagre air forces allotted in Plan GALLOPER to the Middle East would prejudice its defence.' The JPS noted that under present arrangements for war in the short term, the Middle East command would be reinforced by 10 medium bomber squadrons (80 aircraft) from the UK by D+1 month, and by two FGA squadrons (32 aircraft – formerly BAFO but presently in Hong Kong), by D+3 months. Interpreting the JIC assessment rather differently, what was important to the JPS was not that the Russians would not attack the Middle East until D+6 months, but that when they did attack they would be capable of overwhelming British positions in the Middle East if air assets were misguidedly withdrawn. To meet the threat, Plan GALLOPER had allocated, by D+6 months, some 184 fighters (day, night and ground attack), and 140 medium and light bombers. It was by no means certain that all these aircraft would be made available in the time allowed, thereby accentuating Allied disadvantages in terms of the air battle, air support for the ground battle (with only six allied divisions allocated to meet the projected Soviet eight) and medium bomber operations. This, the JPS argued, was hardly the time to consider reducing the level of air forces in the region. The JPS did, nevertheless, acknowledge that the COS had wider problems with which to contend:

> Should the Russians succeed in overrunning Western Europe, the defence of the United Kingdom would be extremely difficult; and the Chiefs of Staff have decided that, while the Middle East is important to allied strategy and the attempt to hold it must be made, the allocation of resources to it must not be allowed fatally to compromise our ability to defend Western Europe and the United Kingdom.

Nevertheless, risking COS objections, the JPS tried to argue their case on the following lines. First, the 32 FGA, which might prove vital in the much lower-scale Middle East battle, would scarcely have any impact in Europe: 'The requirement stated by the Commanders-in-Chief is for 4,200 tactical aircraft and the most that the Allies can hope to deploy by 1951 is 550 aircraft'. Similarly, the re-allocation of bomber aircraft from the Middle East to Britain would have a disproportionate effect on the defence of the Middle East, especially since the Americans had so far declined to base any aircraft in the area but were likely to base some 420 strategic bomber aircraft in Britain.

After discussion, the COS rejected the JPS appeal and agreed to amend Plan GALLOPER to bring it into line with the new Allied Defence Policy and Strategy paper, JP(49) 172 (Final). Slim felt that the JPS were guilty of assuming that a land campaign could only take place in the Middle East. If this proved not to be the case, implied Slim, there would be a need for air support for the land battle in Europe. But even if the JPS were right, then 'the main object in that event would be to defend the United Kingdom against atomic attack. This object drew the need for air forces in the United Kingdom into even sharper relief.' Slessor, Chief of the Air Staff (CAS), took the familiar position that Britain's meagre air forces should not be split in two or otherwise over-committed.

The early months of 1950, marked by a reassessment of the relative importance of the defence of the Middle East and Europe and by the need to keep pace with changes in American views, were clearly a turbulent time for British strategic thinking. A new, general strategy was developed, designed to replace the plan which had been drawn up in May 1947. The strategic review process had begun in late 1949, with the object of assessing the new global strategic situation, deciding whether existing strategic thinking could meet any new demands being placed on it, and making new plans as necessary. The outcome, the last major strategic assessment before the outbreak of the Korean War, was a report entitled *Defence Policy and Global Strategy*, produced between May and June 1950.[81] A slightly amended version of the original COS assessment describes in some detail Allied strategy for both the 'cold' and the 'hot' war with the

Soviet Union, and analyses the possible contribution of the British Commonwealth to the Allied effort. The report also touches, albeit briefly, on the Soviet threat to Europe, Germany and Britain, and therefore amounts to the last pre-Korean War threat assessment undertaken by the British military.

Two types of threat were considered; the first pertaining to the Cold War and the second to its 'hot' successor – the 'shooting war'. During the Cold War there would be a need to guard against Fifth Column activities, the aim of which would be to 'rot resistance from within'.[82] As for the 'shooting war' in the Middle East,[83] the COS openly accepted that 'the full [Soviet] threat is unlikely to develop against Egypt until considerably later than we had hitherto thought probable.' Egypt was seen to be the 'key strategic area of the Middle East', just as the UK was 'the key to Western defence.'[84] The COS therefore expected that in any 'shooting war' in Europe, the UK would be singled out for special attention. Yet the COS did not regard a shooting war in Europe as 'inevitable or even likely'.[85] At first glance, this suggests that in the last months before Korea the COS had relaxed their assessment of the Soviet danger to Europe. Elsewhere, however, the paper shows that the sense of danger was in no way reduced: 'from the purely military point of view, Russia could march to the Atlantic at any moment'.[86] But this was not a sufficient basis for a strategy which could serve in both peace and war, and it is in their awareness of this that the COS demonstrated the subtlety of their thinking. Far from being alarmist and simplistic, their analysis of the 'worst case' of massive Soviet aggression in Europe brought them instead to the conclusion that Allied strategy was as much a matter of political cohesion and steadfastness within the West as military plans and preparation. Soviet aggression was not likely, but it was certainly possible, and this possibility had to be kept firmly in mind if the political and ideological defences of the West were to be maintained. These were the first line of the West's defence, and if weaknesses developed the Soviet Union would be sure to exploit them, thus making war more likely. COS thinking might therefore be described as genuinely strategic, where political and military considerations are interlaced, leading to the familiar conceptual cocktail of deterrence and defence.

SUMMARY

From 1945 to mid-1950, British military threat perceptions revolved around two possible adversaries: Germany and the Soviet Union. In respect of the manner in which these threat perceptions governed strategic thinking about Europe, it is useful to think in terms of three phases. In the first phase Germany was the focus of attention. The second phase saw the transition from the German to the Soviet threat. And the final phase concerned the Soviet threat almost exclusively.

At the war's end, the German problem was essentially one of tidying up and of destroying any pockets of resistance. During 1946 the problem came to be seen more as a matter of civil disorder than outright armed opposition to the occupying powers. This perception gradually became linked to the Soviet/communist political and ideological threat; social breakdown in the Western zones would, it was thought, create the environment most suitable for the peaceful expansion of Soviet hegemony. By the end of 1946 and early 1947 the German threat had almost been discounted and was little more than nuisance value.

The transition from the German to the Soviet threat presents two points of interest. The transition was a gradual one, and took place over several years; it was not as if the German demon was placed on the shelf just as his Soviet colleague was taken off and dusted down. The second point is that for some time the developing anti-Soviet strategy was disguised by anti-German assessments. During this period the German threat was sustained artificially in order to mask the politically awkward, but increasingly gloomy, anti-Soviet assessments which were being made.

The British military were becoming suspicious of Soviet intentions towards Europe even while the war against Germany was raging. These suspicions became more deeply rooted during 1945. In spite of Foreign Office caution, by the end of 1945 the Soviet Union was recognised as the principal threat to Germany and continental Europe, although, militarily, the threat was not thought to be imminent. Within a year the British military had come to the conclusion that the Soviet Union was also the only serious threat to British interests. At this stage British interests were broadly defined and did not, directly, involve Europe. By examining likely Soviet intentions, as well as capabilities, the COS came to the conclusion in 1945 that war was likely with the Soviet Union between 1946 and 1950, probably involving aggression in the Middle East. This type of assessment prevailed in 1946 and 1947, possibly because reliable intelligence on Soviet capabilities was still hard to come by, and possibly also because the COS felt their first task to be a bureaucratic one of overcoming Whitehall's inertia against accepting an anti-Soviet strategy. By 1947 the COS had come to think of war with the Soviet Union as likely in the 'foreseeable future', possibly as the result of a miscalculation on the part of the Soviet Union.

From 1948, the COS and their operational and intelligence staffs became more interested in the military capabilities of the Soviet Union, atomic and conventional. But even with this important change in approach, the COS still found time to address more speculative issues such as the Soviet tendency to expansionism and the danger of accidental war. By the end of 1948, in spite of internal disagreements about both the intentions and the capabilities of the Soviet Union, the COS had accepted the gloomy forecast of the key intelligence paper of the day – JIC (48) 100. This paper, were it available, would probably show that British military fears about Soviet intentions, and knowledge (or assumptions) of their military capabilities, had now come together. Yet the COS still managed to resist hysteria and maintain a measured and objective view of the threat to Europe. The COS position can be explained in a number of ways. There was the conviction that, barring the recognised dangers of war by accident or miscalculation, the main Soviet threat to Europe was cautious, incremental expansionism short of war. Should this assessment prove to be flawed and war break out in the near future, there would in any case be little Britain could do about it. If there was a Soviet military (rather than political) threat, it was assessed to be to the Middle East rather than Europe. Finally, the COS had developed a coherent and convincing response to the Soviet problem – their own, military version of containment, based upon the West's technological advantages and the threat of massive aerial and atomic counter-strikes.

In 1949 the scene darkened, with currency being given to the idea that the Soviet Union might start war deliberately, if it appeared that conditions had become favourable. However, when Soviet air- defence and air power emerged as reliable indicators of the Soviet Union's likelihood or ability to begin war, there was a move back towards the 'war by miscalculation' idea. 1949 also saw the beginning of a move towards a longer-term view of the Soviet threat. The spring of 1950 saw two milestones regarding the British military perception of the Soviet threat to Europe: not only was the defence of the Middle East now thought to be less vital, but the security of Britain was now identified more closely than ever before with the defence of Western Europe. However, in the last strategic review before the Korean War the COS made the distinction between the *possibility* and the *likelihood* of the Soviet threat to Europe, and felt able to question the latter as long as the West's political cohesion was maintained. The COS had finally decided upon a more rounded, political/military posture – deterrence and, with important qualifications, defence. Strategic thinking continued to focus upon the air threat and the air response – a real territorial strategy and commitment of forces was still very much out of favour. Thus, the last major threat assessment before

June 1950 only served to confirm the value of the air power deterrent, without binding Britain in any convincing way to a territorial strategy. However sharp the sense of a Soviet threat to Germany, Britain and Europe, the evidence suggests that, up to Korea, little damage was done to the prevailing and well-established doctrine of 'limited liability' where commitment of forces to Europe was concerned.[87]

2 The Defence Budget, 1945-50

> There is an occasional caricature-stereotype of defence planning which supposes that it is – or if it is not that it ought to be – a basically simple linear process. One starts by identifying one's commitments; one assesses professionally what forces are needed to meet them; one costs these; and then one sends the bill to the Treasury, which pays up. It is not only in the final particular that this model departs from reality.
>
> Quinlan[1]

The desperate condition of the British economy in the immediate aftermath of VE day is well known. Keynes provided a vivid summary of the problem for the new Labour government in the first week of August 1945. Britain had accumulated overseas debts of about £3,100m and had lost about £1,100m worth of overseas income through sale of overseas assets, and about £7,000m (25 per cent of national wealth) on the costs of the war. Between 25 per cent and 30 per cent of merchant shipping assets had been sunk, and although exports were yielding about £400m, the balance of payments was in deficit owing to the need for £1,100-£1,200m to maintain wartime levels of consumption.[2] Following the surrender of Japan, problems were exacerbated within days by the termination of Lend-Lease from the United States and Mutual Aid from Canada. At a stroke, Britain was cut off from £1,350m of vital assistance. The landmarks in post-war economic reconstruction in Britain are equally familiar: from the Washington Loan of December 1945 to the convertibility crisis of 1947; from Marshall's speech and the beginning of the European Recovery Programme, to the devaluation crisis of 1949. In spite of American assistance, Britain remained economically destitute during the Attlee governments, a constant factor in civil and military thinking about Germany, Europe and strategy generally.[3]

In 1945 the Labour Party had offered the electorate a system of national welfare and had promised to prevent regression to the social and economic conditions of the 1930s. A great deal had been pledged. The central problem, however, was the lack of resources with which to achieve all targets.[4] The costs of establishing 'New Jerusalem' in Britain were immense and were to fall on 'a country with a ruined export trade, heavily in debt to its bankers (the Sterling Area Commonwealth countries and the United States), and with huge and inescapable continuing burdens with regard to the war with Japan.'[5] The ambitious plans of the Labour government could only be achieved with an 'economic miracle',[6] which came in the form of the Washington Loan followed by Marshall Aid. The construction of the welfare state dominated government spending plans. The housing policy of March 1945, for example, promised a construction programme of 'three to four million new houses in ten to twelve years'.[7]

While the government battled with the basic inadequacy of the British economy, the tasks facing the forces of occupation in Germany created problems of their own. In an area of 97,000^2 kilometres, some 25,000 British administrators, civilian and military, organised the lives of 22.3 million people.[8] Among these, in the first days after peace was declared, were some one million refugees (generally from the Soviet-dominated areas) and 1.5 million surrendered German soldiers, sailors and airmen. Clothing, food and shelter were all scarce, the civil transport and communications infrastructures were almost inoperative, industry and agriculture were moribund.[9] The daunting tasks facing the British military governor in these months included 'at more or less equal priority the destruction of German war potential, the reconstruction of the economy and the demobilisation of the British forces.'[10] In an attempt to encourage self-sufficiency, economic consolidation took place in the Western zones ('Bizonia' was formed in January 1947) but it was not for several years after the end of the war that the burden of occupying the defeated Germany, in the region of £80m per year, began to be reduced.

With structural economic weakness, reliance on American aid, high domestic spending plans, and the expense of occupation, it might be thought that the government would be disinclined to embark upon a high profile foreign policy and a strong defence policy. The new Labour government, however, took a different view, and its 'conduct of foreign affairs, with its nationalist overtones and surprising self-confidence, appeared the ultimate sign of a movement of protest that had adjusted itself to the realities and torments of power.'[11] And so there developed the unhappy combination of ambitious, worldly foreign and defence policies without a sound economic base, a combination which could only lead to tension between the country's strategic and economic planners. From the Treasury point of view, defence was simply an economic burden, with BAOR and BAFO/2TAF commitments to be trimmed or even shed. Defence spending meant direct costs, opportunity costs in the form of diversion of manpower and resources from industry manufacturing goods for export, foreign exchange losses and an increase of the balance of payments deficit.[12] The allocation of scarce resources in the face of competing claims is the basic problem of economics. With so many contradictions between the aims and capabilities of the Attlee governments, the purpose of this chapter is to show how the COS – charged with planning for Britain's defences on such an ambitious scale – responded to the constant pressure for retrenchment, and how this pressure affected strategic thinking about Germany. Conflicts developed, not only between the civil and military establishments, but also within the COS, and military thinking about Germany was influenced accordingly.

FROM CONSENSUS TO COMPETITION: 1945-46

The minutes of a meeting held in early January 1945 show how the COS and their staffs viewed the task of occupying Germany, relative to other commitments, and provide a base from which the impact of budgetary considerations on defence planning can be gauged. A JPS paper mentioned overall reductions in the armed services of between 500,000 and 700,000, and saw occupation tasks in Europe as just one of four 'Strategic Requirements' which the planners expected to meet one year after the end of the war in Europe (the other three were security of the United Kingdom, the war against Japan and the security of imperial lines of communication, India and the Middle East).[13] The occupation of the British zone of Germany would require the following:

A British contribution of 209,500, comprising;

- one infantry division and one armoured division, forming a 'mobile reserve' of 50,000;
- occupation forces of 141,100 men, in seven 'occupational groups' and five armoured car regiments;
- 'non effectives' (i.e., administrative staff) of 14,400;
- 4,000 civil affairs officials.

Non-British troops totalling 79,300;

- one Canadian occupational group of 19,300;
- three French divisions amounting to 60,000 men.

In arriving at their figures for the British commitment the planners had made three assumptions. The first was that the Canadians would provide one occupational group to the British zone, thereby saving some 19,300 troops. The Canadians later withdrew this commitment. The second was that the French would either provide three divisions to the British zone or would be given a portion of the British zone which would otherwise have required an additional three British occupational groups. The final assumption was that air power would make a crucial contribution to the occupation and would enable reductions in manpower to an agreed target of 255,500:

> Only the course of events and the degree of our success in using air power will show whether we can, during the 12 months after the end of hostilities, reduce the occupational forces to the estimated figure.

The occupation of Germany was not the most important of the four 'Strategic Requirements'; in both its size and its duration the occupation commitment appeared to the military staffs to provide scope for reductions. At this stage, the object of the occupation was simply to ensure that the instrument of surrender was carried out, and to maintain law and order in the British zone and Berlin; short-term, non-operational goals. These goals were not considered to be of the greatest importance and help was to be sought from any source to achieve them.

Throughout the year the COS received requests for information and assessments on force structures and commitments. In mid-August, with the Japanese all but defeated and the new Labour government turning its attention to peace-time uses of manpower, pressure began to mount for a new assessment with a target date of June 1946 and with maximum reductions throughout the services. Without detailed and reliable predictions from the COS, it was felt that the service ministries and the supply departments could not begin to make adjustments to their plans.[14] The COS duly attempted, somewhat indignantly, to reassess the situation. The winter of 1945/46 was felt to be a critical period and one which would determine the level of forces required for occupation in the long term:

> The commitments entailed in the occupation of Germany one year after her defeat were reviewed and approved by the Chiefs of Staff.[15] In this paper it was assumed that full use would be made of air power, to enforce authority, should the situation demand it. The most difficult period of the occupation is likely to be the coming winter. Until this phase of the occupation is over, it is not possible to foretell whether our occupational commitment will be reduced, and no change in our original estimate has, therefore, been made.[16]

As the allocation of operational troops to other tasks makes clear, the occupation of Germany was not considered a priority, operational matter.

British troops to be deployed to India amounted to 23 infantry battalions (with four divisions, five brigades and 90 infantry battalions coming from India). The Middle East was to receive one armoured, two infantry and one airborne divisions, 17 infantry battalions and three armoured car regiments, with a substantial contribution from the Indian Army.

The COS remained under pressure to provide the leanest possible estimates until, a few days before Christmas 1945, they produced their long-term forecasts for 30 June 1946 and 31 March 1947.[17] The estimates for 1946 assumed that one occupational division could now be dissolved (in addition to the Canadian contribution which was to be withdrawn in 1946) and noted that one infantry division (the 3rd) had already left Germany for Palestine. The estimates for the occupation of Germany in 1946 were now as follows:

	Previous Estimate	Revised Estimate
Armoured divisions	1	1
Infantry divisions	2	1
Armoured brigade groups	1	1
Occupation divisions	7	6
Armoured car regiments	5	5

The planners stressed that the winters of 1945/46 and 1946/47 would be critical points in the occupation and that further reductions should not therefore be considered until spring 1947. The longer term estimates for 31 March 1947 were as follows:

Armoured divisions	1
Infantry divisions	1
Armoured brigade groups	1
Occupation divisions	4
Armoured car regiments	3

In these first post-war months, Treasury and military were evidently not deeply divided over the need for retrenchment, at least where the commitment to Germany was concerned. Some other explanation is therefore required for the COS/Treasury rift which was to develop over the coming years.

Pressure mounted in 1946, first for predictions as to the size and cost of forces required at given dates in the future, and subsequently for reductions to be made in those predictions. Without such data, the government felt unable to decide on priorities in apportioning scarce national resources (both financial and manpower).[18] COS estimates were, predictably, too high; in December 1946 Alexander noted that COS estimates amounted to a figure which equated to the entire revenue from income tax for 1946.[19] Alexander was sympathetic, but was in no doubt that the defence budget and size of the armed forces could not be decided simply by strategic factors if the funds were not available: 'The question seemed to be whether we could carry this great burden of defence and, at the same time, achieve that national recovery which was essential to our position in the world and, indeed, to our defence.'[20] Alexander continued to urge the COS to move closer to a figure of £800m. He warned of 'arbitrary cuts' being imposed by the Treasury if estimates were not brought down, an approach which would be the most damaging to the services. Whatever the arguments, the defence budget would have to be made to respond to national economic conditions.

At first, the COS presented a united front to the government. While agreeing that there were too few resources for so many commitments, they did not feel that it was for them to recommend which commitments should be liquidated, preferring to take the high ground:

> The estimates which the Chiefs of Staff had put forward were the minimum which they thought essential if we were to support our position as a great power in the world today, and if we could not do so, there was a danger that we would degenerate into a second-class power.

They tried instead to pass unpleasant decisions back to the government. If commitments were to be reduced, this would be against strategic advice and the government would either have to 'guarantee' a period of no threat to British interests or accept the risk.[21] This attitude surfaced in the summer when Montgomery (later to develop, ostensibly at least, a much greater understanding of the financial difficulties faced by the government) persuaded the COS to advise the Defence Committee that the rate of demobilisation and release should be slowed for the Army and RAF since he no longer expected to be able to withdraw troops from Greece, Italy and Venezia Giulia by the end of the year. Once again, the difficult decision was passed to the government: 'The issue before the Defence Committee, therefore, was either to reduce our commitments before the end of the year in those areas, or to slow down the demobilisation and release scheme in order to provide the numbers required for the occupation forces.'[22]

In spite of COS attempts to present a united face to the government, cracks soon began to emerge. On one notable occasion in December 1946,

Montgomery's absence in Greece led to his RAF and Navy colleagues suggesting that the bulk of the cuts could go on the Army rather than on their own two services given that many small, war-time commitments, to be liquidated in due course, made the Army's budget temporarily over-sized.[23] Government pressure for reductions also soon began to erode the complacency with which the COS had viewed the likely run-down of forces in Germany. The Army's position became especially prominent. In March the COS informed Montgomery (then C-in-C of the British occupation forces) by telegram of 'the drastic manpower cuts decided on by the Government and of the consequential reductions in the Army and R.A.F. manpower ceiling provisionally allocated to forces of occupation in Germany.'[24] The size and duration of the occupation commitment had not so far been a major issue for the COS; it was a commitment which could be trimmed before other, more vital deployments fell under the eye of the Treasury. Thus, Simpson suggested that, by late 1947, 'we should have largely reduced our occupation forces for Germany'.[25] But a very different impression of the significance of the occupation forces was developing. During discussion of the food shortages in Germany, the COS debated a request from the C-in-C (Sholto Douglas, with effect from 2 May) that 'the Military Necessity Clause [a means to delay demobilisation] would have to be applied, in order that the rate of release of forces in Germany could be adjusted to meet the requirements of security'. The COS examined the proposal but accepted that the Government's objections to a suspension of demobilisation would be insuperable.[26] The COS warned that troop reductions in Germany might make it necessary to 'concentrate our forces on a mobile basis, so that detachments can be despatched to any part of the British Zone where trouble threatens,'[27] but by the end of the year found themselves in broad agreement with Alexander that 'there was no prospect of seeing a reduction by 31st March, 1948 in the strength of the occupational forces which had been allowed for in Germany.'[28]

DEADLOCK: 1947-48

Formal discussion of budgets and force structures began again in February 1947 with the COS and JPS commenting on the draft defence white paper and suggesting a number of amendments. Alexander expected an exacting reception in the House of Commons when the white paper was discussed, some time in March, and needed 'material with which to justify the size of the three Services stationed at home and in Germany'.[29] Any possibility that a co-operative relationship between the government and the COS might be sustained was dashed at the beginning of April, when the COS responded to calls for man-power and financial ceilings of 700,000 men and £600m respectively, and later to the possibility that National Service might be reduced from 18 to 12 months.[30] The Admiralty and War Office had each presented papers on the subject, but Tedder, Chief of the Air Staff, insisted that the matter should rather be dealt with by Alexander in conjunction with the service ministers. The COS duly agreed to meet later in the month and to discuss a memorandum from Alexander.[31] Alexander urged the COS to think of 1948/49 as 'the first year of our longer term plans', rather than as another hand-to-mouth, post-war year. He also warned the COS that uncertainty or hesitation on their part might mean that the forthcoming debate on defence policy would be driven by the estimates issue rather than strategic preferences. On 17 April, Alexander reminded the COS that defence policy was still in a 'transitional' period and that 1948/49 was to be the first year of a 'long-term development and reorganisation plan for the armed forces'.[32] He asked that the Future Defence Policy (FDP) report should be ready within eight months and that the COS prepare to discuss each service's estimates for the coming year.

On 23 April the COS discussed whether the FDP report should also cover estimates.[33] There was concern that to do so would be to delay the FDP process. Should, in that case, the service ministries be allowed to produce their own estimates of the size of forces required on the outbreak of war? Or should the COS/JPS deal with the matter? A compromise was agreed whereby the service ministries would produce their own plans for submission to the COS/JPS, to be merged into an inter-service report to be passed on to Alexander. Two months later, the COS examined projections of the strength of the forces for 31 March 1948.[34] This was the first reaction to Alexander's request for indications of the tasks facing the forces in the remainder of fiscal year 1947/48 and for indications of 'the risks involved should the run-down of the Forces be increased'. With current – rather than long-term – commitments now under scrutiny, the COS decided to pass the matter on to the service ministries, the JPS and the Principal Administrative Officers' Committee. Earlier in the year, Alexander had suggested that the 1947/48 defence estimates should be based upon the following man-power ceilings:

Royal Navy		189,000
Army		590,000
Royal Air Force		315,000
	Total	1,094,000[35]

The Navy's ceiling had later been reduced by 7,000 leaving a total of 1,087,000 for the three services, the projection given in the February 1947 white paper for their strength on 31 March 1948.[36] The size of the Army on 31 December 1946 had been 896,710 (about 63 per cent of the total).[37] The War Office had argued that while a reduction to 590,000 could be achieved in the time required, this would be at the expense of the technical efficiency of the Army and would reduce the core of experienced soldiers.[38] The figure of 590,000 was therefore accepted as a minimum, with the War Office arguing that a figure of 672,000 would be a more appropriate estimate for 31 March 1948. By the time of the 21 July meeting, War Office opinion had hardened. It was now argued that the figure of 590,000 could only be achieved by making 'very drastic cuts' and by accepting that 'there will be no deterioration in the situation in Palestine or Germany, and a reduction of approximately 40% in BAOR between 1 October 1947 and 1 April 1948 ...'[39] While withdrawal from India might permit a further reduction to 566,000, it was again stressed that this figure should be a floor, not a ceiling. Redeployment of British troops from India might ameliorate the cataclysmic 40 per cent run-down of BAOR over just 6 months. In a spirit of compromise, the War Office suggestion was therefore 663,000 at 1 January 1948, and 566,000 at 1 April 1948.[40] Within days the COS were facing demands for further force reductions.[41] Attlee had shown interest in an additional reduction of some 150,000 by the end of 1947. Simpson showed how the three services might together achieve a reduction of some 120,000 by the end of the year. From the Army's point of view, any further run-down could only be made at the expense of the position in Germany or the Middle East, where in both areas the planned run-down 'was already considered to be a maximum.' Alexander acknowledged the risks but nevertheless asked the COS to examine the problem further. This they did and the following day produced a revised estimate of a 133,000 reduction.[42]

On 19 August Alexander returned to the theme of long-term planning and to his insistence that Britain was now at 'the beginning of the end of the transitional period'. But there were still important estimates outstanding, namely the size of the forces required to meet peacetime commitments, and the 1948/49 defence estimates. Total expenditure was to be no more than £600m and Attlee had again asked that further reductions be considered.[43] The cracks grew wider. Tedder felt that the WO was not going far enough in paring its estimates, but Simpson fought back. The planned reductions had been tailored to meet what had been assumed to be the key roles of the Army: the maintenance of essential overseas garrisons in support of foreign policy; and the training of the National

Service (NS) intake.[44] In consequence, said Simpson, 'the Army was no longer therefore designed in relation to readiness for war, the only contribution to which would be the Territorial Army.' Further reductions could only be contemplated if certain overseas commitments were eliminated. If, as an alternative, the Army's heavy commitment to the training of NS men were to be reduced, possibly by reducing the size of the NS intake, this would only exacerbate the situation in BAOR where NS men were to provide some 55 per cent of the total occupation force of 68,500.[45] Alexander agreed with Tedder that the Army had not suggested cuts in expenditure on the same scale as the Navy and RAF. He was 'convinced' that unless the services brought their *joint* estimates down to about £600m, 'an arbitrary cut of all three Services would be imposed which would not be related to strategic considerations or the advisability of maintaining balanced forces.' Simpson repeated his defence and the debate then shifted to the possibility of cutting NS. Tedder, Cunningham and Tizard all approved of cutting NS in some degree, perhaps seeing in its retention an excuse for a large Army. The increasingly exasperated Alexander then pointed out that NS would have to be retained for several political and strategic reasons and that, in any case, the scheme had only been introduced on COS advice. He agreed that the implications of the abandonment of NS might, however, be studied.[46] Thinking, perhaps, that the COS were evading the real issues, Alexander 'deplored' the lack of agreement among the COS and, then, accompanied by threats of arbitrarily imposed ceilings of £160m (Navy), £270m (Army) and £170m (RAF), 'left the meeting'. Montgomery condemned the 'imposition of percentage cuts' as a return to 'the old system of arbitrarily cutting each of the original service proposals'; he could not see how an additional £60m could be saved and was furthermore unable to understand how the figure of £600m had been calculated.[47] On 2 September Tedder complained that his colleagues had failed to take the advice he had given in April,[48] to the effect that the JPS should have produced an addendum to their FDP report if the man-power and financial ceilings of 700,000 and £600m had been imposed.[49] At this late stage, the COS at last agreed to issue the JPS with terms of reference to examine the size and shape of the armed forces 'based on the agreed defence policy' (i.e., DO (47) 44). Montgomery still objected: to give the JPS the task of working out a solution to these most difficult of problems could only have meant that the COS wished to avoid the issue.[50] At a staff conference late in November Alexander made another appeal for advice and planning from the COS.[51] He was about to prepare the 1948/49 defence estimates[52] and needed to be able to explain to Parliament why, in spite of plans and promises, 1948/49 would have to be considered 'still a transition year towards normal peace-time conditions'. A somewhat impatient Tedder insisted that, in accordance with the agreed 'five plus five' rule and in response to the principal threats (an atomic attack on Britain which would be devastating but not likely for five years, and conventional attacks which could be repelled by air superiority), a great deal of planning had been done. Unlike the Navy and RAF, the Army, in Tedder's view, had thought little about the future. And so the wrangling began again, with Simpson stressing that the Army's planning for solely peace-time commitments was a reasonable response given that war had officially been deemed a 'negligible' risk for the next five years. Alexander finished by warning the COS, once more, that their advice was needed and that without it hasty decisions would have to be taken.

The RAF/Army competition for resources developed further on 8 December with disagreement over the likely role of the Army at the outbreak of war. Tedder considered that the Army's tasks 'could, in general, be limited to the defence of the United Kingdom and bases abroad, including anti-aircraft defence.' Simpson dismissed Tedder's reliance on the deterrent capability of 375 atomic-capable bombers as not 'realistic' and recommended that 'the only deterrent… to a future aggressor would be the knowledge that they would have to face the combined strength of the United Kingdom and the United States.' Simpson insisted that the threat to the UK and overseas bases would also include airborne invasion and that to ensure the security of these areas a force of 9½ divisions (TA), a small regular army and an anti-aircraft defence command would all be needed.[53] Tedder and Cunningham later spoke out against Montgomery's attempts to get guarantees of increased funding after the five year lull. The Navy and RAF view was that after the lull it would be their two services which would have to expand at the Army's expense.[54]

Alexander was almost pleased with the COS paper.[55] After some questions about the 'five plus five' rule and deterrence, he asked whether it would be possible to achieve balanced forces with a budget of £540-£550m. Cunningham's view was that balance could not be achieved with so little. The COS then rehearsed their disagreements over NS and over the nature of the threat against Britain. Once again the division between the Army on one hand and the Navy and RAF on the other became clear. Simpson defended the Army's adoption of 'level peacetime expenditure' by citing Montgomery's belief that national economic recovery should precede military reconstruction. Attlee himself later reminded the COS of their failure to produce what was required.[56] Their total estimates then stood at £662m for 1948/49. This was too much in excess of the ceiling of £600m, a ceiling which, in any case, might have to come down by £50m or £60m. The Army's position came under increasing scrutiny, and their insistence on quoting peacetime expenditure figures was again questioned. A budget of £662m was unthinkable, thought Attlee, but he deferred discussion of such matters until Montgomery's return to Britain.

For some months, the Army had seen the occupation commitment as increasingly important, as something other than mere 'peacetime military expenditure'. The occupation certainly had low priority in War Office thinking, but there was growing concern that retrenchment might go too far. At one point McCreery had warned that BAOR was in danger of becoming a 'military kindergarten':

> BAOR is in the process of transition from a strong, experienced and efficient field army to a large scale training organisation. This transition will be complete by 1949, by which time Rhine Army will be 70% composed of National Service Soldiers posted to this command with less than three months service.[57]

Both Sholto Douglas and McCreery considered that further run-down would also lead to internal security problems.[58] At the end of July, the COS outlined the reasons for the occupation and assessed the implications of withdrawals:

> British forces are required in Germany for the preservation of internal security, the repression of any signs of German resurgence and as a counter to Soviet influence ... The exigencies of the manpower situation will make it necessary to reduce British forces in Germany from now onwards, but there is no intention to liquidate the occupational commitment, at least until the conclusion of a treaty with Germany... The strategic effects of an accelerated withdrawal from Germany would be to increase the risk of a resurgence of German power ... Any accelerated withdrawal from Germany would also permit the Russians to extend an unchecked influence to the borders of Holland and Belgium.[59]

Later in the summer, the COS received another paper from McCreery on the future organisation of BAOR.[60] McCreery called for a force of one armoured, one infantry and one airborne division (less one parachute brigade), three armoured car regiments and one independent armoured regiment. Any units which had to be reduced to cadre strength would be reactivated after January 1950. BAOR would continue to be organised on a static, administrative basis, but with the ability to move three major units (i.e., a battalion or regiment) anywhere in the zone in an emergency. McCreery gave a concise definition of the tasks then facing BAOR:

> the primary operational task of the [BAOR] will remain as at present, to aid the civil power in the maintenance of law and order and enforcing Military Government orders in the British Zone of GERMANY. In the event of a peace treaty being signed, [BAOR] will assist in ensuring that the terms of such a treaty are carried out, and will enforce sanctions if necessary when this is NOT done. If NO peace treaty has been signed, assistance will be given in ensuring that the provisional government of the Western Zones carries out its obligations. [Emphasis in original].

The type of army units needed in BAOR were 'of high mobility with the ability to search; great fire power is NOT required. It follows that the most suitable units for the operational task are armoured car regiments and infantry battalions'. The RAF would not be needed. Based upon McCreery's recommendations, the War Office produced a revised order of battle for 31 March 1948: one infantry division, two district headquarters (with the minimum necessary administrative troops), one armoured brigade group, one parachute brigade and three armoured car regiments. The bulk of another airborne division would eventually arrive from Palestine and would replace the parachute brigade and one of the district HQs. Montgomery supported the McCreery plan and considered that 'this force, together with the Allied contingents of Belgian, Danish and Norwegian troops, is adequate for internal security duties in Germany.'[61] Yet Attlee remained doubtful as to the need for maintaining a large army, given that in the event of an invasion of Europe the British Army would be unable to put up much resistance.[62] He also wondered how long it would be necessary to station forces in Germany. Alexander advised that the situation was too volatile after the recent breakdown of the London Council of Foreign Ministers (CFM) and that it was important to be aware of 'the danger of creating a vacuum to be filled by other powers'.

The starting point for the 1948 round of Cabinet/COS disagreements over the size and shape of the armed forces is to be found in a 9 March memorandum, in which Alexander asked that a review of equipments and dispositions of the services be carried out prior to the preparation of the 1949/50 defence estimates.[63] This stock-taking review was also to be the preliminary to the organisation of a 'continental strategy'.[64]

In early April Montgomery submitted a paper to his colleagues in which he attempted to lay the blame for the disorganisation of defence upon the lack of an 'impartial Chairman' for the COS, with the result that meetings too often descended into inter-service rivalry. Without a major reorganisation of the defence structure, Britain would make no progress towards a unified defence policy and balanced national forces, and would be denied efficient and expandable command and control systems, essential in the event of war.[65] Hollis disagreed.[66] Similarly, Tedder argued that the failure of the present system lay with the incumbents of the posts, not with procedures. The problem was that the COS had been unable to recommend to Alexander the size and shape of the armed forces, within given economic and demographic constraints. Tedder had warned of this on 2 April 1947 but his advice had been ignored. In due course, 'pro rata' cuts on all the services had been made. The fault was with the individual members of the COS and their inability to agree. He was clear that 'the remedy lies in our own hands' and suggested that 'what was needed to complete the framework of our defence was "a long-term plan for the land forces on the same basis as, and closely co-ordinated with, the plans already outlined for the sea and air forces". That plan we have not yet got and until we get it no useful progress is possible.'[67] Two days later, the First Sea Lord contributed a memorandum in which he laid the blame for the lack of progress towards 'balanced national forces' [original emphasis] at the Army's door. While the Navy and RAF had both been working upon long-term policies, the Army had only been examined 'in the light of present day commitments'.[68] The Army had earlier made its case in the following, not very convincing, way:

> Although the Navy and the R.A.F. have produced a long-term twelve-year plan for the size and shape of their forces, the Army... have adopted a level peacetime expenditure. It is not yet possible therefore to make a firm estimate of Army forces in 1957.[69]

The following month, Montgomery tried to find a way out of the dilemma by reverting to the tactic of passing the problem back to the government. He argued that the Cabinet should be asked to decide whether, in view of present circumstances, war was considered inevitable. If so, when would it occur and what resources would be allocated to the Services to prepare for the conflict? He could no longer accept that war – be it 'accidental' or otherwise – would not break out before 1957, arguing that it was 'unrealistic to work on the philosophy that there will be no war for a predetermined number of years. We are not ready for war and, as a result of economic and manpower stringency, can make no really adequate preparation. We should ask Ministers how long they are prepared to accept this state of unreadiness.'[70] Tedder sought to defuse the situation. In 1947 the Cabinet and COS had already approved the policy of preparing to meet an emergency in 1957.[71] The Cabinet could not be expected to go any further until a long-term plan for the reorganisation of the services was produced. The Navy and Air Force had produced their plans, as requested by the Cabinet, but so far the Army had failed to produce an equivalent:

> The Admiralty and Air Ministry plans had been based on the provision of a deterrent force, and a minimum nucleus to meet war requirements and on which expansion could be based to meet an emergency in 1957, if time and resources were available. The Army plan however, related only to meeting peacetime commitments, i.e. the maintenance of occupation forces, the reorganisation and training of the Territorial Army and of the National Service intake.

Cunningham suggested that, since the COS had agreed to provide the Defence Committee with a long-term plan by the autumn, the Army should work on an order of battle for 1957 designed to meet the agreed three pillars of strategy. Occupation forces, he felt, should be accounted for in a supplementary estimate. Montgomery believed that he had already provided the relevant information. The peacetime Army, he said, would cost £270m annually from 1950. In addition, a staggering £300m annually would be required for five years from 1952 to bring the Army up to the mark by 1957. This would provide an Army of 11 divisions – the minimum necessary to meet all commitments. Montgomery had thus provided the calculations required, albeit somewhat disingenuously. His colleagues agreed that Montgomery's questions should not be put to the government and that they should see whether all the necessary information had in fact now been provided to enable a long-term plan to be drawn up.

In mid-June the COS made yet another attempt to reconcile the formulation of defence policy with the resources available.[72] The COS had before them memoranda by Montgomery and Tedder, both dealing with the size and shape of the armed forces. In his paper, Montgomery spoke of the need to prevent unco-ordinated planning and 'acrimonious' inter-service wrangles.[73] He proposed three principles. First, the only way by which the allies would be able to knock out Russia in war was by 'the development of air power'. Second, to enable the first, the three pillars must be maintained. Finally, to secure an effective air base in the West it was essential that Russia be held as far east as possible, allowing bomber forces to operate from the UK and Western Europe. Once again,

Montgomery seemed to bow to the strength of the air strategy but ensured, as he did so, that the Army was given a crucial role. His priority was to secure the bases and then develop the air offensive:

> Agreement on this would not mean that we must neglect the development of our bomber forces until we have secured our bases. This would manifestly be nonsence [sic]. But we must win the first battle first, if we are to be in a position fully to develop our air power in the decisive battle.

Tedder's memorandum began by referring to the May 1947 defence policy document, the aim of which had been to decide on a basic strategy and allow subsequent planning for the shape and size of the forces to take place.[74] The three pillars had been defined and had come to be accepted as the basic strategy, but so far no agreement had been reached on the disposition of the forces in the long term. The reasons were clear to him: the role of the Army on the outbreak of war had not yet been defined, neither had the method of training and distributing the National Service intake. Tedder then referred to Alexander's memorandum to the COS of 23 August 1947. In it, Alexander had set the annual budgetary ceiling of £600m, had articulated the 'five plus five' rule, and had stated that in an unpremeditated war Britain must 'fight with what we have'. Tedder suggested that the Alexander directive meant that risks would have to be taken: it would no longer be possible to have all the forces which might be considered necessary on the outbreak of war. Limited resources could not be dissipated; only those forces 'which give us the best chance of survival' should be maintained. Alexander had stressed the need for deterrent forces and admitted that 'our policy for the next five years would bear no relation to any state of preparedness for war.' He had called for the competing bids for defence resources to be ranked. So far the COS had failed to meet his requests, pro rata cuts had been made, and more would follow. The recent stock-taking had exposed severe weaknesses, especially in two of the three pillars: defence of the UK (the air defence system was 'virtually non-existent' and the bomber force Tedder described as 'utterly inadequate'), and the maintenance of the Middle East base. Stock-taking in the European countries had disclosed even more alarming weaknesses.

Tedder felt that the only way forward was for each country to concentrate on getting its own house in order. Two questions had to be asked. Should short-term steps be taken now which may undermine long-term plans; was the situation severe enough to warrant this? And 'to what extent should Great Britain commit land and air forces, other than those already on the Forces of Occupation, to a campaign on the Continent?' As long as Alexander's directive remained in force, Tedder believed that no short-term steps should be taken which might undermine long-term planning. As far as the second question was concerned:

> assessments have been made of the Army commitment… and also of the additional sea and air commitments involved… The sea and air commitments can be added to the long-term plans already drawn up by the Admiralty and Air Ministry. The Army commitment however cannot be related to those of the Navy and the R.A.F. in the absence of a long-term plan for the Army similar to those drafted for the other two Services. Moreover, until the plans for all three Services are on a common basis of readiness in 1957/8, it is impossible properly to consider the balance between the Services and their relation to each other or to produce the "properly co-ordinated inter-Service long-term plan" called for by the Prime Minister.[75]

Montgomery then contradicted his earlier position regarding the commitment of troops to Germany and talked of a force of four divisions. Although no addition to Army manpower, this would now involve reinforcing BAOR with two divisions from the UK (the same would apply for MELF). He wanted this plan to be agreed first, and then to assess the cost of it. Tedder replied that, although the role of the Army had been made clear in DO (47) 44, 'since then our policy vis-a-vis Russia had changed and we were faced with the political necessity of giving support with land forces to the Western Union.' In Tedder's opinion, any commitment was of a political rather than strategic kind. He then reversed Montgomery's argument – until the cost of the plan to keep the Russians as far east as possible was known, it would be impossible to decide whether or not it was feasible – and tried to force Montgomery into producing the long-term plan which could, in the contemporary technological and economic climate, only be damaging for the Army.

A break-through occurred in mid-August, during the Berlin crisis. Montgomery presented the COS with a paper entitled 'Role of the Army on the Outbreak of War and Plan for Long-Term Development of the Army to fulfil its Role.'[76] The Berlin crisis was a gift for Montgomery: a role for the Army could no longer be denied, certainly in terms of Western Union defence. The moment was auspicious to enter into long-term planning along the same lines as the other services. He now suggested six roles for the Army:

- the land battle in defence of the WU;
- helping to secure Britain's position in the Middle East;
- garrisons abroad for the defence of sea and air bases vital to the maintenance of SLOC;
- civil defence in the UK;
- air defence of the UK;
- the nucleus for expansion.

He then returned to the point, made earlier in the year, that Britain should deploy to Europe two army corps of two divisions and supporting arms (e.g., artillery) each. This could be done at no extra cost, especially since two of these divisions already existed – potentially – in BAOR. Once again, Montgomery appealed to higher 'political' reasoning: for the sake of the morale of the Western Union, 'anything less would be utterly unacceptable.' His colleagues were pleased with his efforts.[77] Although his paper had not yet given the required costings, Montgomery had at least provided a basis for assessing what peacetime forces would be required to enable expansion on the outbreak of war. The War Office was to be asked to provide the necessary statistics.

On 8 September the COS discussed overall manpower requirements, following another memorandum on the subject from the increasingly emboldened Montgomery.[78] Montgomery had described the current planned ceilings for the manpower of the Army: 1 January 1949 – 371,500; 1 April 1949 – 351,500; 1 January 1950 – 300,000. This would not be enough, and Montgomery proclaimed it his 'duty to inform the Chiefs of Staff that it will not be possible for the Army to carry out its tasks in 1949 with these ceilings.' What was needed for 1949 was a male strength of 400,000, and this could only be achieved with a period of National Service of two years. The COS approved Montgomery's comments. Alexander, however, responded that defence policy – even in the critical short term – had to respond to economic realities, and spoke of 'a knife edge on one side of which was economic disaster and on the other grave military risks.'[79] And if progress towards a national strategy formulated within budgetary parameters was slow, the COS must accept a good deal of the blame.[80] With the new session of Parliament to begin on 25 October, Alexander insisted once more that the COS supply the report, for which he had been waiting since February 1947, by 15 October at the latest.

The data necessary for planning the size and shape of the armed forces were finally collated in early October, just in advance of Alexander's deadline.[81] In his memorandum, Montgomery dismissed previous attempts at costing the size of the Army, either because they had been based on 'a very different role', and had not taken account of the Western Union, or because they had envisaged a 'no war' period and had not provided for preparation for war. The figures Montgomery now provided amounted to 'the first estimate based realistically on a clear definition of the role of the Army at the outbreak of war'. This 'clear definition' was a result of the Berlin crisis. For his part, Tedder explained that projections for the RAF did not include any forces for WU defence other than the TAF already stationed in Germany. Since the RAF would not have time to expand, the RAF in peace 'will be identical with our front line in war.' In this case the RAF, unlike the Army, would have to be 'kept constantly at a high state of readiness.' Tedder listed the tasks of the RAF on the outbreak of war:

- air striking force as a deterrent and as Britain's principal defence;
- protection of the UK against air attack, with the Army;
- co-operation with the Navy to secure the SLOC;
- defence of the Middle East in support of the Army;
- support for a corps of four divisions on the Continent and protection of the LOC from UK to the Continent.

The joint report set out to define three things: the roles of the three services; the forces available at the outbreak of war; and the cost of build-up and re-equipment:

> Now that the relevant information is available for all three Services prepared on a common basis and set out in a common form, it is suggested that the procedure should be first to consider the roles of the three Services ... and secondly to consider whether the planned forces ... make a reasonable provision for carrying out these roles.

The paper gave the standard interpretation of the roles of the services. As far as the budgetary ceiling was concerned, the paper mentioned the Defence Committee meeting of 14 January 1948 where the Defence Committee had '"agreed that for the years immediately succeeding 1948/49, the annual financial provision for defence should not exceed £600 million".' But since January, the Berlin crisis and unsettled conditions generally had meant that 'greater provision has had to be made for meeting existing commitments and against the possibility of an emergency in the near future'. One of those commitments was, of course, the recently formed Western Union for which the January meeting had also not been able to account. The Western Union had changed the situation for the Army in particular:

> As things stood, there would have been a considerable force of the Territorial Army available in the United Kingdom at the outbreak of war without any particular role assigned to them other than the defence of the United Kingdom. *Now that we are committed to giving limited help on the Continent to the Western Union*, the force remaining in the United Kingdom at the outbreak of war (which according to the Army plan will not be equipped to field scales) will not be so big. It may perhaps be considered that this force is not an unreasonable strategic reserve for the kind of war envisaged. [Emphasis added].

Perhaps the most important part of the paper, however, was the compilation of the estimates. That these were considerably in excess of the ceiling of £600m was not lost on the COS, and Montgomery immediately began to draw uncomfortable conclusions: 'it was quite unreal to suppose that the country could afford defence expenditure on this scale during peacetime. If this was so, then it would clearly be impossible, in peacetime, to have adequate forces ready for battle on the outbreak of war.' It seemed financially impossible, in peacetime, to prepare the forces for battle in 1957 as long as the £600m ceiling was maintained. The government was therefore faced with a difficult decision:

> If the Government decided that the forces must be fully ready to go to war immediately on the outbreak of hostilities, then they must be prepared to meet the financial costs involved. If these financial costs could not be met, then it must be accepted that the armed forces could not be made 100% ready to fight on the outbreak of hostilities and a decision must be made of the direction in which risks must be taken.

So, although the three services had finally come to the point of agreeing to prepare long-term assessments using common formats, the main problem had not yet been overcome. The confrontation had now hardened between Cabinet and COS, between budget and strategy: the government's pressure for decision had simply caused the COS to 'close ranks'. It was agreed that a staff conference should be called.

The staff conference took place on 13 October.[82] Alexander suggested that decisions should now be made as to how the commitments of the forces could be met, especially the Army's. He now considered that long-term planning to meet threats, within economic limits, was not so urgent and insisted that the Army should cut its manpower projection of 433,000 for 1949: neither men nor money were available in sufficient quantity. However, the same old problem loomed: which commitments should be cut back? If a 'different occupation policy in Germany' were feasible, there might be manpower savings to be made. But with the occupation of Germany becoming ever more important in political and Cold War terms, Alexander had difficult decisions to make: 'as a personal generalisation he still felt that the provision of Air Defence, including offensive air forces, must be a first priority, the defence of our sea communications being a second priority.' Differences between the Navy and the RAF on the one hand and the Army on the other were discussed. The Army needed its manpower problem to be resolved first: re-equipment and re-organisation could come later. The other two, highly technological services, however, had precisely the opposite view. They both required 'a continuous flow of equipment during peacetime since both services must be ready to play their part in active operations immediately on the outbreak of a war'. As in 1947, the Navy and RAF did not anticipate any warning time, or any time to build up, before their services would be required. The Army could not be a fully equipped, standing force; that would be unsustainable and probably provocative, hence its concentration on methods of expansion.

On 9 November the COS (now Tedder, Slim and Fraser) suggested the establishment of a tri-service working party, the task of which would be to make joint proposals for the strength of the armed forces over the next few years within a total budget of £700m.[83] Slim argued that the Army could not make any further cuts: there was no fat left to trim and the 1949 estimates were already at the minimum. The Army's requirement of £325m for 1949 was based upon 'existing commitments in the present cold war', 'the essential structure of the Army', and 'the ability to "fight with what we have got".' Slim suggested that these should be the basic criteria for all services. If this were done, the Navy might be allocated £185m, the RAF £200m and the Army £310m. With research and development costs, this would amount to a budget of £780m for 1949. Without this, Slim warned, Alexander might be unable to prevent further, arbitrary cuts. To pre-empt the Treasury, Slim suggested that the COS might investigate, as a second stage, what the implications would be of making further cuts. The only likely saving (of about £60m, to bring the total for 1949 down to £720m) would be in the area of short-term readiness, i.e., 'reversing the decisions lately taken to enable us to "fight with what we had got"':

It did not appear that any other substantial saving was possible for next

> year without affecting the essential structure of the Services, for even if it were decided to reduce present commitments, e.g., by withdrawal from Malaya or Berlin or by cutting the forces in Germany, the economies effected would have no great effect on the estimates for 1949.

Later in 19 November, with Treasury pressure mounting, the COS decided to re-examine the situation under something similar to Slim's three headings: the manpower structure of each service, the ability to meet present commitments; and readiness for war.[84] Alexander then dropped any reservations about the working party, provided it had a neutral chairman. The working party, under Harwood, was duly appointed to consider the three year period from April 1950, excluding the estimates for 1949/50. The target was for an average expenditure during these years of £700m. British defence policy was to run in three periods:

- **Present**; current occupation tasks, garrison commitments and 'the necessity to wage the "Cold War" effectively';
- **Near Future**; i.e., an unpremeditated war;
- **More Distant Future**; 'the necessity for a foundation for re-armament programme calculated to enable us to meet a premeditated war effectively by 1957'.[85]

In a later memorandum the new CIGS gave his own views of the future of the Army,[86] and suggested that manpower should be allocated in the following order of priority:

1. "Cold war" troops; internal security, occupation forces and garrisons;
2. Emergency measures in order of priority UK, Middle East, Rhine Army;
3. 'Q aftermath' tasks (i.e., civil assistance following attack);
4. Long-term preparations.

Slim then suggested that the Army's overstretch problem might be tackled by creating a UK-based strategic reserve of three infantry brigades, one of which would have to be taken from BAOR. He also suggested that the strength of BAOR be reduced from 57,000 to 51,000, a decision which would need 'Governmental approval'. In an appendix to the paper the current strength of BAOR was given as 19 infantry battalions and 9 armoured regiments. Their 'existing and possible operational tasks' were described as 'occupation duties'. The 'possible reasons for reinforcement from UK in 1949' of BAOR, with a force of only three infantry battalions, were given as 'internal security'. Slim's 'commitment' was, quite clearly, more a matter of cold than hot war.

On 7 December Alexander once again vented his frustration upon the COS. They had provided the detailed assessments required of the effects on each service of cuts in resources, but had not yet done enough to bring their estimates down. During discussion the COS agreed that the RAF should be cut last since 'neither of the other Services could get on without the Royal Air Force, and furthermore the striking power of the Air Force, was the greatest deterrent to any would-be aggressor'. But the Army and Navy could not be cut either.

The Army's role in Germany was described as one of providing political and moral support, with no reference to Montgomery's earlier idea of preparing to fight on the Rhine:

> our forces in Germany, though they were not strong enough physically to prevent the Russians from sweeping across Europe, were a most important factor in stimulating the moral resistance of the Western Union Nations to Communism, and thus from preventing a war from breaking out.[87]

CONFRONTATION TO COMPROMISE: 1949-50

The report of the Harwood working party was discussed by the COS at the end of March 1949.[88] The terms of reference had been to provide, on a genuinely inter-service basis, a long-term assessment of the size and shape of Britain's armed forces, within the financial parameters of a defence budget of £700m p.a. over three years.[89] The report looked from two perspectives at the problem of an outbreak of war. First was the matter of preparing for accidental or unpremeditated war, second 'the longer term risk of war in 1957 or subsequently'. The COS accepted that the requirements of the Cold War and other peacetime commitments would involve larger land forces than might otherwise be necessary. The problem of unpremeditated war would be met by keeping at a high state of readiness those elements of each service which were designed to absorb the first impact of war. Only after these two demands had been met should any excess capacity be diverted towards preparing for a premeditated war in 1957 or thereafter.

Slim regretted that the report did not make enough of what he called an 'active cold war policy' which could be an additional deterrent to war. Force planning ought, he felt, to reflect the assumption that Britain could conduct 'an offensive cold war policy aimed at separating Russia from her satellites and disintegrating Russia from within.' A disagreement then developed between Slim and Tedder, each trying to show that 'fighting the Cold War' was a vital task performed best by his own service. Tedder resented the assumption that the Cold War was primarily a task for land forces; the Berlin airlift, 'perhaps the most important single factor in the cold war', was a 'severe strain' for the RAF and so, by implication, it was the RAF and not the Army which should be assigned any additional funding. Harwood argued that the Cold War demanded a larger peacetime Army than might otherwise be the case. The manpower allocated to the Army was only 'disproportionately large' if compared to the Army's tasks on the outbreak of war.

Generally, the COS were happy with the report. The report was 'courageous' and 'a tribute to the Joint Service spirit'. But in the end, the report was welcomed mainly for the boost it gave the COS in their dispute with the government. The achievement of the report, therefore, was less that the services had come together and worked out a strategic plan than that they had united in adversity against the Cabinet. The COS were unequivocal: without a larger budget, commitments would have to be cut or re-equipment would have to be limited. The strength of forces in Germany and the size of the National Service scheme were mentioned as likely areas of retrenchment. Cuts would have to be made somewhere unless the budget was increased.

Detailed examination of the report was to take place within each department. The problem of collating the three responses soon presented itself. Alexander was concerned that the three papers did not appear to have been prepared on a common basis.[90] He sensed that all was not well with the COS response, and was 'most concerned that they should not drift back into the old position in which each Service approached the problem with preconceived and fixed ideas.'[91] Alexander warned the COS that the Chancellor of the Exchequer would have to be convinced that their plans were genuinely tri-service, otherwise arbitrary cuts would again follow. He appealed to the COS 'collective responsibility' to advise the Government without interference from 'other considerations'.

Analysis of the Harwood report continued for several days. At one point the COS discussed whether the report should be forwarded to ministers as it stood, or should be accompanied by other comments and reports. One problem was immediately visible: the report recommended expenditure of £750m p.a., whereas the COS had been asked, and had agreed, to produce assessments within the lower figure of £700m.[92] The question of the distribution of the report became more delicate as time went on. The COS were wary of being too critical of the report, both because they had commissioned it and because without it, or something like it, they would be more vulnerable to arbitrary cuts imposed by the Treasury. On the other hand, they wished to avoid any suggestion that £700m was an adequate defence budget. Slim's reference to this dilemma illustrates again the different roles then thought appropriate for each service. If the Harwood report were implemented, Slim would have to ask that the Army concentrate on 'its present peacetime commitments rather than on building up and equipping the forces required for war'. In Slim's view:

> The Army's problem was rather different from that of the other two Services, for though the Navy and Air Force both had inescapable "cold war" commitments, their chief aim must be to make sure that they would ultimately be ready for war. The Army, of course, could not altogether abandon preparation for war - for example they clearly could not abolish AA Command – but he thought that it would be better to accept the fact that the Army would be ill-equipped at the beginning of another war than to allow its structure to be destroyed by a further reduction in size which, in effect, would mean the abolition of some existing regiments. He would not make proposals on these lines, however, unless he actually had to face the fact that the Army's allotment would be no more than that shown in the Harwood Report.

In the end, the COS agreed not to forward the report as it stood but to consider it further and then to get 'Ministerial guidance'.[93]

Slim reiterated his position a week later.[94] He wanted the COS to make clear that the Harwood 'solution', if imposed, would mean that the three problems with which the working party had been concerned – the Cold War, an unforeseen emergency and long-term (i.e., post-1957) preparation – could not all be tackled and that one would have to be chosen as a priority. If, in the end, the annual defence budget was indeed to be no more than £700m, then Slim was clear as to how it should be allocated: 'the decision ought to be that while the Army would have to devote itself primarily to the cold war and peacetime commitments at the expense of preparations for war, the reverse should be the case with the Navy and Air Force.'

The COS agreed to discuss their re-drafted views of the report with Alexander on 10 June, eventually meeting him on 16 June.[95] Slim stressed that the goal of expenditure on land forces should be to ensure that the Cold War was won. Alexander now accepted this point and agreed that the priority for the Navy and the Air Force should be preparation for a 'fighting war'. In the resulting paper, the COS argued that, within its terms of reference, the Harwood working party could not have produced larger forces and may even have been too generous, by under-estimating the cost of some proposals:

> The Harwood proposals confirm our previous opinion that the forces obtainable on £700 million per year would be seriously inadequate to carry out our foreign and colonial policy in peace and the requirements of strategy in war.[96]

If the Harwood proposals were to be taken up, then the Army's necessary concentration on fighting the Cold War would undermine long-term re-equipment and preparation to fight a 'shooting war'. As far as Germany was concerned, the report would necessitate a drop in the strength of BAOR from the current 58,000 to some 47,900 in April 1949. Two years later, there could only be one division (21,600) in BAOR. This would have to be withdrawn into a small area, for ease of resupply from the United Kingdom. For reinforcement of these troops, in response to continuing pressure from the WUC-in-C, the Harwood proposals would permit only a 'relatively small' contribution. Furthermore, the reduction of occupation forces would make a clear statement to the Western Union, undermining any benefits gained from a promise of small scale reinforcement. Even the British air contribution, which had so far been thought large enough to offset the weakness of the commitment of ground forces, was threatened by the Harwood report, a prospect sure to alarm France and the Benelux countries. Even so, involvement in a campaign in Western Europe was far down the COS list of commitments:

1. Defence of the United Kingdom and its development as an offensive base;
2. The control of essential sea communications;
3. A firm hold in the Middle East and its development as an offensive base;
4. The delivery of a strategic air offensive from the United Kingdom and the Middle East;
5. 'Such assistance as we can afford, as a measure of self-preservation, to the forces of the Western Union.'

The Harwood plan made the final commitment particularly difficult:

> Even if we can count on some months' warning of an emergency, we should be unable, with the existing shape and size of our forces, to

> reinforce the Middle East and Western Union in time. The Harwood proposals aggravate this state of affairs. Under these proposals by 1953 the active Army would be so reduced that it is almost certain that all reinforcements would have to be drawn from the Territorial Army, and even the two higher priority divisions would not be fit for operations overseas until some four months after they had been embodied.

In fact, in every area of defence planning – the air contribution to the WU, the strategic air offensive from the Middle East, re-equipment, the speed of mobilisation, the role of National Servicemen and so on – the Harwood report meant penalties. By now, no service was entirely satisfied with the report and the Army, in addition to demanding provision for a 'considerable strategic reserve', felt that the report failed to concentrate on its chief task:

> the Harwood proposals do not give sufficient effect to the statement that the cold war should be covered primarily with land forces. We consider that the Army should give priority to this task. An essential feature of our cold war task is to satisfy the Western Union that we can provide a reasonable contribution of forces from all three services fit for war after a short period of intense preparation. The Army cannot fulfil its share of the task and meet its other cold war commitments without considerably more manpower and money than that allowed under Harwood.

The COS were ultimately unable to recommend that the Defence Committee accept the Harwood report. They made no alternative proposals and shifted the problem onto the laps of ministers: were ministers willing to accept the risks pointed out by the COS, and, if not, what additional funding would be made available?

In late July a new working party was established in succession to Harwood's. The Inter-departmental Committee on Defence Estimates, chaired by Sir Harold Parker, was charged with drawing up a provisional defence budget for April 1950 to March 1953.[97] The committee's terms of reference were a net annual budget of £800 million (with a further £10 million annually as a reserve) and with uniformed strength reducing from 700,000 at 31 March 1951 to 650,000 by 1952/53.[98] Each service department had, as requested, produced their own estimates for each of the three years. The problem was that, as ever, the overall totals considerably exceeded the figures permitted. Parker asked for strategic guidance as to where reductions could be made, and the COS duly met to discuss the matter.[99] Parker's memorandum showed that the total requested budget for 1950/51 amounted to £828.35 million, rising to £860.62 million and £881.85 million in the following two years. Manpower would stand at 703,000 in April 1951, 704,000 in April 1952 and 699,800 in April 1953. These were distressingly out of line with instructions and Parker was at a loss as to how to proceed. Should the services have a common timetable for re-equipment? The Army had made almost no plans for re-equipment for 1957, the Navy was expecting a 'reasonable degree of readiness' by that date, while the Air Force had embarked upon continuous re-equipment, ensuring that it would be the best placed of all the services at any time before 1957. Could the RAF be manned by fewer personnel? Could the Army reduce in size, in view of its Cold War tasks? Lamely, the COS felt unable to provide the necessary information, in spite of the knowledge that the Defence Committee was waiting to make plans for the next three years. Parker was merely advised to see whether any reductions could be made for the following year only. Once again, a familiar COS tactic can be observed: just enough was done to avoid being labelled irresponsible or unrealistic and inviting the imposition of arbitrary cuts, while at the same time ensuring that they were not drawn into making uncomfortable decisions.

The War Office response to the Parker Committee enquiry is worth examining in some detail, for the light it throws upon the Army's view of its current and future roles.[100] 'Victory in the Cold War', the War Office claimed, was the 'first essential'. The Cold War was expected to continue for several years and should be pursued even at the risk of delaying preparation for a premeditated war. As a concession to the possibility of war breaking out, the War Office was prepared to lay the foundations for rearmament for 1957 over the next three years but felt that if an unpremeditated war did break out, the only course of action was to do the best possible with the available resources. To wage the Cold War, an Army of around 355,000 would require equipment and resources to resist Communist pressure, maintain order, provide moral support, arms and other material support and fulfil treaty obligations.

These resources would not require huge expenditure, suggesting that the main objective was a simple one – the largest possible Army. Thus, the War Office listed the orthodox strategic requirements at the outbreak of war, took issue with none of them, but then claimed that the waging of the Cold War also required 'A clear demonstration that we will resist armed aggression, have plans ready for that contingency, and retain a firm hold on those bases from which we would launch our air offensive' and 'the provision of adequate military support for Western Union and the Atlantic

Pact'. Thus was the War Office's plan for the Army – involving a large uniformed strength but little in the way of costly equipment or other resources – tied firmly to concepts which might otherwise have undermined the Army's *raison d'être*. And, as if to dispel any possible accusation of preparing a continental strategy, the War Office gave its plan for the peacetime deployment in Germany:

> The Berlin garrison of one brigade will be unchanged. One infantry and one armoured division must continue to be in the British Zone, *if only from the point of view of satisfying Western Union.* [Emphasis added].

In the weeks following, Alexander managed to avert another COS/Cabinet deadlock over the size of the defence budget. In a letter to the COS[101] he followed up the Parker committee's request[102] for strategic guidance concerning short-term planning for 1950/51. COS reluctance or inability to provide advice had already delayed the work of the Parker committee on the short-term problem and Alexander insisted that this advice should be provided by mid-September. On 9 September, while discussing the allocation of the £800m defence budget, Fraser reported the Navy's willingness to accept a reduced allocation of £201m. The Army was willing to reduce its claim by £5m to £303m, giving the RAF an increased figure of £231m (a further £7m was to be allocated to the Western Union and £58m to the Ministries of Defence and of Supply). Slim commented that in accepting the reduced figure 'he was obliged to neglect readiness for an unpremeditated war and was concentrating on the cold war'.[103] The COS finally agreed, one week later, to provide the following estimates to Alexander:

	1950/51	**1951/52**	**1952/53**
Admiralty	201	201	201
War Office	307	304	302
Air Ministry	233	237	244
Western Union	7.5	4.5	0.5
MoS/MoD	62.5	62.5	62.5
Total	811	809	810[104]

These estimates were eventually incorporated into a full COS report to Alexander.[105] This document illustrates many of the tensions between the services. Britain's first object was to 'win' the Cold War, described as a 'war with Soviet Communism'. If it were lost then the other main enemy – Russia – would also have won without having to resort to the second main danger for the West, a 'shooting war'. But in their efforts to win the Cold War the West might provoke the Soviets into overt military action, unless they were convinced that the West was so strong that they dare not attack. It followed, therefore, that the West should both fight to win the Cold War and prepare quickly and firmly for a 'shooting war' in order to deter it. The bulk of Cold War tasks fell upon the Army:

> The greater part of [the Army's] units are already deployed overseas to meet Cold War commitments. There is little prospect of these commitments being reduced – the tendency is for them to increase... Unfortunately, the demands of the Cold War are, as far as the Army is concerned, largely antagonistic to preparation for a Major War. The Army, on any possible Budget, cannot effectively bear the burden of the Cold War and at the same time prepare fully for a Major War. One must have a preference; this should be the Cold War.

The Navy and the Air Force, on the other hand, should concentrate on preparations for real war. Thus, the position was that the Army would concentrate on trained manpower at the expense of re-equipment, while the reverse would be the case for the other two services. A budget of £810m could be made to work, but it was an irreducible minimum, below which there would be 'unacceptable defence risks' or the inability to meet certain commitments. The budget would prove inadequate in the event either of a surprise attack or of delays or limitations in American aid. The report as it stood, however, represented a 'great advance on the proposals contained in the Harwood report'. The Parker report allowed for the proportion of the Army garrisoned in Germany up to 1953 to be limited to one armoured division, one infantry division and one infantry brigade. The following table shows how this allocation compared with other commitments.

Active Army/Garrisons

	1/1/50	1/4/51	1/4/52	1/4/53
Germany				
Arm'd division	1	1	1	1
Inf. division	1	1	1	1
Inf. brigade	1	1	1	1

Austria				
Brigades	1	1	–	–
Trieste				
Brigades	1	1	1	–
Middle East				
Inf. division	1	1	1	1
Inf. brig. gp	2	1	1	1
Far East				
Inf. division	1	1	2/3	2/3
Br/Ghurka div.	1	1	1	1
Inf. brigade	1	1	–	–
United Kingdom				
Inf. division (- 1 brig. gp)	–	–	–	1
Brigades	1	1	2	1
Guards bns	2	2	2	2
Anti-air regts	24	24	24	24
Home service units (underposted)	16	26	28	24
Parachute brigade (underposted)	1	1	1	1
Total manpower				
	1/4/50	1/4/51	1/4/52	1/4/53
	364,400	339,500	335,750	332,750

In April 1953 the Army would still be facing equipment difficulties, especially with wheeled vehicles. By this date, however, the TA Field Force would have been equipped to war scales. The size of the Regular Army was such that even if Cold War commitments were to diminish, there would be little chance of regular reinforcement of either Western Europe or the Middle East. Reinforcement would have to be the task of the four TA divisions. Since these divisions would need a 'precautionary period' in which to prepare, emergency planning for war in the short term was simply inappropriate; Slim's preference for Cold War tasks and long-term preparation thus appears a matter of necessity as much as choice. As for the RAF, the following comment illustrates their disparaging view of taking on too great a commitment to Europe's defence:

> B.A.F.O. would continue to support B.A.O.R. in its occupational duties and, as our only existing Tactical Air Force, to keep alive the technique

> of Army support. This very small force has had to be depleted by two squadrons in order to reinforce Hong Kong and it is not known when they can be replaced.

With the size and shape of the armed forces to be discussed in Cabinet later the same day, the COS met Alexander for a preliminary staff conference on 15 November.[106] A breakthrough in the budget debate had taken place in the Defence Committee's 22nd meeting, with the Defence Committee having now agreed to a budget of £810m, subject to Cabinet approval.[107]

In spite of this breakthrough, it was just months before the familiar arguments began to surface. At a staff conference on 11 May 1950, Shinwell soon turned to the structure of Britain's armed forces.[108] His comments bore a familiar refrain: 'we must', he argued, 'cut our coat according to our cloth'. The 'present financial position' was a reality which would have to be reflected in decisions regarding Britain's defence: any increases in the defence budget for the coming year would be small, if at all. Were the services 'fully harmonized and balanced'? Was there any 'duplication of effort'? Were there any '"frills" which could be removed'? What would Britain require in the event of war in the short term? 'What was the basic minimum needed to put up some form of effective defence?' What would be needed if war broke out in the slightly longer term, when Britain's allies might be in a position to offer more assistance? As Alexander had done before him, Shinwell was trying to persuade the COS to agree among themselves a strategically coherent, balanced force posture, as a preliminary to removing those tasks and activities which appeared to be on the periphery. As their predecessors had also done, the COS tried to pass the problem back to Shinwell. The COS held that the size and shape of the armed forces was governed by two main considerations: the Cold War and the possibility of deliberate aggression by 1957. These two requirements clashed, especially for the Army. What could not be adequately prepared for was the prospect of war in the near future, in which case 'we should be very hard put to it to defend ourselves'.

Without a 'considerable warning period', Britain's air defences would be inadequate and might last no longer than one month of 'intensive fighting'. Based upon careful assessments of the character and timing of likely threats, Britain's forces could ensure that the best equipment became available at the time that the threat seemed most likely to materialise. If procurement of equipment were rushed then there was a danger that Britain would have inadequate, outdated equipment when the threat developed. Clearly, this meant that if the threat assessment proved to be too complacent and danger loomed in the near future, then Britain would also be ill-equipped. But it was impossible to cater for every contingency, and so the problem returned to the straightforward one of resources and was passed back to Shinwell:

> the Chiefs of Staff emphasised that it was quite impractical to be ready for war on a defence budget of the order of £780M. The present policy was based on the assumption that we would get adequate warning (of the order of eighteen months) that war was coming and that increased financial provision would then be made to enable us to build up our forces and to provide them with adequate equipment.[109]

Shinwell seemed sympathetic. In order to explain to his Defence Committee colleagues the 'hard facts of the position', he asked the COS to initiate a study on the implications of an outbreak of war 'in the near future – say in July 1951 – without adequate warning'. But the following comments suggest that his real intention was simply to paint such a grim picture of Britain's defences that North American aid and the implementation of the North Atlantic Treaty might follow more swiftly:

> He wanted to be able to explain to his colleagues the hard facts of the position and to point out to them just what we would have available to secure the basic requirements of our strategy if war broke out without warning. The report should also show how the position would improve if war came a bit later on, when we could rely on getting more assistance from our Allies. From what the [COS] had said, the paper would probably indicate that if war came at once, when we would be on our own, we should be in desperate straights [sic]. If war came later on the position might not be so bad. This would illustrate the essential need to obtain maximum benefit from our Allies. Much assistance would have to come from the American Continent. This all pointed to the urgency of pressing ahead with the implementation of the North Atlantic Treaty. He would like the [COS] to prepare this report at the earliest opportunity, but he realised that careful thought would have to be given to it. The paper, therefore, should not be unduly rushed.[110]

The COS met the following week to discuss the report requested by Shinwell, and the terms of reference under which the JPS should write the first draft.[111] Slessor felt that much of the information being sought had already been provided by the COS, in an earlier report to ministers.[112] Although a direct comparison was not possible, Slessor suggested that some similarities existed between the situation in 1938, leading up to the 'surrender in Munich', and current thinking about Shinwell's hypothetical war in 1951. If Britain were to improve its preparedness and the likelihood of being able successfully to resist attack, then higher defence expenditure would be required. The following simple message should, in Slessor's view, form the kernel of the new report for Shinwell:

> In presenting the state of our defences if war came by July 1951 it should be assumed that Europe would be overrun by the Russians and that they would set up rocket sites on the Continent for use against this country. There was no doubt about the weakness of our defence and it was time that the [COS] made the position quite clear to Ministers.

Elliot argued for a more subtle approach: the COS should not make the error of seeming to be driven solely by the wish to secure more funds for the services. He recommended an approach more in keeping with Shinwell's original request, one which would enable the minister to impress his Defence Committee colleagues as to the 'true position i.e. that if war came at a time when we would be on our own we should be in desperate straits.' The COS agreed that each service would set out its own likely position in the event of war in July 1951, showing forces available, the tasks these forces could undertake, and their shortcomings. The 'basic assumption', however, was the pessimistic one that 'if war broke out in 1951 the whole of Europe would be overrun and there would be a similar position to that which existed in 1940-41'.

The COS seem to have accepted the danger of war in the near future in an unusual way. The possibility of war in July 1951, just over one year into the future, should in retrospect have been near the top of their agenda. Yet this was the scenario in which they appeared least interested, or about which they thought least could be done. Perhaps the prospect of war in 1951 was thought to be too unlikely. Perhaps also the COS had been overcome by budgetary stringency and had decided to pass the problem of short-term planning, heavy as it was with spending implications and competition from other areas of government, back to ministers. Either way, the COS believed that longer term (1957) planning held better prospects for an adequately funded defence posture which reflected strategic thinking rather than Treasury limitations. Hence, on 19 June, Slessor suggested that a new, two part report should be prepared by the service departments. The first part would cover the short term, showing what level of defence could be produced for the sums likely to be made available in the next financial year, 1951-52. The second part would reverse the process and would 'deal with the sum of money which would be required if an adequate provision was to be made for fulfilling our obligations under the North Atlantic Treaty by 1957. He thought it was important to make an early start on the study of this subject in order to avoid hurried consideration of it in the autumn.' The outbreak of the Korean War on 23 June removed any complacency. Spurred on by Parker, the COS now took the initiative: short-term planning could no longer be determined by the availability of resources. An annual budget of £810m was inadequate: increases would be required, to at least £850m, for the next three years 'even if the size of the forces to be maintained was to remain as set out in C.O.S. (49) 313'.[113] The strategy/resources debate now took on an entirely different character and sense of urgency, as short-term planning for war finally began to move to the top of the COS agenda.

SUMMARY

Pressure for retrenchment in defence spending began to mount as soon as the war with Japan ended. Retrenchment was a reasonable proposition; even as the Cold War developed, few argued that wartime levels of spending should – or could – continue into the peace. The new government called for maximum reductions to be made. Yet it became increasingly obvious that if the government's objective was to be anything more than merely accelerating demobilisation, without incurring great security risks, then a plan would have to be drawn up which made strategic as well as financial sense. Thus the COS and their staffs – as the only officials capable of providing such advice – were expected to assist in their own attenuation, as they saw it. They resisted, and not until Christmas 1945 did they produce any estimates. During these months Germany and its occupation were peripheral issues. Civil and military officials all agreed that the occupation of Germany was not an operational task, was not a high priority in overall strategic thinking, and was not expected to be of long duration. Thus, the view that the occupation was a prime target for savings was hardly disputed on military grounds. The COS/Cabinet rift which was to develop had its roots less in the need for retrenchment than in the manner in which it was to be carried out.

In 1946 attention shifted to the possibility of reductions in forces and commitments in the longer term and a rift developed between civilian and military officials. The COS felt that while the availability of resources was an essential consideration in any military plan, be it at a strategic level or lower, strategic planning could not be conducted solely with a view to satisfying the Treasury – whatever this process could be called, it was not strategy. Yet the COS were even less willing to allow amateur strategists to draw up plans. The COS also shunned political decision-making; however much they could accept that cuts should be made, such decisions were for others to make. Finally, there was the most straightforward sentiment of all – self-preservation in the face of Treasury pressure. This had the effect first of uniting the COS and then dividing them, with loyalty to an individual's service taking prominence as times became harder; rivalry between the COS deepened as 1946 progressed.[114] While the COS had some sympathy for the economic problems facing the government, under pressure divisions developed and, in the end, the COS 'paid only lip-service to the priority of economic recovery.'[115] Earlier complacency regarding the run-down of forces and capabilities in Germany was gradually eroding, especially in the Army's view, although the commitment to Germany was still not of great significance. However, as resources of manpower diminished, there was increasing talk of the troops in Germany adopting a slightly more active role. Flying columns of lightly armoured vehicles could work out of garrison areas and deal with civil disturbance.

Alexander was keen for the 1948-49 financial planning year to be seen as the first genuinely post-war year of reconstruction. Debate with the COS in 1947 dashed any such hopes. The COS refused to allow the Future Defence Policy paper to cover matters of resources on a tri-service basis, in accordance with the general tenor of the paper, and preferred instead to pass the problem to the individual service staffs.

The same was true of the COS reaction to Alexander's request for an assessment of the risks of running down the forces. This lack of co-operation frustrated Alexander's plans, and reflected a deeper problem within the COS. Following an attempt to discuss retrenchment in current, as opposed to long-term, commitments, the Army made plain that such reductions, while certainly possible, would carry great political risks for Britain's position both in Germany and in the Middle East. Interest was thus deflected back towards long-term planning and resources, and it was here that the divisions within the COS were at their deepest. The services – notably the Army and the RAF – were simply not working to the same agenda. The Army sought to frame discussion of its future and its share of available resources, not in terms of long-term strategic plans, which stressed the defensive and offensive value of a strategic air assault, but in terms of current commitments, defined as 'political' and therefore exempt from the normal budgetary/strategic discussions. The occupation of Germany was increasingly seen in a more 'operational' light. This was not in the sense of military operations, which would have challenged contemporary faith in the strength of air power, but was more a matter of peacetime 'political operations' – the fighting of the Cold War. The Army associated itself as closely as possible with a task which was not covered during the debate on long-term planning and retrenchment and which was a much more difficult political matter, especially with the worsening of the Cold War, and it tried to prevent the RAF making a similar association. The RAF and the Navy, however, both thought in terms of building up forces for the point when the threat from the Soviet Union was calculated to be at its most serious.

The rivalry continued into 1948. By mid-June, however, shortly before the beginning of the Berlin blockade and airlift, it began to look as if Montgomery and the Army staffs would finally be drawn into the long-term planning process with the RAF and Navy. This would have been a great success for Tedder. But Montgomery's change of mind, such as it was, was simply a response to the possibility that, after the signature of the Brussels Treaty in March, Britain might move closer to a 'continental strategy'. Yet Montgomery was inspired more by the chance to improve the Army's lot in the overall planning process than by real faith in such a strategy. After the Berlin crisis, Montgomery became far more confident when dealing with his military and civilian colleagues. He was now willing to join a long-term planning process, essentially because a new, irrefutable sense of threat to land forces in Europe had emerged, and because Britain's recent commitment to the Brussels Treaty offered a rationale behind which the Army could shelter for the foreseeable future. The three services thus began to work to a more common agenda, although serious disagreements remained. This did not, however, make the COS more biddable. On the contrary, the COS now reverted to their earlier practice of uniting against the government, with Montgomery bluntly informing ministers that they should either fund strategic plans or face the risks. By the end of 1948 the division between COS and Cabinet was deep, with the chances of either side giving way diminishing. The Army now had its vital role in Europe, both as a current commitment and for the future. The need to maintain a presence in Germany, in order to avoid Russian and communist influence pouring into an ideological vacuum, was now set in the context of the fledgling Western Union.

Disagreements between the Army and the RAF continued into 1949, with Slim calling for more of an 'active Cold War policy' and anxious to prove that the Army was the best service to carry out such a policy. Slim was least content with the Harwood report, believing that it failed to present an indispensable, long-term, peacetime role for the Army. The Army saw its task as 'victory' in the Cold War – one which would take several years to complete – rather than preparation for premeditated war with the Soviet Union from 1957. By the end of the year some progress had been made and the COS at last found themselves agreeing upon the framework of an inter-service budget. The Army was still at pains, however, to stress that it would be unable to reinforce either the Middle East or Europe. The Defence Committee was finally persuaded to accept a budget of £810m, a marked increase on the target of £540m for which Alexander had been hoping in 1947. In early 1950 the familiar pattern seemed about to repeat itself, with Shinwell, the new Minister of Defence, calling for reductions and the COS threatening to pass the whole problem back as a 'political' matter. At this stage, short-term planning for military operations in Germany was not seriously considered. This suited both Shinwell and the Treasury, for budgetary reasons, and the Navy and RAF who saw in long-term planning an opportunity both to diminish the effect of budgetary pressure on strategic thinking and to undermine the Army's position. The Army was in any case not willing to enter into tri-service, long-term planning for military, non-Cold War operations. But then, with the invasion of Korea, the agenda began to reflect much more favourably the Army's position, as the need for short-term planning for military operations in Europe was perceived more keenly. Pressure for retrenchment had led to Britain's involvement in Germany being presented in a succession of different ways: first as peacetime, political, short-term tasks, then as the first stages of a longer-term requirement to be involved in Germany, although still for largely peacetime, Cold War, rather than militarily operational tasks. The shock of the Korean War provided the impetus towards a more military rationale for involvement in Germany. The Army grasped the opportunity to meet the other services on more equal terms.

3 The 'No War Rule'

There must be no return to the "no war for 10 years" assumption which so debilitated the services in the interwar years.

Bagnall[1]

Held to be a crowning example of budget-driven, civilian mis-management of military affairs, and an illustration of the perils of failing to consult professional defence planners in matters of national security, the no-war rule of 1919-1933 has clearly made a deep impression on strategic thinking in Britain. But what is most interesting about the above comment is not that it was made in mid-1990, but that it could also have been uttered in, and of, the late 1940s. During post-war discussion of strategy and resources a variation of the rule was developed which, like its predecessor, still crops up in contemporary defence policy debate in Britain.

The assumption behind the 1919 rule was that Britain would not be involved in a major war for a decade. In 1928 it became a 'rolling rule', when Churchill proposed that 'at any given date there will be no major war for ten years from that date'.[2] The rule originated at Cabinet level and the professional advice of the Foreign Office and the service chiefs was not sought. For some historians, seeking to establish reasons for Britain's lack of preparedness and strength in 1939, the rule was a 'calamitous act of policy' which 'took all sense of urgency and reality of purpose from strategic planning and defence policy', meeting the Treasury's requirement for 'a simple and effective weapon for crushing any service demands for research or development'.[3] Others have argued that the rule was a reasonable reaction to the economic, strategic and foreign policy conditions of the day, with the damage caused by it being 'less than is generally supposed'.[4] Most recently, it has been suggested that 'however questionable its continual rolling-forward may have become', the rule 'was not in itself foolish.'[5] In the early 1970s the *Journal of the Royal United Services Institute* hosted a debate on the origins and effect of the rule. The debate began with Silverman blaming the 'infamous' rule for Britain's impotence and lack of preparedness in the 1930s.[6] Booth responded by rejecting 'diatribes against the rule' as 'uncritical'.[7] Finally, Roskill sought to 'set the record straight' and decided, with some reservations, in favour of Booth's assessment.[8]

The no war rule of the late 1940s has provoked a debate along similar lines, with the bureaucratic origins of the rule and its effect on

Britain's readiness for war coming under scrutiny. Spice is added to the debate by the possibility that the lessons of the past were ignored. The 1940s version is held responsible for 'the slow, almost leisurely, pace with which the Armed Services, industry and the defence research establishments approached the problem of military research and development and future military operational requirements for the years immediately following the war.'[9] Some see the rule as an example of resource-led defence decision-making; an unwelcome situation, whatever the economic circumstances. In one interpretation, the rule was accompanied by a dearth of military planning, with the 'chief factor' being 'financial pressures' which resulted in 'a political rather than military decision, made by the Attlee government and not the Chiefs of Staff'.[10] Others have suggested that, however influential the Treasury, there were also sound strategic reasons for a suspension of threat perceptions and that, in any case, the COS were involved in drawing up the rule.[11] One historian sought, rather like Roskill, to settle the controversy and 'set the record a little straighter'.[12] Grove began by showing that the rule was in fact a 'five plus five' rule; major war was not considered a risk for the first five years, with the risk increasing only gradually in the following five. It was never a 'rolling rule' and always related to the decade after 1947. Budgetary considerations may have been considered, but the 1947 version was essentially the product of COS strategic assessments carried out between August 1946 and spring 1947. These assessments 'confirmed economy in shaping British defence policy in the period 1945-1950.' But when the rule was used as a cost-cutting tool by Alexander, in the summer of 1947, this was unpopular with the COS who had all along intended the rule to be a matter of 'strategic judgment, not a mere budgetary device'. Grove made it clear that the two rules were different in origin, construction, longevity and effect. Nevertheless, for many historians and defence analysts, the two rules and modern equivalents are but manifestations of budget-led mis-management of military affairs by civilians. Rejecting the notion that the 'no war rule' is a cyclical phenomenon, a core deficiency in British defence planning which is reinvented after every major conflict, this chapter examines the origins, course and significance of the rule of the 1940s. The rule is a short-hand expression which says a great deal about defence planning, and it is important to gauge its accuracy. The issue of the no war rule of the 1940s also encapsulates the 'budget, threat and strategy' debate explored in the preceding two chapters and which underlies all strategic thinking in post-war Britain.

THE FOREIGN OFFICE ORIGINS OF THE RULE

Condemnation of the 1919-1933 rule derives in large part from the fact that it was framed without the involvement of the service planners or the Foreign Office. The Foreign Secretary, Balfour, was not even present at key meetings when the rule was brought into being.[13] By the 1940s, of course, the pitfalls of the rule were deeply engraved in the Foreign Office's collective memory. Hence, both Frank Roberts of the Central Department and Robert Hankey of the Eastern Department 'were strongly opposed to any reversion to "the now notorious ten years rule", adopted in August 1919 and effectively only cancelled in November 1933.'[14] In spite of its reluctance to antagonise Britain's war-time ally the Soviet Union, and in spite of uncomfortable memories of the 'no war rule' of the 1920s, the Foreign Office nevertheless found itself drawn towards the idea. In mid-1944, only reluctantly acknowledging that the Soviet Union could be a threat after the war, the Foreign Office was squeezed out of its involvement in the post-war strategic planning process by the COS. Up to this point, the Foreign Office had been represented on the Post Hostilities Planning Sub-Committee (PHP).

The terms of reference of the PHP had been to examine 'non-strategic' aspects of the defeat of Germany, such as the surrender, the occupation and the zonal division.[15] Deliberating upon the wider principles which might guide British policy in Europe after the war, the PHP arrived at an early version of the rule, one based on assessments of Soviet capabilities:

> We consider that the USSR is unlikely to adopt an aggressive policy in the immediate post-war years, and that her main pre-occupations will be security and internal development... It is at present reasonable to work on the assumption that two years warning will be received before the outbreak of a major war ... Both the general and the air staffs have adopted this 2-year period as a provisional basis for post-war planning ...[16]

More evidence of early FO involvement is available in the minutes of the short-lived Committee on the Post-War Settlement, the first of the 'Attlee Committees', which record the following comment from Eden, the Foreign Secretary, in August 1943:

> It is probable that the cure of Germany will take many years and that the patient may undergo another series of paroxysms. It would be foolish to ignore such a danger and unwise to forget that *the danger period*

> *is not immediately, but 10, 15 or 20 years after a great war*. We must not again, as after 1919, let up all our guards just when the danger period is beginning.[17] [Emphasis in original].

Other than his preoccupation with German resurgence, this passage illustrates Eden's sensitivity to the mistakes of the 1920s, and his interest in a lengthy, threat-based planning period. The lesson of the 1920s had been learnt; something very different was now being proposed. The first rule was based on the idea that British interests would not be vulnerable *for* ten years; an open-ended, approximate judgement which could easily be extended, which of course it was. The post-1945 rule, which was always confined to the decade after 1947, was instead framed to reflect the notion that Britain's interests would be threatened *in* ten years, a finite projection based on an examination of the threat.

The Foreign Office, with its ambivalent position on the rule, had some influence on the military planners in whose mind, as Grove shows, the rule of the 1940s was to find its clearest expression. Citing a COS meeting of April 1946, Lewis has suggested that Foreign Office doubts over Soviet intentions 'coincided', in the spring of 1946, with COS fears of Soviet capabilities.[18] While the meeting does record the firmness of COS views, with Alanbrooke insisting that 'our long-term policy must take full account of the fact that Russia is a more dangerous potential enemy than Germany', and while it is known that these views were passed on to the Foreign Office,[19] the coming together of views was possibly more deliberate. The minutes of a meeting held at the end of August 1946 show that the convergence of COS and Foreign Office views was a straightforward, procedural matter, with the COS being informed 'that the pre-war practice has been for the Foreign Office to complete a yearly review of the political situation, on which had been based on the Chiefs of Staff's military review to the Committee of Imperial Defence.' In a letter to the Foreign Office the COS explained that 'without a similar paper from the Foreign Office, they would have no proper basis for setting out the strategical arguments ... the political and military aspects are complementary.'[20] Thus the Foreign Office, with its admittedly mixed views on the Soviet threat and the value of the rule, had direct, regular input to the military planning process. It seems unlikely, therefore, that the rule could have developed in isolation in the minds of the military planners. This observation contrasts only slightly with Grove's account of the military origins of the rule, but also clarifies the difference between the 1940s and 1920s versions of the rule.

THE MILITARY ORIGINS OF THE RULE

Grove has stressed the part played by assessments of the likely Soviet threat to British interests in the development of the rule. While the Soviet danger was clearly perceived, assessments of Soviet intentions and capabilities in the near future suggested that a number of years would elapse before the threat would materialise, thus providing a rational basis for the rule: a 'suspended threat assessment'. Yet even among the COS, calculations of the Soviet threat developed very tentatively during 1946 and 1947, the period when Grove sees the strategy-based rule coming to fruition. Grove found traces of 'no war rule' thinking in early 1946, but chose the *Review of Defence Problems* paper of April 1947 as the formal origin of the rule.[21] The following quotation from COS minutes taken at the end of 1947, however, shows that the rule originated at least as early as October 1946, in the period when the COS view of the Soviet threat was less blunt and hawkish:

> In October, 1946, the Joint Intelligence Sub-Committee had estimated that the risk of war during the following five years was negligible, that this risk would increase during the following five years, after which the risk of war would sharply increase. This estimate was made over a year ago and the Joint Intelligence Committee were now revising it.[22]

Since the rule originated at a time when the perception of the Soviet threat was not at its clearest or firmest, it seems possible that the military origins of the rule could be traced elsewhere.

The experience of the Second World War, with saturation bombing by manned aircraft, the use of atomic bombs on Japan, the success of *blitzkrieg* armoured operations and the development of cruise and ballistic missile technologies, represented a dramatic change in the character of warfare. Strategic thinking would have to respond to – if not be directed by – the new weapons technologies available. The COS were aware of such developments and in January 1947 instructed the Defence Research Policy Committee (DRPC) to examine their impact.[23] As far as the development of the rule is concerned, the COS were influenced by technological considerations in three ways: the general effect of new technology on the conduct and likelihood of war; British vulnerability to air attack; and the timetable for Soviet acquisition of an atomic bomb.

Britain's plan for the beginning of the 1939-45 war, in agreement with the French, was to send an expeditionary force to the continent on the outbreak of war. This force was intended to delay the aggressor, enabling plans to be confirmed and military resources to be built up 'in an unhurried way.'[24] That this strategy ended in the ignominy of Dunkirk was not lost on Montgomery who, as CIGS, was determined not to allow a repetition of the mistake, which he felt had also been made in 1914. He believed there would be no 'period of grace' at the beginning of the next war,[25] and made frequent, vehement attempts to reorganise the British Army into a 'National Army' which would be 'ready from the start'.[26] Modern technology was seen to support Montgomery's convictions. In January 1947 Slim, then Commandant of the IDC, reported to the COS the IDC opinion that in the next war there would probably be 'no time to develop a war potential after the war, using atomic and B.W. [bacteriological warfare] weapons, has begun'. The COS were in 'general agreement' with Slim's report.[27] The next step was to establish the point in the future at which technology, in the form of developing Soviet war potential, would transform a latent threat into an actual one. If, in terms of weapons technology, the Soviet Union was behind the West, then it made sense to try to maintain the gap by, for example, banning the export of machine tools to the Soviet Union, provided this did not provoke conflict. It also made sense to calculate the point at which the Soviet Union would close the gap, and for the West to use those years or months for planning and preparation.

The second technological consideration concerned Britain's vulnerability to air attack. The First World War had left Britain with a radically altered view of its relationship with the Continent and of national security; 'for the first time in her history [Britain] really *was* vulnerable... to a form of attack against which there seemed no possible form of defence.'[28] In the uncertain months after VE Day the COS urgently examined Britain's defences – especially air defences – and tried to calculate the time it would take to bring those defences up to the mark. The results of their examinations were not encouraging: Britain's fighter and anti-aircraft defences were unco-ordinated, ill-equipped and would probably not be able to provide an effective defence against air attack 'in the next few years'.[29] The COS learnt that it would take two years of planning and re-equipment to redeem the situation.[30]

Finally, the atomic bomb posed a problem of a different order and, given the quality of the air defence against manned bombers (at that time the only available delivery vehicle), by far the most alarming. The risks and opportunities of atomic power had a paralysing effect on the COS, certainly contributing to the adoption of the rule. It was argued in 1945 that attempts to plan beyond 1950 would be fruitless 'since the general development of atomic weapons and atomic energy may then produce unforecastable implications.'[31] This view was confirmed some months later by a Joint Technical Warfare Committee report which stated that atomic power would cause 'profound changes' which would not, however, be observed for at least five years.[32] Concerns were deepened by the knowledge that if Britain were to build and deploy its own atomic weapons, it would be necessary to construct an atomic pile which could not produce the necessary fissile material for, once again, some five years.[33] Montgomery, nevertheless, was eager to explore the implications of these new weapons, especially when in the hands of an adversary, as early as possible. He urged that an Army Conference, planned to be held in May 1947, explore the intricacies of an opposed landing against an enemy possessing atomic weapons, and the general implications of 'weapons likely to be in use in ten years time'. His COS colleagues did not disagree, but were inclined to postpone discussion of the effects of atomic weapons until the results of the Bikini Atoll tests could be known.[34]

The new technologies and strategies which grew out of the war clearly shaped COS thinking. Problems were seen in the shape and size of Britain's forces – especially the air defences – which would take a number of years to resolve. Advancements in Soviet weapons technology were constantly in the minds of the COS. Atomic weapons seemed likely to change everything, but so little was known about them that the COS felt it would take at least five years before they would even be in a position to discuss them sensibly. There were, therefore, several good reasons for the COS to have suspended judgement and planning. To some extent the rule made a virtue out of technological necessity: a convenient and above all reasonable means of summarising the circumstances of the day.

THE BUDGETARY ORIGINS OF THE RULE

If the rule was rooted in reasonable assessments of strategic intentions and capabilities, and not, at least initially, a budgetary tool, then the apparent isolation of Britain's strategic planners from economic reality requires explanation. The economic situation in Britain in the immediate post-war years was, in one word, disastrous. At the time – spring 1947 – at which Grove sees the rule coming to fruition, the dollar loan which Keynes had managed to negotiate was quickly running out and the convertibility crisis was on the horizon. It is unlikely that the COS could have been oblivious of the financial problems facing the country, and so the "budgetary or strategic" dichotomy fails to offer a satisfactory explanation.

In mid-October 1945 the COS accepted that 'financial stringency would probably prevent us retaining adequate armed forces.'[35] Any uncertainty on this issue would have been dispelled at the end of the following year, with Alexander making it increasingly clear that the defence budget and size of the armed forces could not be decided simply by strategic factors if funds were not available.[36] Not only were the COS aware of the economic problems, they also responded sympathetically and constructively – if a little grudgingly – to the government's dilemma. Even Montgomery, always at loggerheads with the short-sighted, hesitant planners in the Treasury and Cabinet offices, advocated an interim structure for the Army which could be expanded when the essential economic recovery had taken place.[37] As well as the technological considerations outlined above, their awareness of Britain's economic plight also pushed the COS in the direction of a rule, suggesting that 'strategic versus budgetary' may not be the best way to discuss the rule of the 1940s. 'Strategic' is not necessarily the antithesis of 'budgetary'. Strategy is a matter not only of establishing geopolitical, technological and temporal parameters to national military activity, but also of working within the resources available. The extent and type of these resources were determined by the strength of Britain's economy and what could be afforded, and it has been shown that the COS responded to these restrictions on their planning. The rule as 'budgetary device' may therefore have been less a corruption of COS thinking, than a natural extension of it.

The origins of the 'five plus five' rule of the 1940s present something of a conundrum, explained only partially by the distinction between 'strategic' and 'budgetary' factors. One thing is clear: in terms of bureaucratic involvement and strategic background, the rule bore very little relation to its 1920s predecessor. COS awareness of resource limitations informed their strategic thinking. Roskill described the 1919-1933 rule as 'an entirely empirical formula', for all its faults.[38] The 1940s rule was, similarly, a reflection of the circumstances in which the planners operated. It was a pragmatic framework which enabled decisions to be made, and strategic planning to proceed.

THE RULE IN OPERATION

In April 1947 the COS, along with Tizard and Alexander accepted the 'five plus five' rule as a planning assumption which the JPS were to use in the preparation of the Future Defence Policy paper (FDP).[39] Yet, as far as Alexander was concerned, this was most certainly not a no war rule in the sense of the policy which had governed defence planning in the 1920s:

> We must, I think, resist any tendency to embark upon the kind of policy which was pursued with such detriment to our fortunes between World War I and World War II, namely the "Ten-Year No War Rule". The evils of this policy did not lie so much in the prophecy that no major war would occur for a period of ten years from the time the rule was instituted, but in its cumulative detrimental effect on our defence preparations as a whole by reason of its annual renewal. This is a mistake we must not make again.[40]

Cunningham was also wary of admitting a no war rule, believing that it would 'render us defenceless' for the declared period of five years.[41] But at this same meeting, Tedder declared his open support for the rule: 'Provided we continued to maintain such a force he [Tedder] agreed that the risk of war during the next five years was negligible. Further, he considered that, in fact, we shall be incapable of waging a major war during that period.'[42] Tedder's support for the rule, on behalf of the RAF, might be explained in a way which reveals more of the background to the discussion.

While the Soviet threat had by now been accepted, it was assessed that this threat would not materialise for five to ten years, the time it would take the Soviet Union to recover from the last war and be able to mount another. It was also assessed that the Soviet Union's technological backwardness – especially in the atomic field – would take some years to correct. Tedder may therefore have felt that preference should be given to the service (the RAF) which best represented the advantage (technological) which the West then held over the Soviet Union. But there was more to Tedder's support for the rule. The rule could be interpreted in such a way that first the RAF and then the Navy would receive priority in defence planning over the manpower and cost-intensive Army. The COS were never fully prepared to accept that there would be no risk of war in the first five year period. If the RAF represented the particular strength of the West which the Soviet Union could not match and which would keep them in second position, this might be seen as at best a passive quality of the RAF, insufficient to secure for the RAF a large slice of the defence budget. But if some risk was accepted then the opportunity arose to make an active contribution with no extra effort. A massive offensive strike capability – which the COS had already decided would be required at the end of the 'five plus five' period – could also deal with an accidental war which broke out during the first, 'no risk' five year period. This force would then provide the post-1957 deterrent force. So it seemed that one service could manage the problems of both the present and the future.

Accordingly, during the COS meeting of 14 May, Tedder claimed that what was needed were strong offensive and defensive forces available immediately and that such forces would reduce the risk of war.[43] There would not be a period of months to mobilise and, in any case, if it were seen that Britain needed such a period then pre-emptive attack might be invited in the 'instant war' of the future. The manpower-intensive service – the Army – must have seemed unwieldy, unfashionable and perhaps even an unsafe organisation on which to rely, if it could not organise itself in time to meet an immediate danger. The only possibility for the Army would have been to maintain a large structure on a permanent war footing which, for domestic political and economic reasons, would have been impossible. Furthermore, how would the Soviet Union – the 'two camps' were not yet completely estranged – view such a 'defence' posture? And where would such an Army go? The correct sort of preparations, according to Tedder, were therefore those which were less provocative, less costly, more up to date and fashionable, more easily mobilised and more in keeping with the accepted three pillars of defence policy; the RAF and the Navy, in other words. Tedder's point during the 14 May meeting was that the JPS did not place enough stress on the importance of the Navy and RAF at the outbreak of war and he went on to say that the JPS should use the 'five plus five' idea as long as appropriate (i.e., Navy and RAF) preparatory measures had been carried out. So Tedder supported the 'five plus five' idea as a way out of the economic and demographic dead-end which defence planners faced. The risk could never be entirely removed but could be managed by the deterrent force which the RAF would, in any case, be expected to provide in due course and would certainly not be of the scale to justify the retention of a large Army with an appropriate tranche of the defence budget. With this subtle interpretation of the rule, Tedder managed to undermine the Army's position and strengthen that of the RAF. The competition for resources was essentially one between these two services; the COS and government had accepted that one of the pillars of defence effort should be the defence of SLOC and it was clear that only the Navy could satisfy that requirement. The Army could not be kept in waiting for the possibility of a war. The RAF, on the other hand, would not only obviate the need for a large Army but could also provide the basis for Britain's future defence policy with its emphasis on technology.

That the rule was being used both to set the parameters of Britain's technology-based defence planning, and as a forum for inter-service competition for resources, is shown by Montgomery's reaction to the 'five plus five' idea. At the meeting in May when Tedder complained that the JPS report did not make enough of the idea and did not place enough stress on the need to prepare offensive and defensive forces which could operate immediately on the outbreak of war,[44] Montgomery approved the same report. At a meeting in August, when Tedder again presented his interpretation of the rule, Montgomery agreed with the rule against Cunningham's opposition. Montgomery referred to 1957 as the threat date and seemed willing to abandon caution altogether by disregarding the threat of war for at least the first five years and possibly all ten.[45] An explanation of Montgomery's position emerges from the minutes of the following meeting when he asserted that 'The risk of war during the next five years must be ruled out, as until our economic and industrial strength had recovered, we would be quite incapable of taking part in a major war.'[46] In a memorandum produced by Montgomery in December and discussed by COS at their 143rd meeting, he emerged as the advocate of economic and industrial recovery as the *sine qua non*: 'if we fail in this, all other preparations will be of no avail.' Defence policy should be a matter of long-term planning and must stress research and development leading to eventual rearmament (i.e., at the end of the 'five plus five' period). Interim forces should be no more than what was required to support foreign policy.[47] It may be that Montgomery was more sensitive than his colleagues to Britain's economic condition. An alternative explanation is that Montgomery was trying to break out of the 'technological fix' which had not only helped to frame the rule, as an expression of Soviet capabilities, but which had also provided an answer to the problem: the creation of a large air force which could both deter and defend (by taking the war to the enemy) from the outset of the next war, accidental or not. The wisdom of the day, it should be remembered, was that the next war would be immediate and that a slow response would be worthless and perhaps provocative. Montgomery could not argue against the implications of the new technology; Hiroshima and the 'V-Bombs' were memorable examples of what was now possible. Nor could he suggest that a huge Army should be maintained. But if he accepted the Tedder/Tizard axis then he accepted a minor role for the Army – probably nothing more than the air defence of Britain and the defence of overseas garrisons – and a low priority for the Army in the allocation of defence resources. So his answer was to leave this middle ground altogether and to propose a rule which stressed economic recovery in the longer term, as the key to Britain's strength, rather than the construction of an offensive/deterrent air force of some 1,250 aircraft. This approach would undermine the RAF's case for a large tranche of defence spending. The Army, while being unable to avoid contraction and run-down as demobilisation proceeded and resources dwindled, would remain one among equals in the services. As long as the difficulties were shared by all, when the country had recovered sufficiently to make rounded, well-informed decisions on defence spending (rather than those driven solely by budgetary reasoning), and when the threat was more predictable, the Army's position would not have been weakened in relation to the other two services. Forced into a corner, Montgomery was trying to fend off the most obvious and tempting deduction to be drawn from the economic, political and technological considerations of the day – that the Army was no longer supportable or even necessary.

Whatever the rationale behind the rule, it was to be short-lived. The 1948 papers show that the rule quickly became discredited as an instrument for strategic planning, and at the same time lost any value as a weapon in the inter-service struggle for resources. The year began with a clear affirmation of the place of the rule in strategic thinking. The first mention of the rule occurs in the third meeting. Cunningham was anxious that, given the 'insecurity' of the French, with whom military discussions were about to take place, they should not be told that 'our policy was based on the fact that the risk of war during the next five years was unlikely', since 'it would be most detrimental should it reach the ears of any potential enemy.'[48] French sensitivity was not, however, sufficient reason to question the rule itself. A JPS briefing paper, drawn up at the end of January for use by the COS representative to the Washington Discussions, shows that 1957 was still very firmly a long-term planning date: 'Our examination is related to the increasing danger of war up to 1957 and is likely to remain true for some years thereafter.'[49]

Within months, however, the COS were beginning to suspect that the rule might not provide all that was needed. On 9 March, just weeks after the Prague coup, with the first session of the London Conference just concluded, and with negotiations progressing towards the Brussels Treaty, a wide-ranging discussion of defence policy took place. The COS had some reservations about the state of readiness of Britain's defences. They noted that although major war had been discounted for five years, they were still faced with the problem of fighting a war if one broke out during that time. Faced with such a prospect, the rule seemed at best dated and at worst dangerous. The accepted answer to the problem of an unplanned war had been to 'fight with what we had'. The COS now began to question this solution. What was available to fight? Could any reinforcement be achieved without mobilisation? 'What long-term steps could be taken to reduce the long period of unreadiness implicit in our present plans?' While budgetary justifications for the rule no doubt retained their meaning, by spring 1948 the strategic rationale of the rule was clearly looking frayed. The COS seem to have realised that a possible threat must either be treated as a real threat, or ignored; confidence in Alexander's 'five plus five' rule was evaporating.[50]

On 17 March 1948 the COS discussed a memorandum by Hollis in which it was suggested that a new examination be carried out, based on agreed principles, before the COS became too involved in discussions with the West Europeans.[51] In Hollis' judgement the rule was becoming less and less appropriate:

> The time factor for this examination must be amended from our present anticipation of war after 1956, and firmly related to present realities, i.e. if war should occur –
> (i) between now and 1950;
> (ii) between 1950 and 1956;
> (iii) when both sides have Atomic and Biological Weapons.

Montgomery's rejection of the rule followed soon. In early May, Montgomery minuted that while it was 'unlikely' that Russia would be able to wage war before 1957, and while 'available scientific evidence' indicated that the Soviet Union would not have weapons of mass destruction before 1957, there could still be no guarantee that war would not break out. In that case, he argued, 'It is ... unrealistic to work on the philosophy that there will be no war for a predetermined number of years'.[52] Cunningham also later rejected the rule. At the end of July, with concern mounting over the Berlin crisis and with some apparent hesitation on the part of the government to set in motion emergency or short-term planning, the First Sea Lord insisted that preparations could not be held up while formal investigations and surveys were carried out, and that 'the situation which had now arisen meant that the five-year rule for a future war was completely dead.'[53] Montgomery agreed, although Tedder hoped that a more subtle approach to the problem might be taken.

In early August, while discussing the need to ensure that the National Service Bill should not be based upon a twelve month period of service, the COS agreed that the situation in Germany was now so stressed that the five year rule should be abandoned, with Cunningham noting that 'In the Minister of Defence's report [DO(47)68] to the Defence Committee in 1947, it was stated in para. 8 that the risk of war in the next five years must be ruled out. The course of recent events had shown that this was an unacceptable basis for defence planning. He [Cunningham] thought the Chiefs of Staff ought, as a first step, to point this out to the government.'[54] The advice was passed to the Cabinet, as a note by the Secretary to the Cabinet explains:

> At recent meetings of the Defence Committee, Ministers have expressed the wish that all possible steps should be taken to bring our paper plans to the highest possible state of readiness, subject to the two provisos that nothing should be done without specific authority which might have a serious impact on our economy.
>
> The Defence (Transition) Committee met this morning to consider the tempo at which these preparations should proceed. To continue as at present, working on the assumption that an emergency was unlikely to arise before 1952, was obviously out of the question.

The Committee

> agreed that an immediate emergency would have to be dealt with on an ad hoc basis, and that the right course to adopt was to concentrate all efforts on preparations to meet a possible emergency on 1st October 1948 ... [55]

The COS later endorsed this approach, stating that 'the experience of the last few months had shown that the existing basis for defence planning seemed no longer tenable.' The 'existing basis' was the plan under DO (47) 68, whereby the ability of the forces to meet an emergency was to deteriorate over the next few years until long-term plans for build-up and re-equipment could take effect.[56] Although comments made at a meeting in early November, to the effect that certain types of threat could reasonably be 'ignored for the time being in order that proper provision could be made against the more serious ones', suggested a possible return to 'no war rule' thinking, the concept had by mid-1948 been thoroughly discredited in the minds of the COS. [57]

SUMMARY

The origins of the rule were broadly based. Both the Foreign Office and the COS were directly involved in the development of the rule, thus distinguishing it from its 1920s predecessor. From the military point of view, the rule reflected perceptions of the Soviet threat and the technological assumptions of the day, principally of the value of air power and of the primacy of the atomic bomb. But the COS were also very sensitive to Britain's economic situation, and seem to have accepted, for a time, that their strategic thinking should take account of such factors. This suggests, again, that the 1940s rule was rather different from its predecessor. More significantly perhaps, it can also now be said that the origins of the rule were more than simply a function of a contest between budgetary (Treasury) and strategic (COS) imperatives. The rule was based upon reasonable assessments of the prevailing and fast-changing situation and it is not clear that the military planners were short-sighted or ignorant in making those assessments.

With the rule becoming accepted as a planning framework, the COS remained no less aware of Britain's economic weakness and the impossibility of funding large defence programmes. This was not, however, a continuation of COS consensus on budgetary matters which had been seen while the rule was being drawn up. Economic stringency, as manifested by the rule, now dictated rivalry and competition among the COS for scarce resources. Each service chief presented an interpretation of the rule which seemed most likely to further (or at least maintain) his own service's position. Thus, the rule not only became a weapon to be used by the Treasury against the military, but also one to be used by the COS upon their colleagues. This had the effect of distracting attention from real strategic thinking about Germany and Europe; each member of the COS was preoccupied with jostling for position and with devising convincing strategic arguments for a larger portion of the defence budget. During 1947 and into 1948 Germany and the Soviet threat were still not high on the strategic agenda. From about the middle of 1948, pressure began to mount for a planning process designed to meet the growing likelihood of conflict in the short term. As this pressure grew, the need for strategic thinking about Germany moved into the limelight while the 'five plus five' rule was edged out.

4 Fragile Logic: Strategic Plans, 1945-47

> The immediate problem that now faced us was terrific. We had in our area nearly one and a half million German prisoners of war. There were a further one million German wounded ... about one million civilian refugees ... and "Displaced Persons" were roaming about the country ... Transportation and communication services had ceased to function. Agriculture and industry were largely at a standstill.
>
> I was a soldier and I had not been trained to handle anything of this nature.
>
> Montgomery[1]

With Germany's defeat, Britain's relationship with its former adversary immediately took on an entirely different character. In its zone of occupation, Britain now became wholly responsible for social, political and economic affairs. While many military tasks attended Germany's defeat, tasks which were carried out using military resources and Montgomery's command structure, the whole panoply of civil affairs planning and organisation, which had been in preparation for so long in Britain, was now brought into effect.[2] The military had also been preparing for some time for Germany's defeat. Yet VE Day did not mark a complete and sudden change of attitude on the part of the COS and their planners. With the exception of a tentative involvement in US planning for war in Germany in the short term, British military thinking and strategic planning for Germany in the immediate aftermath of the war were characterised more by caution and incoherence than by anything pro-active and far-sighted.

1945 – THE AFTERMATH OF WAR

For some months after the defeat of Germany, the British military were preoccupied by the question of the redeployment of troops either for the continuing war against Japan, or for demobilisation and return to Britain. Decisions as to deployments and the rate of demobilisation could not, however, be made without investigation of the military commitments which would face Britain after the defeat of Germany. The essential foundation of any deployment plan was an accurate and coherent assessment of the source and character of military threats to Britain. As earlier chapters have shown, however, the early development of threat perceptions was a rather tentative process. As a result, British military thinking about Germany in this 'pre-Cold War' period lacked clarity and sense of purpose. In spite of this, the papers for 1945 do show that although the occupation of Germany was not a major concern in strategic planning, the occupation nevertheless had a place in wider planning discussions.

In January 1945, while discussing French proposals for the control of German means of war production, it was agreed that although the control of Germany would require long-term planning, this was not to begin until after a phase of intense and comprehensive control described as 'total occupation'. Although it was essential to destroy or isolate Germany's means of war production, the COS and their planning staffs were anxious to avoid being drawn into additional commitments of troops which might delay the demobilisation programme. That said, it was recognised that a permanent and heavy commitment of occupation troops in the Rhine-Ruhr area 'might enable the period of occupation of the rest of Germany to be terminated at an earlier date.'[3] The transition from war to peace was later described as taking place in three stages: the assumption of control by the Control Commission (Stage 2) would take place at the conclusion of military operations (Stage 1), and would eventually give way to control by the Foreign Office (Stage 3).[4] The COS asked the PHPS to assess the forces which Britain might have to contribute to German occupation, and suggested that the use of air power, and even a United Nations force of some sort, should be considered as possible ways to reduce the commitment. There was, clearly, a sense of duty on the part of the British military to assist in stabilising Germany, but also a sense that this duty did not carry with it – and should not be allowed to develop into – a commitment with unlimited liability. British occupation forces were to be responsible for 'the disbandment of the German armed forces, and for measures of demilitarisation, destruction of material etc. They will also be responsible for Military Government and for the maintenance of law and order.'[5] It was felt that 'main operations' would be over by early June and that any remaining opposition would have been eradicated by the end of that month.[6]

The emerging picture is one of a non-operational, or at best quasi-operational, occupation of Germany in which British troops were simply to police the defeated country and enforce the decisions of the Military Government. This picture is complicated by one reference in the papers. At a meeting in May, just over one week after VE Day, with both Eisenhower and Churchill present, Churchill is reported to have 'envisaged the control of Germany being exercised from a number of cantonments, scattered throughout the country, on which air forces and armoured flying columns would be based.'[7] The role of air power in the occupation of Germany had been discussed on many occasions, and seemed to offer an opportunity to reduce the number of troops deployed to Germany. One possible role for the RAF had been outlined in March:

> The main role of these [British] Air Forces in Germany will be that of a central striking force to support the Army of Occupation anywhere in the British Zone.[8]

Quite how this 'central striking force' would have operated is not explained. Analysis had been made of the accuracy of aircraft machine guns against civilian targets, such as a rioting crowd, but it is unlikely that air power could have been perceived as a substitute for ground forces; this would have been contrary to the basic operational doctrine of the day. Moreover, if the role of the 'central striking force' was to support the occupation forces anywhere in the British Zone, this presupposes an Army with sufficient numbers of mobile troops and equipment. In contrast, the Army in Germany had static, largely non-operational 'policing' tasks, suggesting that the notion of 'air control' would have been unsupportable in practice. It would appear, therefore, that the idea of air control was entertained only casually, and may have been no more than an attempt to mask the numerical and equipment deficiencies of British ground troops in Germany. To an extent, air control was also a function of the prevailing preoccupation with air power, and was an attempt to show that air power provided solutions not only on the strategic level (i.e., with bombing raids), but also on the tactical level.[9]

Until August 1945, the occupation of Germany was considered less important than the other strategic requirements of home defence, the war against Japan and the protection of the Middle East, India and imperial SLOC. Unless it could be achieved with the smallest possible number of troops, the occupation of Germany threatened to hinder the creation of the Imperial Strategic Reserve, the centrepiece of immediate post-war strategic planning, such as it was.[10] One plan, discussed shortly after Japan's surrender, illustrates the low status which the COS and their planners attached to the presence of British troops in Germany. This was the plan, known as Operation 'Signpost', to deploy one infantry division from Germany to the Middle East. The plan would have given the division a warning time of just six days before deployment to the Middle East; this state of readiness would have undermined the division's effectiveness as far as occupation duties were concerned, and would also have made it barely useful on arrival in the Middle East.[11] On this and other occasions the COS made clear their view that Germany was less in need of operational troops than India and the Middle East.[12] The role for the Army in Germany was simply occupation, described as a peacetime activity in a mid-October meeting.[13] This role would require many troops initially but these troops would be deployed in occupational, not operational divisions. It was not intended that occupation would last longer than two years after the defeat of Germany, at the most. Forces assigned to occupation tasks were therefore in temporary positions and were understandably not highly valued by the defence planners.

1946 – A QUESTION OF PRIORITIES

As for 1945, the COS and JPS papers for 1946 demonstrate that British military thinking about Germany was only gradually becoming more coherent and certain. Mounting pressure for reductions in military spending, particularly on the Army, presented the prospect of 'drastic manpower cuts' in RAF and Army manning levels in Germany.[14] The COS were being forced to make hard choices, and it appeared to them that sacrifices in the size of the occupation forces would have to be made if other, more vital, commitments were to be protected from the Treasury. Hence, Simpson was of the opinion that occupation forces in Germany would have been 'largely reduced' by late 1947.[15] During 1946 the COS were on the verge of accepting that the occupation forces in Germany should be either thinned out, or rearranged in some way. The implication of all this is quite clear: Germany had not yet become a vital issue in the minds of Britain's military planners and thinkers. Shortly after assuming his appointment as CIGS, Montgomery recorded that the situation in Germany had 'altered little' since his departure from Germany at the beginning of May. Before leaving Germany, Montgomery had recommended that the occupation forces be reduced to four divisions, an armoured brigade and ancillary units; 'in his opinion this force would suffice to perform the tasks required of it'.[16]

If Germany was not at the forefront of British military thinking in the early post-war period, the Middle East certainly was, and the priority accorded to this region in strategic thinking was made clear on many occasions. In April, the COS considered that the garrison in the Middle East, wherever it may end up, must be big enough to defend against a major threat and 'to operate long range strategic air forces'.

As well as defending Britain's SLOC, a base in the Middle East would enable Britain to attack the Soviet Union's 'soft under belly' in time of war, providing a form of deterrent against Soviet adventurism in Europe.[17] Later in the same month, while discussing revisions to the Anglo-Egyptian treaty, the COS reiterated their faith in the value of a Middle East base, insisting that a British withdrawal from Egypt should only be contemplated if the Egyptians accepted the idea of a British regional base being established in the Canal Zone (Palestine being considered too unstable) and, more significantly, if the Egyptians agreed to make certain concessions to the RAF.[18] The stability and security of the Middle East was of vital interest to the COS, so much so that the deteriorating situation in Palestine threatened to disrupt a wide range of plans. In mid-May Simpson commented that disorder in Palestine could mean that planned reductions in manpower would be difficult to meet and that other commitments might have to suffer. In the same discussion, while listing the commitments he expected to see liquidated by the end of 1947, he noted that 'in addition we should have largely reduced our occupation forces for Germany'.[19] For the Army, the Middle East was far more important than any thought of 'commitment' to Europe. At the end of the year Montgomery, pointing out the deficiencies in projections of Army man-power strengths, gave his understanding of the three fundamental bases or 'pillars' of British defence policy: the defence and safety of the United Kingdom main base; the defence of sea lines of communication (SLOC) between the UK and, in order of priority, the Atlantic, the Mediterranean, and the Indian Ocean; and, finally, 'A firm hold on the Middle East area. It was from this area that we could retain the ability to take the offensive, particularly at the initial stages with heavy bomber forces.' He went on to suggest that only a small Regular Army would be necessary, with two divisions in the Middle East and the balance in the United Kingdom. The balance would be made up with the Territorial Army:

> This meant that the United Kingdom force would be too small for operations on the Continent in the early stages of war, and the extension of the Army to meet the needs of a major war could only be based on the Territorial Army Organisation.

Montgomery dismissed the idea of an expeditionary force against 'an enemy who possessed almost unlimited manpower'. In Montgomery's opinion there was no merit in committing ground forces to meet the Soviet threat.[20]

A subject closely connected with thinking about the Middle East was that of the strategic reserve, a matter which had been discussed in 1945 but which received more attention as the Middle East became more turbulent. While there was some debate as to the preferred location of the reserve, there was no doubt that it should be somewhere in the Middle East. In March, Attlee suggested that the reserve should be moved to Kenya, instead of maintaining it in Egypt or adjacent countries. Alanbrooke dismissed this suggestion on the grounds that communications would be made too difficult and that, in any case, the accessibility of the reserve to the Middle East would be seriously restricted by being so far away. He did, however, instruct the JPS to prepare a study on the implications of such a move.[21] The JPS argued that the despatch of air and ground reserves to Africa would place them too far from naval forces in the Mediterranean, thereby undermining the overall British presence in the area. Alanbrooke insisted that the Canal Zone would be the most appropriate location for the reserve, which should be of at least a brigade group with air support. An additional division might be located in Africa, perhaps made up from those troops presently deployed in Palestine and unable to be used elsewhere at that time, but the reserve itself could not be stationed so far away from the eastern Mediterranean area.[22]

SPRING 1947 – THE LAST MONTHS OF UNCERTAINTY

In early 1947 the COS continued to wrestle with the problem of producing a coherent Future Defence Policy, a task made difficult by the number of strategic and technological demands on their attention, by financial stringency and scarce manpower, and by a political and diplomatic (though not military) atmosphere which, in the early months of the year, was still only tentatively anti-Soviet. As this review of strategic priorities progressed, the lack of commitment to Germany on the part of the COS went unchallenged and may even have been reinforced.

On 8 January reference was made to the 'recently approved aide-memoire on Future Defence Policy'.[23] This document was an attempt to establish a consensus among COS and Cabinet as to the bases of defence policy, and was considered again on 13 January at a staff conference chaired by Attlee.[24] This conference has been cited by Bullock as the point at which the three key ministers (Attlee, Bevin and Alexander) accepted the COS view of the necessity of maintaining a 'firm hold in the Middle East'. This, Bullock suggests, signified the end of Attlee's insistence that a British position in the Middle East need not be considered crucial.[25] The final version of the paper lists the 'factors' governing Future Defence Policy and the 'principles' of Commonwealth defence, with which it should be possible to decide on the size and structure of the armed forces. Both were to be 'governed by political and scientific development, and therefore subject to continual review'. The factors were given as

- The United Nations Organisation;
- The Commonwealth;
- The vulnerability of the UK and the need, therefore, to avoid war;
- The role of the British forces in deterring aggression and safeguarding the UNO and Commonwealth interests against attack;
- The identity and reliability of Britain's allies;
- The structure and capabilities of Britain's forces, exploiting technological resources to offset any manpower disadvantages wherever possible.

Deterrence, the fourth factor, was to 'meet the needs of the future' and forces were to be refashioned accordingly. Yet there could be no breathing space during which this reorientation could take place unhindered. In other words, deterrence was to become policy immediately, however fragile it might be in its first years. As far as Britain's allies were concerned, the fifth factor, the Commonwealth, was considered the most reliable, the United States was 'likely' and India was 'open to serious doubt'. Since Britain could not stand alone, 'It must be our aim... to build up a strong Western region of Defence with France as its key stone'. The first of the principles was to be the defence of Commonwealth resources until an all-out offensive could be developed. Next, there would be a requirement to maintain and defend bases from which an immediate offensive could be launched. Third, although the main threat to the UK was 'attack from the air, long range bombardment and attack on sea communications', 'the possibility of an invasion' could not be 'entirely discarded'. Fourth, the services would be required to provide for air defence, civil defence, a bomber force and naval/air superiority around the UK and along SLOC, and make preparations to develop a 'heavy air offensive'. Fifth and finally, the UK would require a 'firm hold in the Middle East area', without which 'our war capacity will be dangerously weakened':

> The Middle East is the only area from which if we are attacked, an active and immediate defence can be applied in the form of limiting the aggressors' weight of attack.

As strategic thinking progressed, it was becoming clear that there was little likelihood of the Army being given a pivotal role in Britain's future strategy and defence policy, either in Britain, in Europe or globally. According to the new strategic thinking, the Army could expect to be given only relatively minor tasks such as civil defence and the protection of Britain against the possibility of an invasion.

The Army and its presence in Germany remained low on the COS list of priorities, as the minutes of the very first meeting of the year indicate. Slim, the commandant of the Imperial Defence College, provided an outline of the broad conclusions reached in an IDC study into 'general policy governing Commonwealth defence in 1947.' The COS found themselves in 'general agreement' with Slim's paper, which could therefore be taken as a fair summary of contemporary COS thinking about a commitment to the defence of Germany. The IDC considered that future war between the Great Powers would make use of air power and would be launched from one centre against another; war would no longer involve large armies jostling for position on the European – or any other – land mass. When an air attack was made, it would be massive and would involve the use of atomic and biological weapons and rockets. Not only would war be a remote and highly technological activity, it would also be so devastating that it would be over in an instant: there would be 'no time to develop a war potential after the war... has begun'. Unlike most of the Commonwealth, the United Kingdom was 'peculiarly vulnerable' to the new style of warfare. Yet in spite of this, the IDC found themselves able to recommend that some risks be taken:

> The first defence requirement of this country is considered to be its morale, physical and economic rehabilitation. If defence risks have to be taken to ensure this, the present moment is as good as any to accept them.

The IDC report was an attempt to make the best out of a bad situation. Given the likely nature of future war, the quality of Britain's air defences was vital. Yet these defences were currently ineffective: 'It is true to say that for the next ten years at least a large proportion of the attack will penetrate any defence'. Having decided that 'defence by the shield will not be effective', the IDC recommended the following:

> Real defence in the atomic age must lie in making an aggressor realise that while he may wreck the nation he attacks, he will at once be subjected himself to such a counter blow that, whatever success he gains in his initial attack, will be purchased too dearly. Our main defence

> should be a counter offensive force, in readiness to deliver such a counter blow the moment we are attacked, and the knowledge that it exists.

It is in conjunction with the above recommendation that the IDC's earlier comments on the need to accept 'risks' must be read. The IDC were merely recommending that the quality of Britain's air defences need not be a cause for alarm, provided that a 'counter-offensive' force (of perhaps 50 squadrons of 25 aircraft each, eventually to be replaced by rocket forces) be created: 'The first charge on our defence resources should therefore be the formation, maintenance and improvement of this force, and the collection of intelligence that would ensure its most effective employment to destroy Russia's war effort.'

With this in mind, the prospects for the Army – certainly that part of it based in Germany – were not good. Other than the creation of the counter-offensive air force, Britain's defence commitments were: the security of the UK 'main base'; the security of the Middle East ('the main source of our oil supply and an offensive base from which to strike with the counter-offensive force, or part of it'); and the security of bases on the SLOC (the Azores, Iceland and so on). To meet all these commitments, the IDC had listed the tasks of the services in the following order of priority:

1. Counter-offensive force (mainly air).
2. Defensive force (mainly anti-air).
3. Anti-submarine forces.
4. A research and development organisation, spread throughout the Commonwealth, to support the above tasks.
5. An increase in the intelligence effort directed against the Russians.

Not only was a traditional role for the Army conspicuously absent from this list, the IDC review went on to recommend, ominously for the Army, that 'Every military activity that does not fit into this pattern must be objectively examined, without service or traditional prejudice, and, if possible, ruthlessly and quickly cut'. This recommendation was given further emphasis: 'our commitments in areas other than these essential areas should be examined objectively, with a view to appreciating if commitments in these areas did not fit into the foregoing foundations of defence, they should be discarded.'[26]

The prescriptions made by the IDC seem to have had direct influence on the COS view of a 'continental strategy', i.e., one which would involve the stationing of operational, as opposed to occupational, forces in Europe and which would give the 'ground battle' priority over the maritime and air strategies. The COS were increasingly wary of becoming entangled in some form of defence commitment to Europe: 'The fact that our forces were already on the Continent might tend to commit us to a continental strategy, which might, in the circumstances, be incorrect.'[27] In this context, progress towards an agreed strategy paper was fraught with difficulties, especially as pressure mounted for cuts in manpower and spending.

The COS hoped to submit a consolidated report to the Defence Committee, incorporating the paper on factors and principles, a JPS study,[28] and papers from the War Office and the Admiralty.[29] At their next meeting, a staff conference chaired by Alexander, discussion was mainly procedural, with the minister trying to impress upon the COS the need for a swift conclusion to the planning process, for the sake of his Parliamentary and Cabinet position as the services' principal representative. The COS report was to be just one of the documents used to decide Britain's long-term strategy. Scientific developments would have to be accounted for, as would Foreign Office opinion on the 'likely trend of future events'.[30]

The following week, the COS discussed the possibility of incorporating estimates of the size and shape of the future armed forces – one of the objects of their original aide-memoire – with the policy report which the JPS were to produce by 8 May. This incorporation would delay the principal report and so the COS agreed to ask the separate service ministers to draw up individual estimates which could in turn be collated by the JPS into one, additional tri-service report. This, of course, was precisely the sort of approach to the problem which Alexander did not want: Alexander's aim was for the COS to incorporate both policy and budgetary aspects in one report.[31] In the end, the terms of reference for the JPS made it clear that they should, in the present report, avoid the question of the size and shape of the armed forces:

> All that was required was an indication of the relative importance of the principal tasks of the armed forces, in order to assist Service Ministries in their estimate of the size and shape of our peace-time armed forces.[32]

The Directors of Plans agreed to produce a short report. They believed that the only way to produce a simple and brief report would be to name the main enemy – the Soviet Union. The COS accepted the recommendation, but not without some diplomatic padding, noting that 'The main strategic arguments ... would be unaltered if either Russia or a resurgent

Germany was regarded as the potential enemy.' The COS also discussed a consolidated version of the War Office and Admiralty reactions to the existing JPS study of defence problems, JP (46) 164.[33] Judging by comments made in discussion, the JPS review contained a list of factors and principles very similar to that found in the COS aide-memoire.[34] Annex 2 of the consolidated paper contained a series of questions regarding these factors and principles, and in their answers the COS revealed both their role in the planning process and something of the content of JP (46) 164:

Question: Since defence policy must respond to a number of foreign and domestic 'constituencies', would it not have made the planning process easier if the COS made their aims clear?

Answer: The role of the COS was to advise HMG of their aims 'from the military point of view' which it was then the job of HMG to place in the wider political context.

Question: Was 1956-1960 the critical period?

Answer: 'Planning should proceed on the assumption that the likelihood of war in the next 5 years will be small. The risk will then increase gradually in the following 5 years, and increase more steeply after 10 years. The risk of war at any time will be comparably lessened to the extent that we and our potential allies show strength.'

Question: Must war with Russia be avoided?

Answer: 'There may be circumstances when initially we alone became involved in war with Russia.' The answer to this dilemma was to ensure material help from the US and have atomic bombs available.

On 14 May the COS were at last in a position to discuss the final JPS report on Future Defence Policy.[35] The report, JP (47) 55 (Final) is still closed, but COS discussion of it is revealing. Cunningham, for example, considered that the report lacked conviction and that 'the need for immediate defensive action to be undertaken, particularly by the Royal Navy and the Royal Air Force on the outbreak of war had not been sufficiently emphasised.' He also asked for stress to be placed upon the need to defend Middle Eastern sources of oil. Tedder approved of the report but believed that it should reflect the 'five plus five' idea. That JP (47) 55 does not seem to propose the rule is curious since it is clear that one of its principal foundation documents – JP(46) 164 – does. This apparent omission begs another question: why would Tedder be keen for the rule to be given a place in the FDP report? The answer may be that it suggested an element of risk – not too much, but enough – which the RAF was in the best position to manage. As discussed in the previous chapter, Montgomery's support for the JPS report suggests that the 'five plus five' idea was not only a response to the technological environment but also a weapon in the rivalry between the RAF and the Army. On 21 May JP (47) 55 was discussed again, having been redrafted as COS (47) 102 (O) (Draft).[36] This was the final discussion of the paper prior to its submission to the Defence Committee. A number of amendments were approved and the document finally went to the Cabinet as DO (47) 44. Since COS (47) 102 (O) was never actually issued as a memorandum, it would be fair to assume that the only difference between the two documents is the file designation.[37]

SHORT-TERM PLANNING: THE AMERICAN INITIATIVE

For so many reasons the COS and JPS found it inappropriate to consider Germany as a first order problem during the first two years after the end of the war in Europe: pressure for retrenchment pushed Germany down the list of priorities; the occupation was intended to be a short-term matter; and, finally, the COS were more interested in ideas such as air power and air control and in problems such as the protection of the SLOC and the Middle East and the location of the strategic reserve. Yet, in one case, the COS were not entirely protected from pressure to take a more serious and longer-term view of Germany and Britain's presence there. The one – American – initiative to prepare contingency plans for the Allied occupation forces in Germany was launched in the summer of 1946 and the COS reaction to it serves to summarise their 'pre-Cold War' view of Germany.

The possibility that Britain and America entered into some sort of *realpolitik* conspiracy in which they planned to desert Germany in the event of war with the Soviet Union, while at the same time exhorting European countries (especially France) to contribute more to their own defence, has provoked a certain amount of interest in the literature:

> the Europeans felt helpless in the face of the large number of Red Army divisions based in Eastern Europe. Britain felt she could do nothing to help stem a Soviet invasion of the Continent, and planned to evacuate her occupation forces in Germany to the United Kingdom in that event.[38]

The code-names which were chosen do indeed convey a sense of indecent haste on the part of the British and Americans to get their occupation troops out of harm's way as soon as possible. Many plans were drawn up, each with variations for the British and Americans and even Canadians. Each plan was given an individual code-name. While the selection of code-names should have been at random, the use of terms such as FLEETWOOD, DOUBLEQUICK, SPEEDWAY, and GALLOPER may have been more than coincidental. And the fact that, in Britain, many of the relevant planning and intelligence papers have not yet been released for public scrutiny, only adds to this sense of mystery. As far as the occupation of Germany was concerned, short-term planning revolved around two ideas which were usually – though not necessarily – related. The first idea was that, in the event of war with the Soviet Union, occupation troops should be evacuated from Germany, a 'straight withdrawal scenario' known as plan PINCHER.[39] The plan was reminiscent of the evacuation from France in 1940, hence the frequent reference to 'Dunkirk plans'. The rationale was that the occupation troops would be ineffective against overwhelming Soviet superiority in ground forces; a threat which would, in any case, be countered with the preferred strategy – air power. The second idea, which developed subsequently, was that after an interval for regrouping and preparation the Allies would fight back into Europe and push the Soviets back to the East. The interval might be as long as three years and the campaign might be launched from a bridgehead or 'lodgement', if the Allies had been able to retain one. Thus would the successful Dunkirk to Normandy formula of World War II be repeated. The development of this second idea suggests, interestingly, that there were already doubts creeping in to the theoretical rationale for air power and the strategic air strike, or at least that air power alone was no longer thought to be capable of bringing the conflict to a suitable conclusion.

The history of the Anglo-American short-term planning process is, however, somewhat complex. In the first place, the process developed in fits and starts. It is useful to think in terms of two phases. The first, in 1946, saw an American approach to the British to take part in emergency planning, and a lukewarm British reaction. The second phase began in late 1947/early 1948 and developed into a comprehensive Anglo-American planning process which lasted until 1950. The British position on Germany and the occupation troops also took some time to clarify, and until it did the British and Americans were simply not employing the same terms of reference.

The American initiative of the summer of 1946 come to nothing, largely because it was deemed politically unsuitable. From a more military perspective, however, the documents suggest that even had the idea been politically acceptable, the developing British military view of Germany and of the role of the occupation forces was such that the American approach could only be met with indifference, or faint support at best. In the summer of 1946, alarmed at the possibility of a Russian surge westwards, the United States Control Commissioner in Germany, Clay, approached his British counterpart, Sholto Douglas, with a view to considering *sauve qui peut* plans for an exit from the Continent. By March 1946 the American Joint War Plans Committee was calculating that, in central Europe alone, the Soviet Union would be able to muster some 91 divisions, with a further 152 divisions in strategic reserve in the Soviet Union. In addition, a further 61 divisions would be available from satellite countries. Air support could amount to some 2,000 fighter/ground attack aircraft. Against this force, the Western Allies might be able to impose some delay on the Rhine, but 'for a short time only', before the attacking forces swept through to the Channel ports. The JWPC concluded that the Soviets simply could not be matched on the ground, and recommended the withdrawal of occupation troops 'as rapidly as possible' in the event of aggression.[40] Sholto Douglas was instructed by the COS in London to reject this approach.[41] The reluctance of the COS to become involved in discussions of this sort was prompted by the intervention of no less than Attlee.[42] American short-term, emergency planning therefore proceeded without formal British involvement.

The COS were thus prevented from joining the Americans in formal planning for a strategy of emergency withdrawal from Germany, but they did nevertheless discuss the subject, usually as the scenario for an exercise. The COS also discussed – far more openly – another matter closely related to the presence of occupation troops in Germany: the question of controlled withdrawal in order to redeploy or demobilise occupation troops. COS discussions of these two matters – especially the latter – served to complicate their position on Germany and the role of the occupation troops, to the extent that the American approach was simultaneously attractive and inappropriate. To understand how the COS position developed, it is necessary to turn back to the closing months of the war in Europe.

Complete withdrawal from Germany was simply not considered in COS and planning staff discussions in 1945. Continued occupation of certain areas was thought essential for the purposes of managing the defeated Germany and in order to deter Soviet aggression. In this context, the American offer of emergency planning discussions would have been inappropriate. Similar ideas prevailed in 1946. In February 1946 the COS met to discuss a JPS paper and noted that, if proposed cuts in the size and strength of the Army were to go ahead, there would be 'inevitable withdrawals from occupational commitments' and that such withdrawals would cause 'dangerous weakness' in Germany.[43] This was hardly fertile ground for the American proposal, which was to be made only months later. The management of the defeated Germany still presented serious problems and in early 1946, less than twelve months after the end of the war against Germany, the threat of resurgence was still keenly felt. Less than two months later, the picture became more complicated. Early in April the COS informed the Foreign Office of a fundamental change of emphasis: Germany was no longer considered to be a threat and the main problem in military intelligence and planning circles was declared to be Russia.[44] This change of emphasis had a dramatic effect on the COS attitude to the role of British forces in Germany. On 10 May 1946 Simpson commented that, in his view, occupation forces in Germany would have been 'largely reduced' by the end of 1947.[45]

While Simpson's comment does not amount to an espousal of anything as firm as the 'Dunkirk' doctrine, ideas of this sort were by now beginning to receive more serious attention. A meeting of the COS in August was informed that Montgomery was eager to organise another Army Conference at Camberley, to take place in May 1947, to address the problems of 'an overseas expedition' and opposed beach landings.[46] It may well be that Montgomery was thinking widely and generally, and that amphibious operations in the Middle East were in his mind. It may equally be the case that he was thinking about Europe and about a repeat of the Normandy invasion following a Dunkirk-style evacuation; it would after all be reasonable to assume that amphibious operations in Europe would only be necessary if the Continent had first of all been lost. If the latter was the case, was this a reaction to an American suggestion? Interestingly, if Montgomery was thinking about a campaign in Europe, there is a certain irony given his subsequent determination, when holding his Western Union appointment, to have 'Dunkirk' plans dropped. Five days later, the subject of the 1947 Army conference was again aired, this time with direct reference to atomic matters. The VCIGS, Simpson, had been considering the possibility of an 'opposed landing' (i.e., a Normandy-type operation), against an enemy armed with atomic weapons. It is highly likely that Simpson was not speculating wildly but that he had the Soviet threat in mind, especially the threat to Europe.[47]

The COS seem to have pushed themselves into something of a dilemma during 1946. Having begun the year fairly clear that Germany was not to be evacuated, by August they had begun to address the matter of an opposed landing by an expeditionary force, with atomic weapons being used by both sides.[48] It was no longer possible for the COS to ignore the idea of emergency evacuation from the Continent; by the summer of 1946 they had grasped the fact that, whatever their views of the dangers of German resurgence, if the Russians decided to invade Europe the British and other Western armies would be pushed to the West. Yet at the same time that they made this uncomfortable appraisal of Soviet strengths and British weaknesses, they also became more aware of the prospects of a British atomic capability. It appeared that Britain's atomic potential might serve to offset uncomfortable imbalances being perceived between British and Soviet military capabilities. Further evidence that this 'technological fix' may have enabled the COS (or at least Montgomery) to develop a rather dismissive attitude towards European defence, and a casual view of the American emergency planning process, can be found in the minutes of the December 1946 conference between Alexander and the COS.[49] Implicit in Montgomery's plan was that Britain's army would be too small to undertake operations on the Continent in the early stages of war, and he accepted that British troops could not contribute much to the fight in Europe, at least in the early stages. Whether this equates to a recommendation for a Dunkirk-style evacuation from the continent is questionable. What is clear, however, is that by now Montgomery had no time for the other half of the idea – large scale operations to fight back into Europe – since he felt that a British expeditionary force could not and should not be expected to take on an enemy 'who possessed almost unlimited manpower.'

In 1946 the COS were evidently aware of the enormous difficulties sure to confront the Western Allies in the event of a Soviet invasion of Western Europe, but were faced with something of a dilemma. If the Soviet Union chose to invade Western Europe there would be little, if anything, that British forces in Europe could do about it; planning for an emergency withdrawal might therefore have seemed sensible. However, just as the Dunkirk evacuation of 1940 had not been presented as a solution to the problem of German aggression, so the abandonment of Europe in the face of Soviet aggression was not a credible option without a parallel plan to re-invade Europe and push the Soviets back to the East. Yet it was felt that 'Normandy'-style operations against an enemy with 'unlimited' manpower and industrial resources would be suicidal. If the allied 'strategy' amounted only to withdrawal, then this was in effect no strategy. The COS had thus worked themselves into an impossible position as far as Germany was concerned. Germany did not have high priority on the list of British strategic interests, and was therefore lacking in manpower, equipment and plans for war. Yet low-key occupational tasks required that Britain maintain some sort of occupational presence in Germany;

Germany was therefore bound to have some small claim on British strategic thinking. As it became clearer that the Soviet Union could invade and overrun Western Europe with ease, so this residual link with Germany in the minds of the COS and the planners became ever more awkward and uncomfortable. While the possibility of a British atomic weapon provided the COS with a way to avoid, if not solve, this dilemma, the American proposal for emergency planning was an unwelcome reminder of the fragile logic of the British position in Germany.

SUMMARY

For the first two years after the defeat of Germany, British military thinking about Germany was governed by three main considerations. First, there was the overall defence policy review process, which was not to reach a conclusion until May 1947. To some extent, this process had the effect of stifling planning, for both the short and long term and for all aspects of Britain's defence interests, and created a cautious, incrementalist atmosphere. As far as Germany was concerned, decisions and ideas were short-term and largely reactive; the official papers do not suggest that the COS had very much of a long-term vision for Germany, or indeed very much interest. The second set of considerations were those relating to budgetary matters, principally in terms of constant and growing pressure for retrenchment and demobilisation. As chapter two shows, this pressure tended to force the COS and their planning staffs to draw up a list of priorities, with commitments at the bottom of the list more likely candidates for rationalisation. Germany, and Britain's occupational commitment there, was consistently at the bottom of the list. Finally, the COS and their planning staffs considered other defence commitments to be more important and to offer more prospect of achieving a sound national defence posture. It is probable that the COS would have expressed these preferences even without the budgetary pressure to classify commitments in order of importance. The commitment to the defence of the Middle East and the SLOC, the need to organise and deploy an effective Imperial Strategic Reserve, and the fascination and faith in air power and the inchoate doctrine of deterrence through massive atomic retaliation, all took pride of place in British military thinking during these months. In this context, not only the type of commitment which the Army might make, but also the Army's very existence were subject to some awkward and uncomfortable scrutiny. By May 1947, the COS and their planning staffs had not yet come close to the idea of a 'continental strategy', and were not even being nudged towards a 'continental commitment' for political reasons. The British military view of Europe was, in every sense, minimalist. There was no emergency planning for war in Europe in the short term with the Americans or even nationally. Britain's military presence and interest in Germany during these years was, finally, an occupational and policing matter and not 'operational' in the sense of erecting a defence posture against the Russians or any other potential enemy.

5 Consolidation of the Cold War: Strategic Plans, 1947-48

> As it was not envisaged we should send an army to hold off the enemy in Europe and since there was little risk of this country being invaded the necessity for maintaining a substantial army equipped with modern weapons and equipment appeared arguable.
>
> Attlee[1]

From the end of 1947 military thinking about Germany became more certain, albeit in a negative sense: there was now even less willingness to entertain a continental strategy. The basic budgetary, technological and doctrinal prejudices against military involvement on the Continent went largely unchallenged and were even given something of a boost during interventions by Attlee at the end of 1947. The Future Defence Policy paper (FDP – DO (47) 44), which provided the framework for strategic thinking during 1947 and beyond, implied further movement away from military involvement in Germany.[2] From early 1948 Britain was involved in new planning discussions – most notably those with the Americans – which, again, postulated movement away from Germany both conceptually and physically.

THE THREE PILLARS

For the remainder of 1947, after the adoption of the FDP paper in May, the prejudices against military involvement in Germany or on the Continent remained intact, with discussion usually reflecting divisions over the allocation of resources. There were, however, also pragmatic arguments against such a commitment – the argument advanced by Cunningham at the end of the year being a good example – as well as a compelling technological perspective presented by Tizard. Referring to the huge armies with which the Soviet Union could threaten Europe, Cunningham provided a more reasoned slant to the otherwise doctrinaire aversion to a continental strategy and argued that 'we should avoid planning on the conception of a Continental war against an enemy such as

Russia with unlimited manpower resources.' Without India, Britain simply could not compete.[3] At another staff conference some days later, Attlee took the antipathy towards a continental strategy to its logical conclusion, when he 'agreed that at the outbreak of war there was no hope of providing an Army capable of holding an attack directed against the West European Coast.'[4]

Tizard's point of view developed earlier in the year. Within one month of the Cabinet's adoption of the FDP paper, the COS had switched their attention to more detailed matters, namely the forces which Britain would require on the outbreak of war.[5] The priorities for ground/air battle planning were the Middle East and the defence of the UK. The FDP paper spoke of impeding 'the enemy build-up in Western Europe' and of 'opposing the spread of Russian influence by adopting a firm attitude to further Russian territorial and ideological expansion'. Generally, however, DO (47) 44 paid very little attention to Germany, and even less to a possible military role for Britain there, hence: 'We must encourage the building up of a strong Western Region of Defence, with France as its key-stone, and ensure that Germany does not become a Russian satellite.'[6] Although the Soviet threat to Europe was clearly perceived, the best response to that threat was still considered to be one which provided for massive atomic air strikes against the Soviet Union, and for the defence of the Middle East and the imperial SLOC. With Tizard's frequent attendance at COS meetings throughout 1947, the COS became more aware of the technological possibilities and risks which now faced Britain. Tizard stressed the fundamental lessons of the war, as he saw them: the vulnerability of Britain to attack by manned aircraft or by rockets; the potential of the atomic bomb; and the vulnerability of SLOC to submarine attack. Britain's defence policy should be shaped around these three impressions and, more importantly, should acknowledge that technology was not static, but dynamic and had to be constantly reviewed to take account of new developments. The COS agreed that the principles of defence policy could no longer determine technological developments; the two must now interact.[7] An air/atomic strategy offered a means of compensating for weaknesses in Britain's armed forces and national economy. But the possibilities being offered by new technology were not viewed merely as a means to paper over the cracks. The air/atomic strategy seemed to offer the optimum use of scarce resources, satisfying all known defence requirements. Furthermore, the strategy was dynamic in that it embraced what was thought to be the strategic future and could therefore provide a base upon which to build.

Any interest and faith in an air/atomic strategy could not, however, overcome the awkward problem that Britain would be unable to produce the weapons with which to threaten massive atomic destruction for about five years. Tizard suggested that there were two possible options for the interim period.[8] First, Britain could abandon conventional weapons and forces completely for the next five years and concentrate instead on economic reconstruction. Alternatively, Britain could give immediate priority to atomic research and development, and prepare to use atomic bombs as soon as they became available. Tizard favoured the second course which would provide not only a firm direction to defence planning, but would also mean that Britain would be able to practise atomic deterrence sooner rather than later. His argument was persuasive: if an air/atomic strategy was preferred choice for the future, then current planning should be made to reflect that preference.

The implications for the Army – and hence for a continental strategy – of Tizard's proposals would have been clear, thus explaining Montgomery's frequent insistence on a suspension of planning and preparations for budgetary reasons. If the available technology led to the sort of deduction Tizard was making, then it would have been in the Army's interest to find a different rationale; it was not just a matter of changing the agenda, the discussion itself had to be postponed, so precarious was the Army's position. Hence, Montgomery advocated a suspension of decision-making in order, ostensibly, to allow for economic reconstruction. Tedder, however, adopted Tizard's argument. Even if the 'five plus five' rule was accepted, there could still be no guarantee that the first five year period would be risk-free.[9]

During 1947 the strategic planners sought answers to three main questions. By what means could war be deterred? How should Britain respond if deterrence were to fail? How should Britain plan to fight a war once deterrence had failed? Only a heavily technological air/maritime/atomic strategy seemed able to meet all these requirements. Reliance on a technological strategy might also allow significant reductions in the size of the armed forces, a claim which would appeal to a government anxious to reduce the size of the armed forces and divert manpower back into industry:

> A political decision barring the use of atomic energy in a future war, would mean a considerable overall increase in the strength of the armed forces. Conversely, a political decision that such weapons would be used in future wars, would ... allow the size of our forces to be considerably less.[10]

Clearly, the most man-power intensive and expensive service, the Army, would have the most to lose in an atomic/technological strategy. Even when, towards the end of 1947, Tizard appeared to accept that Britain should prepare to fight a conventional war in the next five years, he declined to see an offensive role for the Army, and preferred to think in terms of the air/atomic strategy being carried out without atomic bombs.[11] By now, however, the COS had come round to the view that any effort spent on preparing to fight a conventional war would be wasted; by moving as soon as possible to the level of preparedness and technological ability needed in 1957, when an atomic attack on Britain was thought likely, there would be an incidental benefit of deterring small attacks and aggressions before that date.[12]

With the failure of the London CFM in December 1947, the pattern of thinking in Britain concerning a military involvement in Europe became influenced by two distinct forces: movement towards greater political involvement in Europe; and a similar movement towards a more intimate global strategic relationship with the Americans. These two forces were established by January and created immense tensions, the first within the COS over the question of committing troops to Europe, and the second by involving Britain in planning to abandon Europe, knowledge of which would have given Britain a far worse press in Europe than merely a hesitant, cautious commitment.

THE EUROPEANISATION OF BRITISH STRATEGY

That the 'Europeanisation' of British foreign policy was to have strategic implications became clear on the first day of the new year. In December 1947, Bevin had promised military talks with the French and on 1 January Sargent contacted the COS to say that the forthcoming visit by senior French officers was to be taken seriously and that France should be given the impression that Britain was committed to France's security.[13] Doubting the loyalty of communist elements within the French government, the COS were not keen to enter into full discussions. Yet France clearly needed help and advice, and so the COS accepted the discussions while insisting that they should be anodyne, limited to land forces and to such general subjects as training a modern conscript army and standardisation of equipment. The principal concern, however, was that Montgomery's talks with the French, and wider staff talks with the Europeans, might lead Britain into making some form of commitment, involving land forces, to the defence of Europe. Once again, the possibility was quickly dismissed, with Cunningham observing bluntly some days later: 'it was not the intention of His Majesty's Government in a future crisis to send a land expeditionary force to the Continent.'[14] This dismissive tone was reiterated later in January, during discussion of a JPS briefing paper for Britain's representative at the forthcoming discussions in Washington on political union in Western Europe.[15] Defence policy consisted of the familiar 'three pillars': defence of the UK base, control of SLOC and defence of the Middle East. The aim of defence policy was the prevention of war, to be achieved with a 'large deterrent air force'. As for a 'Western European Union', if this organisation could minimise military and economic weaknesses then it would help to achieve the aim, not through any real military defence contribution, but by denying the Soviet Union excuses for intervening. Militarily, a European system would also support one of the three pillars – the defence of the UK base – simply by making Britain less vulnerable to attack from Europe. This paper also provided a careful assessment of three possible strategies for Britain in Europe: a 'Continental Strategy'; a 'Strategy Entailing a Foothold in Europe'; and an 'Air Strategy'.

The continental strategy was, the COS recognised, the one Western Europe would like Britain to adopt. This option could prevent an enemy from overrunning Western Europe, provide early warning of attack and ensure a maximum contribution from the Western European countries themselves. But there were disadvantages: the Soviets would have the advantage of interior lines; they would have more forces and resources; the UK and US would have to provide 30-40 divisions with air support, available in place from the outset, which might prompt the Soviets into pre-emptive action; finally, there were doubts that Western Europe would accept such a strategy. Unless the countries of Western Europe improved their economic and military strength, and unless Germany was rearmed, the 'continental strategy' would be 'militarily impracticable'.

If a 'foothold' could be selected and defended, through which regrouped Allied armies would pour back into Europe, then demanding Normandy-style landings would be avoided and the enemy might be diverted from attacking the UK and the Middle East. Curiously, the JPS also felt that this option would provide encouragement to the Europeans. The JPS could not in the end recommend this option; it would be very costly, would pass the initiative in land operations back to the enemy and, in any case, it was 'always difficult to conduct operations on the Continent on a limited liability basis'. The final option was the 'air strategy', by which 'the main Anglo-American offensive effort would be in the first place only the strategic air offensive.' Given the size of Soviet armies, an air strategy was the one most likely to avoid defeat. It would not require the costly deployment of land and air forces to the Continent, and its success would not be contingent upon the strength and will-power of the West European countries. The disadvantage was that the same Europeans might be so little encouraged to provide for their own defence that there might not be time for Britain to prepare and initiate an air strategy, with the result that 'on political grounds', Britain might have to send an ill-equipped expeditionary force to the Continent.

The JPS argued that it would be 'morally indefensible' for Britain to wash its hands of Western Europe, an act which might encourage the Americans to do the same to Britain. But a choice clearly had to be made and the JPS preferred the 'air strategy' since it offered 'the best chance of preventing war and achieving ultimate victory and provides for at least some support to the countries of Western Europe.' On one point the JPS were in no doubt:

> In any case, we recommend most strongly that in the forthcoming talks [in Washington] we should enter into no commitment to send land and air forces to the Continent.

Montgomery's reaction to the JPS paper was explosive: 'I blew right up, saying that I disagreed completely with the conclusions of the report. What was meant by the expression "the best strategy appears to be the air strategy"? We must defend Western Europe, not liberate it; if we allowed it to be overrun from the East, there would be all too little to liberate.'[16] The next COS meeting descended into a row between Montgomery and Cunningham, with the latter arguing that a Western European alliance could realistically only be a political, rather than military grouping. Montgomery rejected the notion that sea or air action alone could hold back the Soviet invaders: 'The only way to prevent them overrunning Europe was to contain them behind the most suitable line, and for us and the Americans to assist the European nations to do so.'[17] Much was to depend upon the meaning of the word 'assist'. Montgomery found support from an unexpected quarter: Tedder also saw the need to strengthen European defence in order to protect the air bases in Britain.[18] Given that Montgomery had initiated talks with the French and that in mid-January he had disagreed with another JPS recommendation that Anglo-American talks on the Middle East should take precedence over those on Europe,[19] his reaction to the JPS paper and his heated discussion with Cunningham have fuelled the idea that a dichotomy was emerging within the COS and government, between proponents of the three pillars strategy, and Montgomery, the champion of the continental strategy. S. Dockrill describes Montgomery as 'a lone voice in advocating in February 1948 that Britain should send two divisions to the Continent to encourage the morale of her European friends', and Hamilton saw these events and arguments in late January/early February 1948 as the beginning of 'Monty's struggle to make Western Union and the Atlantic Pact a military reality'. Somewhat more cautiously, Kent and Young describe Montgomery as 'the one British military figure who was genuinely interested in continental co-operation,' but point out that he was wary of allowing his enthusiasm for Europe to lead him into making any promises of committing British troops to the Continent.[20]

Montgomery's position was indeed rather complex and subtle, and more than a simple matter of advocating a continental strategy. Not content with the manner in which strategic thinking about Europe appeared to be developing, he produced his own plan.[21] The ideological struggle in Europe would increasingly be focused upon Germany. To resist Russian pressure, Germany should be reunited and reconstructed. It was unlikely, although not inconceivable, that the struggle would develop into war before 1957. When it came, a Russian attack would be sudden and massive and would be directed against both the Middle East and Europe. It was therefore vital, argued Montgomery, that Britain's defensive plans be wide and flexible in their scope. The defence of Europe should not be seen as a discrete option, but as one element of an overall defence plan which would protect the three pillars. Montgomery was effectively trying to change the terms of debate. If a Russian attack could be held 'as far East as possible e.g., on the Rhine' [emphasis in original], then Britain would be granted the necessary defence in depth to allow air forces and air defences to operate effectively. The value of the Rhine in defence terms is explained in precise terms in a recently released JPS document:

> Except for a short stretch on the River Elbe there is no tactical feature East of the Rhine upon which a good defensive position could be based ... The Rhine runs through confused mountainous and forested country in its upper reaches and in the northern plains presents a formidable water obstacle. The area between the Rhine and the Zuider Zee can be flooded to provide an obstacle covering the west of Holland and assisting in the defence of Antwerp. [22]

Thus, defence of Europe would not only contribute to the agreed overall defence plan, but would also support the doctrinal orthodoxy in that a well-defended home base meant 'the retention of air bases from which vital areas of Russia can be reached'. Plainly, Montgomery was seeking to define a role for ground forces with which his colleagues could not disagree.

With deadlock over the fundamental aspects of British strategy, discussion was deferred until a staff conference could be held with Attlee, Bevin and Alexander on 4 February.[23] Bullock describes this meeting as a milestone in the development of Bevin's policies towards Europe. Although moving closer toward the idea of political and even military involvement in Europe, Bevin was adamant that '"We do not want any more Dunkirks."' He thus came to the staff conference as an 'anti-continentalist', and in this was supported by Tedder and Cunningham.[24] The conference ended in compromise. Bevin now accepted that Montgomery's position would merit further research, although with one important qualification:

> It was finally agreed that, while the case for sending British troops to the continent at the outbreak of war could not be accepted without further study (it was not finally accepted until May), Bevin's approach to the problem should be adopted. The COS were to examine the ways of forming the Western European national forces into a single force, and to work out the extra cost of providing two British divisions.[25]

Tedder and Cunningham argued for the established three pillars approach and demanded that the tragedies of Mons and Dunkirk should not be repeated. Attlee agreed, having recently been made dramatically aware of the importance of the Middle East in British strategy: in January 1947 the COS had threatened to resign over Attlee's lack of commitment to the Middle East. Ironically, this 'revolt' had been led by Montgomery. Attlee could not therefore accept the idea of military commitment to Europe and was unhappy at the prospect of building up Germany. Somewhat artfully, Montgomery now stressed that he was talking about the defence of the Continent, not of an offensive strategy for the Army. He agreed that 'overwhelming air power' must be the main weapon. But this weapon could only be effective if it had bases from which to work, within range of Soviet targets, and which could be prepared in time. He estimated that Russia could have 33 divisions on the Rhine 14 days after the outbreak of war and 73 divisions after one month. To hold this force on the Rhine, the West would need 23 divisions by D+14 days and 48 divisions by D+30 days (where 'D' is the outbreak of war in Europe). France alone could provide 30 divisions on the outbreak of war. The British contribution would be only two divisions, which could be allocated out of current 'stocks', i.e., with no additional expense.

With Montgomery apparently advocating greater continental involvement, and Tedder and Cunningham – the arch anti-continentalists – seemingly ranged against him, there is substance to the image, found so often in the literature, of a final struggle between these two competing doctrines: 'the debate between the two strategies raged through March and April, and it was only on 10 May, in a meeting between the Chiefs of Staff and the Minister of Defence, that it was finally agreed that Britain should plan to fight a campaign alongside its allies in Western Europe.'[26] Certainly, Montgomery's own version of events supports this interpretation:

> We must agree that, if attacked, the nations of the Western Union will hold the attack as far to the east as possible. We must make it very clear that Britain will play her full part in this strategy and will support the battle with the fullest possible weight of our land, air and naval power.
>
> Unless this basic point in our strategy is agreed, and is accepted wholeheartedly by Britain, the Western Union can have no hope of survival, and Britain would then be in the gravest danger.[27]

But Montgomery's position was rather more subtle than this view of events would allow. He was, in fact, recommending no change of strategy as such; the requirement was the political one of persuading the Europeans to organise their own defence. Montgomery was simply unable to come up with a real alternative to the overwhelmingly attractive and popular air strategy. And as for his claim that he had 'routed the Pyrenean strategists!'[28] (the advocates of a withdrawal of forces to the Iberian peninsula), it is ironic to note that in a memorandum written in October on the subject of Western European defence, Montgomery was adamant that any withdrawal from the Rhine defensive position would be on his command and would be in a south-westerly direction.[29]

A clearer exposition of Montgomery's view came in a paper produced after the staff conference, showing that he was thinking more in terms of a political commitment than a military strategy:

> I consider that no single operation [defence on the Rhine] can produce a greater contribution, directly, to the security of the United Kingdom and the maintenance of our sea communications and, indirectly, to the maintenance of our position in the Middle East.

> The main land forces contribution must come initially from France, Belgium and Holland, but Britain must help in this too, although the chief British and American initial contribution must obviously be offensive air support.[30]

Having stressed earlier in the year that the suddenness of a Russian attack would require Britain to be ready for the battle on the Continent from the outset,[31] Montgomery now insisted that the force of four divisions to be provided by Britain would not have to be ready until D+28. Even so, these divisions would hardly be crack troops: 'two of these divisions will come from the British forces of occupation in Germany, which will have been withdrawn west of the Rhine and will require to have been made up in administrative units and supporting arms. The remaining two divisions will have to be found from the forces available in the United Kingdom.' These deployments might result in weaknesses in Britain, but Montgomery argued that Britain's fighter and radar defences would be less vulnerable and so more effective and that there would be no need to deploy so many troops on Civil Defence tasks and against the threat of invasion. Having previously been keen to play up the possibility of invasion, it is interesting to observe the alacrity with which Montgomery now dismissed the prospect; a more convincing rationale – one of shoring up the Western Union as East-West relations declined – was now appearing, and so Montgomery embraced it. Montgomery's solution was also possible at no extra cost: 'the United Kingdom's share of the land forces required for the defence of the Rhine can be provided without increasing the size of the peace time Army during the next few years.'

Within weeks, the COS came under renewed Cabinet pressure to co-ordinate their plans and expenditure forecasts. On 17 March the COS discussed a memorandum from Hollis which called for 'broad strategic policy to be made clear', 'with particular reference to the employment of land forces on the Continent', before opening serious discussions with European allies.[32] Discussion quickly became entrenched. Once again, Montgomery showed that his understanding of 'commitment' was more political than strategic, a distinction which he also applied to the occupation forces with their policing tasks:

> Our own contribution on Land in Western Europe could not be very great but we already had an army on the Continent which Lord Montgomery thought must inevitably be there at the beginning of another war for, if we or the Americans ever withdrew the forces we now had in Germany, the whole idea of Western Union would collapse.

Yet the COS also took pains to ensure that too much weight was not attached to the occupation:

> We are in no position at the moment to reinforce our occupational garrison in Germany, neither should we commit ourselves to fight on the continent until the military recovery of the Western European Countries has been established. The land forces we possess would be required for the defence of the United Kingdom and the Middle East. Nor in these circumstances should we send any air forces.

Indeed, any arrangement should be so worded 'as to avoid committing forces to the Continent'.[33]

Cunningham and Tedder argued that broad policy decisions should be decided first, followed by the allocation of resources and, finally, the appropriate strategy. They were sceptical that the three pillars could be served with a military commitment to the Continent and were adamant that, in the event of war, Britain must not again make the mistake of committing 'inadequate forces to the Continent'. In the end, however, Hollis' memorandum was circulated, almost in its original form, as a COS policy document,[34] and was used in negotiations with the US and European allies during much of 1948, with Tedder protesting all the while against the logic of trying to decide upon a strategy for ground forces in Europe without first establishing what resources were available. The Hollis paper described the need to prevent war as the prime aim of British defence policy, along with the capacity to meet a challenge should one be made. With its allies, Britain would aim to halt the Soviet advance at a 'stop line' and, of course, defend the three pillars. Following the suggestion made in Montgomery's paper of late January,[35] Hollis' paper suggested that strategy should be built around both 'the defence of the Middle East' and 'the defence of Europe as far to the east as possible.'[36] Conspicuously absent was the claim that these 'desirable strategic objectives' could or should be achieved by British forces. Where Germany was concerned, what was declared was increasingly falling short of what was practised or intended. This impression is confirmed by a paper produced in mid-April in which the War Office finally caught up with the Navy and RAF and produced statistics showing the availability of forces on the outbreak of war, in both the immediate and the slightly longer term future. If war should break out before 1956/57, the Army would have very little to offer. The following comments are particularly revealing:

> [Up to 1957] the primary roles of the Army will be confined to defence

> of the U.K. Base and reinforcement of M.E.L.F.
>
> None of the formations are administratively capable of going to war. They are all dependent on static installations and German Labour and could not operate outside Germany.[37]

Given these remarks, even the most cautious interpretation of Britain's military intentions towards Europe seems exaggerated:

> On the key question whether British land forces would fight on the continent, Montgomery won a partial victory. On 19 March the Chiefs of Staff agreed that the aim of the alliance should be to defend Europe as far to the east as possible and, in an emergency, to 'fight with what we had' – meaning the British occupation troops in Germany.[38]

PLANNING FOR WITHDRAWAL

During the mid-January meeting mentioned above, reference was made to the 'Dunkirk Talks'.[39] The US had approached Cunningham and suggested talks on an 'operation of withdrawal' from Europe.[40] The JPS stressed the delicate nature of the talks; even the FO should not learn of them. The major problem, however, was that knowledge of the discussions would create the wrong impression in Europe. The JPS described 'the extreme danger of embarking upon talks of this kind just at the moment when we are doing everything possible to bolster up the determination of the Western European Powers to oppose and eradicate Communist influence in their countries.'

The issue of emergency withdrawal planning resurfaced in the spring. In April the JPS met their American counterparts in Washington. It was hoped that the meeting would serve to deflect American interest away from emergency planning in favour of the preparation of a 'long-term plan for action in an emergency in 1957'.[41] The American short-range emergency war plan was known as BROILER (later FROLIC). The plan assumed that, with insufficient land forces, the loss of Western Europe and the Middle East in the early phases of war would have to be accepted, with recovery possible only after D+10 months. The plans placed great emphasis on the strategic air offensive, launched from bases in Britain, Japan and Egypt or Pakistan. HALFMOON and FLEETWOOD were later adaptations. Once again, shortage of forces meant that the oil resources of the Middle East could not be secured. As for Western Europe:

> Because no serious effort could be made to hold Western Europe, allied occupation forces would immediately fall back to the Rhine. Thereafter, they would offer what resistance they could to advancing Soviet armies while withdrawing to French and Italian seaports for evacuation.[42]

Much to Montgomery's disappointment, and to a lesser extent Cunningham's, the JPS had been unable to divert American interest and had begun preparing comparable plans. DOUBLEQUICK planned for the emergency withdrawal from Europe of British and American forces in the event of a crisis in the coming 18 months. Recently released papers show that DOUBLEQUICK was centred upon a strategic air offensive, that British occupation forces were to be withdrawn to the Rhine, and that the plan had been approved by the COS at their 12 May 1948 meeting.[43] However, two other papers, which probably provide more detail on the plan, are still retained within the MoD.[44] The JPS were to continue with their combined planning work, even in the face of Montgomery's deep misgivings.

Disagreement among the COS came to a head at a staff conference on 10 May.[45] Once again, and in spite of the claims made for this meeting,[46] the minutes might be interpreted as falling far short of commitment to the defence of Europe. Montgomery argued that while 'it was essential that we should co-operate with the Americans in the preparation of Plan "Doublequick" – and their intention was to provide for a withdrawal', Britain had nevertheless 'got to prepare joint plans with the Brussels Treaty countries and it would clearly be fatal to the Western Union to start on the basis of withdrawing the Allied Forces in an emergency.' As an emergency plan for Europe, DOUBLEQUICK was therefore unacceptable, not for strategic reasons, but for the sake of the fledgling Western Union. But as an American plan it had to be accepted. What grew out of this dilemma was a compromise and it is this which lies behind the heavily circumscribed commitment which was then made. While Montgomery maintained that the 'fighting spirit' of the Western Union should be nurtured, Tedder and Cunningham could only accept that withdrawal should not be made within the next 18 months. Tedder had hardly been converted to the continental cause, however, stating that there would be 'virtually no close air support' – a deficiency which would quickly have rendered Britain's 'fighting' forces in Europe useless. More importantly, there was to be no reinforcement of the occupation forces, 'other than the necessary administrative backing'; they should simply move to and fight on the Rhine. The COS, and especially Montgomery, were thus all aware of the operational inadequacies of the occupation forces, and the lack of close air support. The problem of being involved in contradictory planning processes was answered by removing references to withdrawal from the British plan.[47] By omitting reference to withdrawal from their paper, the COS hoped that the Americans might see the reasons themselves and 'might also give up their planning for a withdrawal'. Although a withdrawal might have to be planned ad hoc 'if it were forced on us', the priority was to 'imbue the other delegates with the determination to resist all attack.' Accordingly, the British delegation to the recently established WU Military Committee was instructed to make no reference to the possibility of British withdrawal. It was this heavily qualified commitment to the Continent which was subsequently accepted by Attlee and Bevin. During discussion of the commitment, a frank comment made by Cunningham showed just how limited the British contribution must be: 'the police duties of [BAOR] meant that they were deployed in small and scattered units... such dispositions were not compatible with an operational role ...'[48]

Tortuous attempts to find a compromise between Anglo-American and Anglo-European planning conversations also led the COS and JPS to take more interest in what had hitherto been rather peripheral military discussions between the three Allied Military Governors in Germany. These conversations had been taking place for some months, with the object of co-ordinating an Allied withdrawal to fight on the Rhine.[49] The US position in these talks was in some doubt, as was the planned extent of their withdrawal; the continental allies were especially sensitive to the possibility that the Americans were, in fact, planning to withdraw west of the Rhine. Unencumbered by contradictory and secret agendas, these discussions seemed to offer some hope of success, of planning which was both militarily realistic and politically acceptable. The occupation of Germany began to take on a new significance: the essential elements of a Euro-American, rather than Anglo-US or Anglo-European, strategy for Europe all seemed to be falling into place. Even so, the COS were adamant that the European allies should not be told that British emergency planning, although now stopping short of withdrawal from the Continent, recommended that reinforcements should not be sent to the Continent. The COS agreed that the Military Governors should work out an emergency plan, but stressed that the Germans were not be told that a withdrawal to the Rhine was being contemplated. The British representative to the WU Military Committee later told the COS that the Germans may 'turn to Russia' if it were known that plans existed to withdraw from 'Western Germany'. Any movements of stores and equipment must not be allowed to create suspicion.[50]

When, later in May, the COS agreed to give Robertson firm instructions on emergency planning, they made clear that he was to fight with the resources at his disposal, with no reinforcements other than small administrative units. He should plan, in conjunction with the French and Americans, for 'a withdrawal to the Rhine and for a stand to be made there'. This instruction led to some confusion as Robertson promptly began planning not only the withdrawal but also the defensive battle on the Rhine – this had not been the COS intention. The battle on the Rhine was to be orchestrated by the Western Union Chiefs of Staff (WUCOS), as a Western Union (WUDO) operation. Robertson had clearly exceeded his authority and his directive was rejected.[51] Subsequently, however, after a meeting between Montgomery and Robertson, the Military Governor's directive was accepted as a foundation document on which the WUDO Combined Planning Staff could build their plans. Montgomery had in fact been issuing withdrawal orders to Robertson since the spring. For some time Montgomery had considered certain dumps and bases in Germany to be too 'sharp' and had instructed the War Office to decide what equipment was needed for war reserves, and what for normal, peacetime use. The latter should be pulled back towards the Rhine, while 'all the rest should be removed from Germany'. This process, which would take about 12 months, would result in Britain's fighting capacity being held in Britain, not on the Continent.[52] In due course, in order to remove any inconsistencies between the various plans, a sanitised version of DOUBLEQUICK was prepared.[53] The purpose of this exercise had been to remove reference to evacuation from Europe for fear of destroying the inchoate Western Union, even though Britain would continue to consider emergency withdrawal. Furthermore, the plan would only operate up to the end of 1949; the 'continental commitment' of May 1948 was thus not only duplicitous but also of limited life expectancy.

Yet, whatever their misgivings, the COS were not in a position to undermine or ignore the talks being held at the WU, however inconvenient they may have seemed strategically. Following instructions issued at the 19 May meeting, the JPS produced a paper on the defence policy of the Western Union.[54] Montgomery quickly took exception to the report, rejecting the selection of 1955 as a long-term deadline, and insisting that 1957 be kept as the planning target for war with Russia. With defence in depth essential for the effectiveness of Britain's air defences, he was also unable to accept the JPS comment that 'Western Union frontiers would not give the necessary depth with Russian forces established in Western Germany; more particularly as normal air attack might be augmented by rockets and flying bombs.' These defeatist comments 'would be most unpalatable to the Western Union Powers since *though it was true, it might be taken that our intention was not to attempt to prevent Russian occupation of Western Germany*' [emphasis added]. In a rare moment of inter-service harmony, Cunningham also felt that the paper might give the impression that the defence of Western Union territories was a secondary requirement; 'it was in fact a primary requirement', albeit not a task for Britain.

The 'revised final' version of the JPS paper was discussed on 30 June.[55] Aimed directly at the WU Military Committee, the report sought both to lay the foundations for a WU defence policy and to deflect European interest into long-term problems and planning rather than 'the short-term, but less serious, threat'. WU defence policy should be based upon deterrence and a genuine readiness to fight. Russia was the only serious threat but, in spite of a short-term risk of war through accident or Russian miscalculation, a Russian challenge would not be feasible until the end of the second post-war five year plan. The WU, supported by the Americans, should demonstrate their determination to protect Europe and their interests, but should avoid antagonising Russia. Given the extent of Russian industrial and military resources, the JPS argued that a quick conclusion to war might be achieved with the use of mass destruction weapons. However, eventual Russian acquisition of such weapons and the increasing danger of a surprise attack meant that 'the chances of achieving an acceptable standard of defence by purely defensive methods within the time available are slight.' The familiar options were then examined. A 'long and extremely costly' land campaign was dismissed in favour of the air offensive, 'the best prospect of bringing early pressure to bear on the enemy.' The air threat was such that 'depth' would be required to enable air defences to be prepared and to operate effectively. This required that 'the Russians should be held on land as far to the east as possible', a strategy which would also deny the Russians the opportunity of exploiting their numerical advantage in land forces. To deter Russian use of mass destruction weapons, or destroy them before they could be used, the West should possess a large bomber force equipped with atomic bombs. Such a force would be 'the most effective deterrent to war and, should war nevertheless break out, offers the best method of bringing early pressure to bear on the enemy.' Provision of forces within the WU was also suggested. The JPS suggested that France and Benelux should contribute primarily to the early European land campaign, as well as air defences and protection of SLOC in their areas. The UK should concentrate on a 'full contribution' to WU air defence; control of essential SLOC; defence of the Middle East in conjunction with the US; and contributions to the strategic bomber force and 'The European land campaign in conjunction with all the Allies'.

Montgomery had little to add to the revised report. Defence in depth was vital and to that end he suggested one amendment to the report, putting any British interest in a continental strategy for Europe firmly into context:

> there could be *no question of attempting to bring about the final defeat of Russia by means of a land campaign* culminating in the invasion of Russia. It will however, be essential to our final victory that we fight successfully the land battle *for the defence of certain vital areas*. In the conduct of these battles, we must plan to engage the enemy in conditions which will offset his numerical superiority as far as possible and every effort must be made to use our technical lead to counterbalance Russian numbers. [Emphasis added]

Cunningham, however, felt that even this cautious language might imply more 'continentalism' than Britain was prepared to accept. He suggested that the UK contributions should be listed in priority, to make things clear. The defence of the UK, SLOC and the Middle East were still the principal tasks (i.e., the three pillars). The remaining contributions (including, therefore, that to the land battle) were 'secondary ones'. Montgomery resisted this suggestion, arguing that what was 'secondary' for the UK was in fact 'primary' for the WU. His compromise, which the final version of the report reflects, was that no contributions – from either France, Benelux or UK – should be ranked in importance. Eventually the revised report was approved by the COS and submitted to Alexander.[56] It was also sent to the delegation to the WU, with instructions to withhold the paragraphs dealing with national contributions if necessary.

THE BERLIN CRISIS

By the time the COS had agreed their WU defence policy paper, the Berlin crisis had come to dominate all strategic thinking and planning. Robertson returned to the UK on 12 July to meet the COS, by which time they were to have decided how to answer his questions concerning 'the future situation in Berlin if the airlift could not be built up.'[57] At a staff conference on the same day,[58] Alexander suggested that the problem now was two-fold: should Britain go to war over Berlin, and should a command and control organisation be established now for running 'the battle in the West'? The conference could not yet be certain that the Berlin situation would constitute a *casus belli*. At the same time, however, it was felt prudent to assume that there might be a war, and to plan for it. Alexander informed the conference that DOUBLEQUICK plans would provide all necessary information and, without a firm decision being made in any direction, the COS were duly 'directed' to plan on the assumption that war 'might' begin over Berlin. The COS pointed out that although Robertson had made preparations for a withdrawal to the Rhine, arrangements for a Western Union battle on the Rhine were not yet adequate. To make progress in this field, the intentions and support of the Americans must be known: Bevin agreed to make hurried arrangements for this support, without which the British might have appeared to be precipitating the crisis.

The record of Robertson's discussion with the COS has recently been released and shows that he was confident that the tri-nation emergency plan was now viable, but was concerned that 'the German people' might 'get the impression that they were being left in the lurch', and that the quality of British troops in Germany was questionable.[59] The COS also considered that, in preparation of any emergency plans, it should be possible to bring forward DOUBLEQUICK planning from a 12 month warning time to a matter of the next few weeks. The Army and RAF were to draw up lists, similar to that already provided by the Navy, to show what steps would have to be taken to enable Britain to 'fight with what we had got'. These assessments were duly circulated and the COS agreed that these and other relevant reports should be pooled and sent to the Chancellor of the Exchequer to enable him to inform the government of the economic effect of taking these steps.[60] The Berlin crisis was clearly a catalyst for inter-service co-operation in the short-term, as well as exposing Britain's weaknesses in Germany. The RAF, for example, despaired of the tactical air forces in Germany being of any real value in supporting the defensive battle, fearing instead that they would be 'swamped' by Russian support air forces.

As the Berlin crisis deepened, Montgomery was tempted to present the government with an ultimatum.[61] In a memorandum to the COS, Montgomery indicated that he had asked the government the 'crunch question': '"Is it the intention of the Government to resort to War if we are forced out of Berlin by any means?"' Claiming that Berlin was a 'first class military liability', and that every interest in Berlin would have to 'written off once the shooting starts', Montgomery appeared anxious that attention should not be diverted to saving Berlin when the much more important plans for withdrawal to the Rhine had already been made by the three allied Military Governors/Commanders-in-Chief. The defensive battle that would then follow had, however, not yet been prepared; there was thus even more reason not be drawn into fighting for Berlin. With the lack of command and control, the lack of forces '"in being"', and the absence of 'will power' and 'fighting spirit', the WU did not seem up to the task. Britain's allies in Europe were in fact 'quite useless from the military angle'.

The purpose of this tirade was to set the scene for his demand for a 'Grand Design' or 'master plan' for the strategy of the WU, with the US involved. The starting point was to be the establishment of a command structure with one supreme commander running 'the whole front in the West from the Baltic to Trieste' [emphasis in original]. He recommended that the release programme be stopped, that the reserve be called up, and that the TA be embodied:

> It is possible that we may have to fight in the near future. As things stand at present, the British Army is not in a fit state to be launched into a World War.

The COS coolly agreed that 'the short-term strategic objectives at the outbreak of war, for the employment of Allied Forces in Western Europe', would merit examination by the JPS.

The meeting then went on to discuss another memorandum by Montgomery in which he hoped that the sense of long-term perspective should not be lost by the rush to make short-term arrangements.[62] He felt that, having taken a firm line over Berlin, Britain had in fact '"drifted"' into a dangerous situation whereby there was no national plan for the outbreak of war. Given that 'Full peacetime conditions do not exist, nor are they likely to occur within the near future', a 12 month period of National Service, due to come into force on 1 January 1949, was now inadequate and should be stretched to 24 months. On 25 August the COS learned of a Cabinet recommendation to suspend releases from the Armed Forces up to 31 March 1949.[63] Montgomery argued that this was not enough: what was needed was two years of National Service and general mobilisation.

But the short-term crisis was, understandably, never far from the top of the agenda. On 1 September, Tedder stated that short-term plans were still not adequate, that the JPS had not given enough emphasis to 'the risk of war before 1952':

> Our present policy that if war was forced upon us within the next few

> years we should have to fight with what forces and weapons we possessed was unrealistic in that we did not possess at the present time the necessary balanced forces with which to fight.

He wanted the JPS to examine the idea of 'balance' in national forces and to accept that peacetime commitments would continue for as long as the '"cold war"' lasted and should therefore be included in their report. Tedder had thus come to accept something of the position which Montgomery had been arguing for some time; air power and technology could not provide all the answers in the long as well as the short term.[64] But any suggestion of a doctrinal compromise was short-lived.

On 8 September the COS met to discuss the results of JPS deliberations on short-term strategy for Europe, and on Montgomery's 'Grand Design'.[65] The paper described the 'strategic aims' of the WU. In Europe, these were to hold the enemy as far east as possible and to provide air defence of WU countries. Elsewhere, the aims were to defend the Middle East and North Africa and to control SLOC, especially in the North Atlantic and Mediterranean. Since resources were not sufficient to meet all demands, some preference would have to be made. For Europe, the priority should be to defend on the Rhine; a position further east would not be tenable:

> We do not consider that Western Germany will be in a position to assist in any way towards checking a Russian advance Westwards for many years to come. Under these circumstances, there can be no question of planning to hold Western Germany with the Allied forces available. *Allied forces must therefore be withdrawn to assist in the defence of the Rhine on the outbreak of hostilities*. [Emphasis added].

The withdrawal to the Rhine was not expected, however, to solve many problems:

> Though not specifically stated in the paper *for political reasons* it must be accepted that should war occur in the immediate future, Allied resources will be totally inadequate to fight successfully on the Rhine against the scale of attack which the Russians are capable of mounting; and therefore if the Russians attack in Western Europe it will be overrun. [Emphasis added].

Forces in indefensible Berlin would not be assisted in any way and would have to make their own way back to the Rhine. Vienna and

Trieste could not be defended and forces there would have to find their way to Italy. Yet in spite of all this, the JPS still found themselves able to issue a rallying call:

> Allied forces of occupation in Western Germany should, if possible, assist in the defence of the line Yssel-Rhine-Switzerland-Franco-Italian Frontier on the Mediterranean.

In late September Montgomery began to move away from his earlier view that the long-term planning process should not be overwhelmed by the short-term crisis. Responding to a call from Alexander for a joint report, awaited since February, on the long-term size and shape of the armed forces,[66] Montgomery now described earlier efforts at long-term planning as 'old history':

> The papers were written against a background of "no war for five years and risk increasing gradually for the next five" and of "diminishing peacetime commitments". The Naval and R.A.F. contributions were over a year old and probably required revision: for instance, the Royal Air Force paper made no provision for the R.A.F. contribution to Western Union.

Long-term planning should now take second place, and had in fact ceased in the War Office on 4 August. What was essential was to organise the Army to meet its peacetime commitments and enable it to expand in time of war. Montgomery thus seized upon the opportunity offered by the Berlin crisis and the inadequacies of WU short-term planning, to make a case for abandoning the long-term planning process, under which the Army was faring so badly. While future strategy would involve new weapons, such as the atomic bomb, and new concepts, such as strategic air deterrence, the immediate crisis in Germany showed that land forces were still needed. The COS, however, felt that since both short- and long-term planning processes were in hand, both should be kept going.

A glimpse of what little Britain might be able to offer the WU by way of land forces was seen in a memorandum from Hudleston, the British representative on the WU Military Committee.[67] The Committee was of the opinion that 'the forces available to the Commanders-in-Chief in the immediate future would be only those now in occupation zones of Germany.' At that time, the order of battle of BAOR was as follows:

1 infantry division
1 infantry brigade
1 armoured brigade
1 parachute brigade
4 armoured car regiments
4 infantry battalions

'None of the forces in the BAOR', however, were 'administratively complete for war'. Thus, even with the provision from the UK field force of one infantry brigade group, one infantry brigade, two armoured regiments and one infantry battalion, it would not be until three months after mobilisation that a total force of two infantry divisions, one armoured brigade and one armoured regiment would be made available.

MONTGOMERY AT THE WESTERN UNION

Montgomery's departure from the War Office to assume the appointment of Chairman of the Western Union Commanders-in-Chief Committee was the point at which military thinking about Europe began to change, in two important ways. First, the War Office began to move away from the idea of fighting in Europe, in favour of operations in the Middle East. On 29 October, after Montgomery's departure to Fontainebleau, Templer dismissed any possibility that, on the outbreak of war in the next two or three years, the two divisions currently earmarked for the Middle East would be sent to Germany:

> If war broke out in the immediate future, it was his opinion that it would be strategically most unsound to divert to Western Europe reinforcements intended for the Middle East.[68]

It would thus seem that Montgomery's personality and presence may have influenced earlier War Office views on this subject. Second, a shift took place away from WU planning and discussions to talks between the Americans, the British and the Canadians, known as the 'ABC' talks. Once again, the circumstances suggest that Montgomery's interest and involvement in WU planning may have shaped British policy.

'ABC' planning staff talks took place at the Pentagon 18-26 October 1948. On 10 November the COS discussed the JPS report of the meeting.[69] The main points on the agenda had been revision of DOUBLEQUICK command arrangements and the development of a long-term strategic concept.[70] SPEEDWAY, the revised version of DOUBLE-

QUICK, was presented to the COS in late November.[71] This version differed from the original in that a 28-day warning period was no longer assumed. Tedder, commenting on similarities between SPEEDWAY and a recent JIC paper,[72] felt that the plan over-estimated the air threat to the UK and the ground threat to the Middle East. Slim, however, like Templer, agreed with the plan's Middle East assessment. SPEEDWAY covered the possibility of war up to 1950, and was confined only to the opening months of war. The authors confessed that the plan did not provide 'adequate assistance to the countries of Western Europe', and that 'Occupation forces being withdrawn [to the Rhine] can expect no reinforcement to their fighting strength' (emphasis in original).[73] There were other weaknesses: force projections were 'optimistic'; the plan relied too much on an unknown quantity – American atomic bombing; the Western Allies would be unable 'to withstand a Russian advance in Western Europe, even with the full defence co-operation of the Western Powers'; the defence of Britain would become 'critical' after about 6 months; and 'critical shortages of vehicles and equipment, particularly in the Army' would make the defence even of the Middle East a problematic undertaking.[74] Thus, in late 1948, with the Berlin crisis underway, Britain's commitment to continental defence, insincere and temporary as it was, seemed increasingly to be a political declaration with no basis in reality. Britain's military plans were still centred upon the three pillars and DO (47) 44, and upon the American atomic air offensive.

Against this background, Montgomery's canvassing of the COS on behalf of the WU military organisation seems rather futile.[75] He had made three general defence plans. The first was for an emergency in 1949/50. The forces required, which would have to be ready by January 1949, were some eleven divisions (from the French, Belgians and Dutch, and from the British and American forces then in Germany). The British contribution to this force could be no more than two 'equivalent' divisions. Only one division (the American) was considered to be battleworthy. Montgomery pleaded for at least one British division to be made battleworthy before autumn 1949. His second plan, beginning in January 1951, would require 25 divisions: three Dutch; four Belgian; two US; 14 French; and, still, only two British. The third plan called for 37 divisions and was based upon the maximum number of forces which it was thought possible to assemble in peacetime: three Dutch; four Belgian; two US; 24 French; and four British. So the maximum peacetime commitment Montgomery considered Britain could make to Europe was four divisions, and even then not for several years. His request for a peacetime commitment of forces has a ring of tokenism to it, since: 'in his opinion [French] morale would never recover until they could be convinced that Britain would really contribute what the French considered a fair quota of land forces to the defence of Western Europe at the outbreak of another war.' If the Middle East were given priority for reinforcement over Germany then the Continent would receive no additional troops for about six months, instead of the two month gap which might otherwise be possible. This was an important point:

> Unless the French were assured that this additional contribution would be forthcoming, he thought there would be no effective resistance. The battle, in fact, would be lost before it had begun.

Slim's reaction was somewhat sceptical:

> there was much to be said for making the troops we already had in Germany battleworthy. It might be better to have one battleworthy division than two equivalent divisions who [sic] were not battleworthy, as at present. The question of whether we should agree to reinforce our troops in Germany in the event of war was a much more difficult one. Apparently there was not much chance of holding Western Europe with less than about 40 divisions. In this case it meant that if war broke out in the next few years, any additional troops we sent to Europe would almost certainly be lost.

Montgomery's almost desperate response was to argue that 'the promise of reinforcement was so important that *it ought to be given even if we could not be sure that we should be able to fulfil it when the time came*' [emphasis added]. When Montgomery had left the meeting, Slim explained that he did not like the idea of making false promises and, anyway, still doubted that two divisions would make much difference. The COS agreed, but asked that he discuss the matter with Tedder and North.

Slim's non-committal response to Montgomery's suggestion soon gave way and he was to agree that the 'Occupation Forces in Germany should be made battle-worthy'.[76] But his 'commitment' still erred on the side of caution:

> Our intention should be primarily to make our Occupation Forces in Germany battle-worthy. As a first step one Division should be reorganised and trained. Subsequently it might be possible to reorganise and train a second Division in Germany ... No reinforcements should be sent to the Continent at least until there was a good chance that [the WU] could hold the Russians on the line of the Rhine ... *Our*

> *main effort in any war on the Continent would, however, lie in our contribution to naval and air forces.* [Emphasis added].

Slim's statement was accepted as a statement of policy to be passed to the Defence Committee, and so the year ended with little real change having been made to the bases of British defence planning.

SUMMARY

The air/maritime strategic orthodoxy, as enshrined in DO (47) 44 of May 1947, remained potent throughout the period covered by this chapter. Time and again, faith in air power and the atomic strike was confirmed and the three-pillared defence policy underlined. This orthodoxy was rooted not only in doctrinal and technological preferences but also in severe limitations on resources. Britain's 'commitment' to Europe began and ended with the occupation of Germany, a commitment which was certain to be run down.

From early in 1948 Britain's military planners were pulled in opposing directions.[77] In one direction lay Anglo-American planning for an emergency withdrawal from Europe, the contingency most compatible with current British military thinking. In the other direction, however, lay the integration and reconstruction of Western Europe, encouragement of which necessitated some form of defence commitment. Strategic thinking then deteriorated into a series of attempts to find a compromise and to divert European interest into less difficult areas – long-term force planning, for example. The image of Montgomery championing the 'continental strategy' in the face of the scepticism of his colleagues and the government is not the most complete representation of what occurred. There was never a 'debate' between two equally viable, competing strategies: the primacy of the air/maritime orthodoxy was unassailable. Furthermore, Montgomery's motives and actions were more subtle than might be supposed. He never set out to challenge the doctrinal orthodoxy, but sought instead to establish a stronger position for the Army within that orthodoxy and to manipulate the planning and resource allocation processes to the Army's favour. Thus, in 1947, he stressed the strain imposed upon the Army of the National Service training programme, of the need to defend overseas commitments (especially those on the SLOC), and of the need to meet a possible invasion. But more significant was his attempt in 1947 to arrest the long-term planning process altogether, ostensibly for the sake of the nation's economy but actually because the Army could only fare badly in such a process.

The development of the Western Union and the requirement for some form of military commitment by Britain, ought to have provided Montgomery with an opportunity to strengthen the Army's position. Instead, he advocated no more than a token commitment of land forces which he accepted would be sparse, ill-equipped and late in arriving. Equally, the effect of the Berlin crisis on Montgomery's thinking and on the continental cause, was not straightforward. Montgomery emphatically did not see the defence of Berlin as providing an immediate, key role for land forces. Rather, he was concerned that involvement in Berlin – which he had 'written off' – would detract from the more important and realisable goal of withdrawal to, and defence on, the Rhine. In response to the crisis, Montgomery reiterated his calls for a British commitment to a strategy of defence for Europe. But the commitment he sought, once again, neither challenged the orthodoxy in Britain nor laid any particular stress on the value of land forces. Having first been concerned that the crisis would overshadow long-term planning, Montgomery finally saw in the crisis the long-awaited rationale for abandoning the long-term planning process and the concentration instead upon more favourable peace-time considerations and deployments. Even then, his argument fell noticeably short of challenging the strategic verities of the day.

British military interest in Europe during 1947 and 1948 might best be described as a vast exercise in public relations. The events of 4 February, 19 March, and 10 May 1948 are often presented as evidence of steady progression towards a continental strategy. This is difficult to accept, not least because after Montgomery's departure for the Western Union the War Office began to focus more on the Middle East rather than Europe, and on Anglo-American rather than Western Union planning discussions. Slim's response to Montgomery's pleading was merely the vague promise that occupation troops in Germany would be made more battleworthy. British military thinking about Germany and the Continent was in fact a complex response to several different pressures, and in large part attributable to Montgomery's equally complex personal objectives. Above all, it is now clear that 1948 ended with a wide disjunction between the developing political commitment to Europe and its defence, and the strategic thinking of Britain's military.

6 Token Forces: Strategic Plans, 1949-50

A firm and immediate promise of a token force.

Chiefs of Staff[1]

In mid-December 1948,[2] Slim conceded that the occupation forces should at least be made 'battle-worthy', by reorganising and training first one division, but had been reluctant to make any promise of reinforcement. He wanted to stimulate the Europeans into providing for their own defence, and was convinced that Britain's 'main effort' in any war in Europe would be at sea and in the air. The first COS meetings of 1949 show that Slim's view reflected something of a consensus within military planning circles. Defence of the WU seemed a lost cause and it was important not to create 'the impression that if a big enough land contribution could be made, the position would be satisfactory'. Britain could make no contribution to WU defence without additional effort coming first from France and the Benelux countries. But then, even had it been possible to fund a large-scale commitment of land forces – which it was not – the strategic thinking of the day would rule out such an option in favour of action in the air (the strategic air offensive) and at sea.[3]

THE REINFORCEMENT ISSUE

It was to this unsympathetic climate of opinion that, on 5 January 1949, Montgomery brought his requests for reinforcement. Montgomery had requested this meeting some weeks earlier,[4] when he had explained his goal of 'a firm guarantee' to reinforce BAOR in the event of war with 'no more than one Infantry Brigade Group'. Such a promise would do much to improve the confidence of the continental allies, demonstrating Britain's faith in the defence of Western Europe. Without a guarantee of reinforcement the 'will to fight' of France and the Benelux countries would, he believed, 'be irrevocably impaired'. Given that British and Allied forces were still in the process of being made more battleworthy – a process which would not be complete until the end of 1949[5] – the promise of an infantry brigade group would, in fighting terms, be a token gesture but a very popular one. In any case, he argued:

> the likelihood of war in the next year or two was not great and if sufficient time elapsed before the outbreak of war, then the forces of the Continental powers would be more nearly ready to meet the threat and more aware of the value of the British air and naval contribution.

Fraser and Slim, however, at first believed that there could be little 'military justification' for making the guarantee; the troops thus committed would certainly be lost, merely for the sake of boosting morale on the Continent. But within two days, Slim began to speak of 'wider considerations', and Fraser too showed interest in Montgomery's argument 'in spite of the military disadvantages'. For the moment, even Tedder found that 'on balance' he agreed with the need to guarantee reinforcement.[6] But within weeks, it became apparent that a new consensus was not in fact at hand: while Montgomery was attempting to improve the WU's force posture in the short term, the COS were still able only to consider the matter in the long term, where strategic thinking still precluded continental involvement, or as a political rather than military matter.

After the rebuff given to Montgomery, the WU soon resumed its campaign for a commitment by Britain, but now switched its interest to planning for 1957. On 14 January WU Ministers of Defence had instructed WUCOS to prepare estimates of the size and sources of forces needed for Western defence.[7] This inevitably raised the subject of national contributions and the COS duly discussed a request from the UK's representative to the MCFP (Hudleston) to provide no more than a hypothetical list of British forces available in 1957.[8] Tedder's response was now more typical:

> It had already been decided by H.M. Government that in the short term we should not send any land reinforcements to the Continent. H.M. Government would later have to consider whether or not we should send land reinforcements to the continent in the long term.

Fraser and Templer were less at ease. With some sense of where honesty in this subject might lead, Fraser felt that an open projection of figures could only result in Britain's contribution to, and the sincerity of the belief in, the defence of Western Europe being questioned.

Pressure from the WU mounted, and on 2 March the COS discussed short-term planning within the WU for the defence of Europe. The WUCinC (with Montgomery as chairman) had submitted a plan for consideration by the WUCOS.[9] The plan made gloomy reading. With each allied division facing a likely three to eight Russian divisions, each aircraft facing seven to fifteen, and each tank five to ten, the message they gave was that the security of the Western world could not be guaranteed:

> The various Governments should therefore know that the present Forces do not even represent and are far from representing the strength necessary to contain a Russian attack launched by surprise without reinforcement or mobilisation, still less an attack after reinforcement and mobilisation.
>
> The Commanders-in-Chief Committee therefore stress most strongly that the troops at their disposal should be reinforced as a matter of great urgency.

By 1 July 1949, when the plan would become operative, it was assessed that, even without preparation, the Soviets could amass 25 divisions with 5,000 tanks and 2,000 tactical aircraft in support. The aircraft strength could be doubled within days. But with one month of preparation the Soviets could parade a massive force of 75 divisions, 5,000 tactical aircraft and 800 heavy bombers. Against this onslaught in central Europe, the Allies would be able to provide some 140,000 men in about ten divisions with 950 tanks. Tactical air support would be limited to 294 fighters, 69 reconnaissance aircraft and 32 bombers. The JPS acknowledged the demand for urgent reinforcement but commented that no 'substantial' reinforcement would be possible in the near future.[10] The JPS continued to think in terms of making the best with what was available until long-term plans came into effect, rather than drawing up separate short-term plans.

Montgomery resumed his campaign the following day, asking for no more than a planning figure for the number of British divisions which would be available in the future.[11] He wished to know whether he could rely on the figure discussed the previous summer of two corps, each of two divisions with supporting arms, with two of these divisions already existing, in embryo form, in BAOR.[12] Slim confirmed that this was indeed still the basis of planning within the War Office. But even long-term predictions could not be guaranteed:

> There might be some difficulty in obtaining this approval by the 1st April, 1949 since the size of the British contribution was bound up with the long-term plans for the size and shape of the forces which were being reconsidered.

The COS then passed the problem back to Montgomery and the WU, deciding to defer their decision on the provision of forces for Europe until plans for Europe were known.[13]

Pressure from the WU was relentless, and on 6 April the COS learned that the idea had gained ground that Britain would be in a position to supply ten divisions for Europe's defence by 1951.[14] But the WU had misunderstood; British policy was to contribute no more than the one and two thirds divisions (not even the full two divisions which Montgomery had taken to be the irreducible minimum) currently in Germany, explained Alexander. The figure of ten divisions represented the total British land forces, to be distributed among all commitments. Slim, however, sensed the delicacy of the European problem:

> it would be necessary to make a promise of additional land forces to the [WU] before long. He did not see how we could maintain our influence in the [WU] without doing this. Furthermore, it was greatly to our strategic interest to prevent the Russians from over-running Western Europe: particularly in view of the threat to the [UK] that would arise from rockewts [sic] attack mounted from the Channel Coast.

Slim's suggestion was to tie a promise of a further two divisions to an undertaking by the French to supply 15 effective divisions. Tedder, still unhappy at the prospect of being drawn into commitments to major land campaigns in both Western Europe and the Middle East, was adamant that decisions about land forces should not be taken without the allocation of tactical air resources having first been decided. This review was in progress and so Tedder asked that no specific undertaking be made. So the meeting ended, with growing awareness that, in spite of earlier Cabinet and COS decisions, the issue of reinforcement would soon have to be faced.

Later in April, with the WUCinC having decided to draw up its next plan (to be effective from 1 June 1951), some indication was sought as to the likely British contribution.[15] Slim reiterated the argument that there was little military value in increasing the land forces contribution to Europe, especially since it might detract from the far more important task of defending the Middle East, but noted that there were 'serious political objections' to such an approach. Expanding upon his earlier suggestion, he acknowledged that an increased contribution would have to be offered. But he would make any such offer conditional upon the contributions made by the European Allies themselves. When the Allies were able to provide more, effective divisions, then the British might agree to increase their contribution by two divisions. These two divisions would not, though, be ready until D+3 months and would only be made available if a tactical air support element could be provided, a matter which was still under review.

The report of a joint War Office/Air Ministry review of the forces which might be made available for operations in Europe was produced in mid-May.[16] This paper assumed that the allocation of finances for re-equipment would meet the following order of priority: the Cold War; premeditated war from 1957; and unpremeditated war before 1957. The proposed timetable for reinforcement of Western Europe within the first three months of war shows that the bulk of any reinforcement would probably be from the reserve forces, requiring six months to prepare for war. By the end of one year it should be possible to send two infantry and one armoured divisions. The report finished with a precise summary of the shortfall between what Britain could provide and what its European allies would expect:

> To sum up, the land and air forces which could be sent to Western Europe in time under present conditions would be very limited and would fall very far short of what the Continental Countries are likely to consider as a fair contribution. It must also be emphasised that the size of the land forces and of the air forces are complementary; it is valueless to contribute divisions unless provision is also made for equivalent strength in the Air Forces which protect and support them.

Slim suggested that Britain had two choices: either to contribute to a plan designed to match the Russians on the Rhine; or to concentrate on the Cold War and allocate to Europe only those resources surplus to the need to improve readiness for war.[17] The choice was not easy:

> Course A would mean that we were committed to a major war on the Continent with obvious repercussions on our ability to defend the Middle East. Course B, however, amounted to telling the Western Union countries that we were not making any material contribution to the defence of Western Europe apart from the forces now promised; and this would have a most serious effect on the solidarity of the [WU].

Tedder reiterated the basic tenets of Britain's agreed strategy: defence of the UK, the Middle East and the SLOC. Nothing should be allowed to compromise these aims. Edelsten was wary that involvement in Europe could develop into 'a "snowball" and we would find that we would inevitably have to send very substantial forces to the Continent'. Slim's newest solution was to think in terms of TA rather than regular divisions. Deployment of regular divisions could not be reliably predicted, but a promise to send to Europe two out of the first four TA divisions mobilised would require no immediate action.

EMERGENCY VERSUS LONG-TERM PLANNING

With WUCOS due to meet on 1 June, the 30 May COS meeting showed that whatever priorities the COS may have decided, pressure from the WU was now forcing them to consider joint, short-term or emergency planning more than they would have liked. The COS felt the problem to be largely an Anglo-French matter, given that the other four Brussels Treaty powers 'well understood that we were not yet in a position to make any commitment'.[18] Yet with another WUCOS meeting due on 23 June and a WUDC meeting on 15 July, the COS were aware that the WUCinC would need more detailed information on the forces available for war in spring 1951.[19] The joint War Office/Air Ministry paper[20] had now been re-drafted.[21] Among the differences recorded between this document and its predecessor, it was now assumed that there would be no American aid and that there would be no field forces in Britain at the start of an emergency from which a strategic reserve could be formed. The new draft assumed a three month transition to war period during which emergency measures could be taken. Divisions would be equipped for 'tactical' but not 'strategic' mobility. Training would not be fully complete. The new mobilisation plan was spartan:

Infantry divisions
1 in 4 months or more
1 in 5.5 months or more
1 in 6.5 months or more
1 in 7 months or more

Armoured brigades
1 in 4 months or more
1 in 10 months or more

All the above, the report noted, would be in 'a low state of operational readiness'. Furthermore, without a period of six months in which to prepare for war, Britain's land forces could not be 'sufficiently trained and equipped to meet fully mobilised Russian forces on level terms'. Nonetheless Templer, representing Slim, accepted that for 'political reasons' it might be 'desirable to stick to this more encouraging estimate'; the Army Advisory Committee to the WU had assessed that Britain could provide four infantry divisions and two armoured brigades within three months of the declaration of an emergency, calculations which bore no resemblance to WO/Air Ministry ideas. Developing a point made by Montgomery at the beginning of the year, Templer suggested a way out of the dilemma:

> the right course of action was to promise to send the first two Divisions and an Armoured Brigade to the Continent. In the event of war in 1951 the land forces available initially to the Western Allies would be quite inadequate to hold the enemy on the Rhine and operations would probably develop so swiftly that it would not be practicable to send additional forces to Western Europe.

Fraser agreed: if a promise of this nature could avert the collapse of the WU then the problems of fighting on the Rhine might not have to be faced. Furthermore, such a promise might even persuade the Americans to help in the defence of the Middle East. Tedder did not agree. He resisted the seductive logic of reinforcing the occupation troops, a decision which would have unintended implications and which would undermine current defence policy. The earlier War Office/Air Ministry paper[22] had said that no firm decision could be made until the likelihood of tactical air support had been investigated. Rejecting hollow promises which could not be met, Tedder now said that no substantial addition to the tactical air forces currently in Germany could be made. He described the idea of a commitment of land forces as 'completely out of touch with modern developments'; air and sea power were where the future lay. The COS duly requested a new report on the subject, showing precisely the implication for British strategy of offering any additional forces to Europe.

When, six days later, the COS returned to the subject, they came directly to the point, asking 'whether the right military advice to Ministers was that it was in our broad strategic interest to increase the British contribution to the defence of Western Europe.'[23] Fraser and Slim, by now unable or unwilling to consider the problem as a purely 'military' one, and thus to dismiss it, agreed that a commitment of forces made little military sense. In a war in 1951 the Western Allies would simply be unable to hold back a Soviet attack on the Rhine and any additional forces assigned to this hopeless task would, therefore, be lost. The loss of the Rhine would be a 'severe tactical setback', but not 'calamitous'. The real strategic disaster would occur if the WU were to fall apart through lack of support. If this Cold War victory were to fall to the Soviets then, once again, the fear was that the Allies' performance in a 'shooting war' would be 'prejudiced beyond repair'. Tedder at first fell back on his argument that Britain's agreed defence policy did not involve or require holding the enemy in Europe. But, finally, he softened his stance and in so doing allowed, for the first time, a measure of consensus within the COS that the reinforcement of BAOR might be wise. The Defence Committee was to be informed of the following view:

> if the political assessment was that the Western Union would be seriously weakened unless we promised to send more forces to the Continent, it would be right to commit ourselves to reinforce the British Army of the Rhine in spite of the inescapable risk entailed.

The reinforcement of Europe was clearly not to be a first charge on Britain's strategy.

Eventually the WU Military Committee accepted that the British mobilisation programme on the outbreak of war could be no more than four and two thirds divisions within three months.[24] This would be disappointing enough for the French, but even more so when, as Templer explained, it was made clear that this projection would only apply from 1951. Furthermore, the subject of reinforcement and strategy for Europe was still open to debate, if not in WU circles. Following a Defence Committee decision[25] to discuss Britain's land forces contribution with American defence chiefs 'in the context of the overall plan for war', the JPS were requested to prepare a report on Britain's preferred strategy. The JPS paper duly appeared,[26] to be updated when the JIC paper on Soviet intentions and capabilities had also been revised.[27]

In the JPS view, the Allies' broad strategic aims were to dissuade Russia from further military and ideological expansion and to create conditions conducive to world peace. There were three possible ways of achieving these aims: by destroying enemy forces on land; by land and sea blockade; by direct air attack on Russia. The second of the three options was rejected; Russia would be 'self-sufficient in all essential requirements' by 1957, so blockade would be indecisive. For two reasons, a land strategy was also rejected:

> A strategy aimed at the destruction of the enemy forces on land would mean that we were engaging Russia in the field most favourable to her and in conditions in which the Russians fight best. We are of the opinion that the effort involved would almost certainly be beyond the

> resources of the Western Powers and, even if successful, would so strain the economies of the Allies that they might well never recover.

This left the air strategy – 'the only military means capable of achieving the Allied war aim' – from which there could be no deviation:

> deviations of policy involving, for example, a land campaign into Russia or an attempt to impose unconditional surrender, may lead to demands for a strategy that would be beyond our military resources.

To achieve the air offensive, jet bombers in service in 1957 would be expected to have an operational radius of 1,500 to 2,000 miles (placing the Urals almost within bombing range of bases in England). It has been suggested that the operational range of aircraft was extended by planning 'one way trips', whereby aircrew would complete a bombing mission at maximum range and then abandon their aircraft.[28] Whatever the case, the UK was without doubt the base 'most vital for the launching of the strategic air offensive'. Reiterating statements made in January,[29] and in the April paper giving a logistic background to plan SPEEDWAY,[30] selected air bases and MSAs would need to be secured by defence in depth and it is again only in this context that the ground defence of Europe was mentioned in this central, long-term planning paper:

> Western Europe, west of a line from the Zuider Zee to the Mediterranean, is most desirable.
>
> Scandinavia, Denmark and the western zones of Germany east of the Rhine are also desirable, but less so than the territory west of the Rhine.

The paper finished with a list of assumptions, a list which would be brought up to date prior to the secret Anglo-American discussions: Allied occupation forces would remain in Germany, but their strengths by 1957 would be no greater than at present; the armed forces of the WU would have been regenerated but only to the extent that they could achieve the rather limited aims of 'fighting an effective delaying action against the Russians and of retaining at least a foothold in Western Europe'.

Having dealt with the problem of war in the long-term, the JPS then turned to short-term Anglo-American strategy and deployment for war in 1951.[31] The COS had so far used the progress of the Atlantic Pact negotiations and the uncertainty of the US contribution as reasons for delay.

American support would be vital: the defence of Europe in 1951 would require 34 divisions of which the French would supply 20, largely unequipped without American assistance. The COS could consider providing assistance to a serious defence effort, but would not pour troops and equipment into a force posture which was doomed. But the real problem was an emotional one, and concerned the morale of the French, who must not suspect that 'we intend to desert them in the event of Russian aggression.' The first section of the JPS report examined the availability of British and American forces for war in 1951, giving, in an appendix to the main document, a plan for deployment and mobilisation of the Army in 1951 which shows that Germany was still not a priority matter:

	Armoured Division	Infantry Division	Brigade Group	Regiment/ Brigade	Battalion
Germany	1[A]	1[A]	-	1[B]	-
Trieste	-	-	-	1	-
Mid. East	-	1 1/3	-	-	-
Far East	-	2[C]	-	1[D]	-
UK	-	-	1	-	25[E]
W. Indies	-	-	-	-	1
Gib'tar	-	-	-	-	1

Key
[A] British Occupation Zone
[B] Berlin
[C] Including one British/Ghurka Division
[D] Commando Brigade based in Hong Kong
[E] 24 AA and one armoured regiments

The mobilisation timetable, much less optimistic than that presented in June, was as follows:

Mobilisation (M)

M + 2 months:	1 infantry brigade group
M + 4 months:	1 infantry division
	1 armoured brigade
M + 6 months:	1 corps (1 infantry and 1 armoured division)
	1 infantry division

After the outbreak of war in 1951, the plan for Germany was simply to provide 'Reinforcements and administrative units to bring the regular divisions in Germany up to strength'.

The second section of the document covered likely peacetime deployments of British forces in 1951. Such deployments would be, in order of priority: to support foreign and colonial policies; as occupation forces; to 'arrest' the spread of Communism; and 'to be ready for war'. Occupation troops would still be required in Germany in 1951 where they would 'by their presence, act as a deterrent to the spread of Communism.' Even this minimal task might draw troops away from the defence of vital areas in war (especially the Middle East). However, with the prospect of war before 1951 considered 'unlikely', the JPS were 'prepared to accept this as a calculated risk.'

The concept for the main strategic battle formed the third part of the paper. The JPS referred to 'a plan' which had been drawn up in late 1948 by British and American COS to deal with the possibility of war in 1949/50.[32] In parallel with long-term thinking, the plan determined that, in the early stages of war, the Allies' only strategic action would be from the air. All other forces could be expected to do no more than defend air bases, MSAs and SLOC. This concept had appeared in several other papers. Plan SPEEDWAY, however, accepted that the lack of forces meant that not only Europe but also the vital Middle East might be untenable. Although 'Anglo-American forces of occupation in Germany [would] fight alongside the other forces of Western Europe', SPEEDWAY did not allow for the reinforcement of these forces, nor for the defence of Germany to be considered essential in its own right. A land campaign in Europe would be militarily impossible; 34 divisions would be needed at 'D Day' and an additional 22 by D+1 month. With 20 divisions from the French and about four divisions of British and American occupation troops, along with all that could be mustered from the Benelux countries, the best that might be achieved was 34 divisions by about D+1 month. This was inadequate. The same prospect applied to tactical air support. The WUCinC had indicated a need for some 4,200 tactical aircraft at full readiness at the beginning of the war, but the projection of 400-550 aircraft fell rather short of this requirement. Even if all Anglo-American forces destined to bolster up the defence of the Middle East – 'already an irreducible minimum' – were to be diverted to Europe, 'the defence of the Rhine would still prove impracticable'. Britain and America would therefore have to prepare for 'the early collapse of the defensive system in Western Europe with the probable loss of any forces committed to the battle'. The inference was clear:

> Thus on military grounds it is fundamentally unsound for either the [UK] or the [US] to enter into any binding commitment to reinforce Western Europe at the expense of the Middle East.

Once again, however, the political dimensions of the reinforcement issue were recognised; 'some gesture towards the [WU] countries' could help to rebuild public morale and, in consequence, military strength. There were three possible courses of action. The first was to promise small reinforcements to be available after mobilisation by D+5 or 6 months. This option was rejected: the forces suggested would still be insufficient and, in any case, 'the critical battle will occur during the first three months of war'. The second option was to promise small reinforcements by D+1 month, drawing them from the Middle East reinforcements. This option was also rejected; it would reduce the Middle East posture without making an appreciable difference to Western Europe's defence. The third option was to make no promise at all, and to explain the reasons to the WU powers. The French, in particular, would have to understand that the principal factors in the avoidance of war were the exclusive Allied possession of the atomic bomb and the industrial potential of the United States. The JPS concluded that the third option should be adopted and that, therefore:

> there should be no alteration to the agreed overall concept for war in the near future in respect of the action to be pursued by the [UK] and [US] forces of occupation in Germany.

The Middle East was to remain, in 1951, the top priority for build-up and reinforcement, and 'no Anglo-American reinforcements should be sent to Western Europe in the early stages of the war'.

THE NEW AMERICAN 'CENTER STRATEGY'

The meeting between Tedder, Fraser, Slim, Elliot and the American JCS took place on 3 August,[33] beginning with 'an exchange of views on the Strategy to be adopted in the event of war breaking out during the next few years'. The full minutes of the meeting were recorded in a confidential annex which remains under a fifty year closure rule. Subsequent meetings of the COS do, nevertheless, give some indication of what was discussed. The minutes for 10 August show that the US JCS had surprised their British counterparts by proposing a 'strategic concept' which recommended greater British involvement in Western Europe in preparation for war in 1951.[34] The COS were concerned to explain the implications for

British strategy of the American proposal, especially in terms of Middle Eastern defence, and determined to make 'every effort' to alter the Americans' perspective. The meeting then went on to discuss the issue of Western European defence and, specifically, the COS response to a letter from Montgomery in which he had asked again for reassurance on the reinforcement issue. The COS referred once more to the key Cabinet meeting where it had been decided that a promise of reinforcement should not be given.[35] The novelty of the Americans' 'new overall strategic concept', however, meant that 'the whole question of the British contribution to the defence of Western Europe would have to be reconsidered.' Montgomery would have to be informed of the situation and be told that there would have to be yet more delay before a decision on the size of Britain's contribution could be made.

The COS discussed JPS assessments of the US proposal early in September, and in so doing provide more clues as to the progress of the 3 August meeting.[36] The Americans' 'Center Strategy' had three elements beginning with a series of agreed basic defensive tasks.[37] The next phase would be the strategic air offensive. In a new twist, the Americans had now decided to use their strategic air forces in a tactical role, in order to blunt any Soviet invasion. The JPS commented wryly that this was a 'new conception' for Britain's planners, not least because some 25 per cent of the American strategic bomber force would be diverted from the all important air offensive to tactical operations. The reason for this proposed switch becomes clear in the third phase of the plan. The Americans now proposed a full-scale strategic offensive in Western Eurasia along with a strategic defence in the Far East. Given that British thinking had to date seen land forces in Europe providing no more than a defensive screen from behind which the war winning strategic air offensive would be launched, the American proposal was certain to raise British eyebrows.

The Americans accepted that the most appropriate way of securing Europe for operations against the Soviets was to maintain a defensive line from Britain on the left flank, along the Rhine to a right flank in the Cairo/Suez area. However, this position was at present untenable; the Rhine and Western Europe would in fact be overrun.[38] With the difficulties of 'Overlord' still fresh in their minds, the Americans were adamant that the Allies should retain a bridgehead or lodgement in Europe, from which the 'major land offensive in Western Eurasia' would be launched, albeit not for two years after the outbreak of war. Without a lodgement the delay would be for three years. Britain would remain a vital base for land, sea and air operations in Europe. The defence of the UK and of the lodgement would both take priority over defence of the Middle East, ensuring that there would be no US forces assigned to the defence of the Middle East, although there could be some naval and air assistance. If the Rhine were not appropriate then the lodgement would be in either the Pyrenees or southern Spain and the Gibraltar Straits; the Americans had already begun to consider the deployment of their troops to Morocco.

The British had several objections to the 'Center Strategy'. The plan envisaged land and air forces requiring the first six months of a war for preparation and deployment. With the Washington Treaty only recently signed, this delay could only have a disastrous effect on the morale of France and the Benelux countries as they sought in vain to defend the Rhine, supported only by four Anglo-American occupation divisions. From the national perspective, the American plan would mean that the defence of the Middle East – one of the three vital pillars of Britain's defence policy – could not be guaranteed. The build-up of defences in the Middle East would be severely retarded to the extent that, after the first six months of war the defence forces would be deficient by some three divisions (of a minimum requirement of eight) and 260 aircraft (of a minimum requirement of 636). The absence of American troops and aircraft would put additional pressure on British forces which in turn would mean that the forces of occupation, having withdrawn to defensive positions along the Rhine, would have no support or reinforcement whatsoever. To complete the vicious circle, this would further impair the Europeans' willingness to fight, making disaster in Europe more likely. The American concept made no attempt to answer the political dimension of the European defence problem, and could lead to the collapse of the defence posture in the Middle East. From a purely military point of view, the plan was also, politely, labelled 'unsound'. The deployment of American forces to Morocco would entail complicated amphibious operations in order to bring them over to European soil – 'Overlord' might have to be repeated, rather than avoided. The notion of a break-out from a defensive position in the Pyrenees was also treated with some scepticism.[39]

Having taken such pains to discredit the American concept, the JPS were however anxious that the practice of joint Anglo-American strategic planning be nurtured. To that end, they recommended that an adapted version of the American idea should be pursued for short term planning. With air and naval assistance from the Americans, Britain and its Commonwealth allies would assume the responsibility for the defence of the Middle East. For their part, the Americans would be expected to provide for the defence of Western Europe. This was a division of labour which the Americans would accept since they had, on 3 August, presented the defence of Western Europe as a vital national interest. However, the

British had in mind something more concrete than withdrawal to a foothold and a break-out some years later. This was the main problem; the Americans would have to be persuaded to satisfy the political requirements of European defence, rather than viewing the matter as a purely military matter. If the Americans' enthusiasm for the defence of Europe could be shaped to the British image then the situation might look a little more hopeful, even though the defence of the Middle East would remain a huge task. The JPS were to examine ways to persuade the Americans to look at other, more suitable bridgehead sites such as the Brittany/Brest area, and to plan to hold the Rhine:

> Knowledge that the Americans were planning to hold the Rhine would be of immense benefit to the morale of the Continental countries and thus assist in winning the 'Cold War'.

But, in the end, the COS returned to the vital nature of the defence of the Middle East:

> It was generally agreed... that our attitude must be that we would continue to hold the Middle East at all costs. We must, however, press for the maximum assistance from the [US] naval and air forces for the defence of the Middle East.

There was also a sense in which the defence of the Middle East was vital to reduce the size of the threat to Britain. In mid-September the COS discussed the 'implications of certain aspects of United States strategy for war in 1951.' The basis for this discussion was a JIC paper (not yet released) which, it seems, had examined the consequences of a British withdrawal from the Middle East and the consequences of the Middle East being overrun in the early stages of war. The COS accepted the report as the basis for further studies, but agreed with Tedder that it should be revised slightly to mention 'the effect that it would have on the [UK] if the Russians were not engaged in the Middle East. This would mean that they would be able to concentrate their air effort on Western Europe and the [UK].'[40] The amended JPS reports were accepted by the COS as the basis for forthcoming talks in Washington, but the JPS was also asked to examine further the possibility of a bridgehead in the Brest/Brittany area. This paper was also produced in mid-September, and found that the bridgehead could not be held in 1950/51. The COS decided to use this adverse report as another weapon with which to 'shake the faith of the Americans in their new strategic concept'.[41]

Under renewed WU pressure, the COS remained adamant that firm answers could still not be given.[42] The fact that the COS had just been discussing the American 'Center Strategy', which made quite clear that no American troops would be immediately available for the defence of Western Europe, suggests that the COS were both confident that the American position was not yet firm and that they were determined not to let the Europeans have any indication of the Americans' morale-shattering proposals. Slim felt, however, that, especially with WUCOS and WUDC meetings imminent, further procrastination would be wrong and suggested that the French be informed of a number of tenets of British policy.[43] The first was that there was 'no prospect' of a successful defence on the Rhine for the next two or three years. However, the danger of war was so remote, given American atomic monopoly, that the West should resist the temptation to rapid rearmament and the economic retardation which would ensue. Britain's active army was already fully deployed 'resisting the spread of Communism' and only some four TA divisions could be made available. Even if a war were to break out unexpectedly in the near future, there would be no value in throwing this force into Europe where it would certainly be lost. With the Rhine indefensible, rapid rearmament unwise, the chance of war remote given America's atomic monopoly, and the size of Britain's reserve forces so small, Slim suggested that the French be given an honest explanation of British plans:

> We propose therefore to concentrate on the defence of the Middle East, a course which we consider would result in a shorter war and hence offer more prospect of an early liberation of occupied Europe.

He anticipated some difficulties with this; the Europeans might be uneasy about a strategy which would see their homes being overrun. But only if the situation on the Rhine were to improve, to the point where a 'successful defence' was a 'reasonable prospect', could Britain afford to change its strategy and consider 'the re-alignment of our whole military policy'. Finally, Slim also recommended a complete revision of Britain's defence policy, then embodied in DO (47) 44. Templer took up this cause early the following month. With so many developments – the Brussels Pact and the North Atlantic Treaty, for example – the context of strategic planing had changed significantly. While the original report had stressed the importance of the defence of the Middle East, the 'present American attitude' was such that an up-to-date appreciation was required (Templer did not say whether he expected this new appreciation to support or undermine the emphasis on the Middle East). The Vice Chiefs of Staff agreed to postpone further discussion until the outcome of Tedder's and Elliot's recent meeting with the US Joint Chiefs of Staff was known.[44]

The record of the Tedder/Elliot meeting with the US JCS on 5 October was discussed by the COS in mid-October.[45] The American view was that no more than a small force would be deployed to Europe during the first months of war. In the unlikely event of the Rhine being held for two or three months, they would then consider sending ground forces directly to France. Gradually, the American position softened as they appreciated the need to encourage the French and saw some value in agreeing to reinforce the Rhine position if it were successfully defended. But British lobbying in this respect also reflected calculations of self-interest:

> If the [US] forces could not be in Western Europe on the outbreak of war, there would be a demand from the French for all available [UK] forces to be sent there.

As the meeting came to an end, the Americans seemed to have accepted more responsibility for Western European defence.[46] Agreement was not, however, reached on the idea of Britain assuming exclusive responsibility for the Middle East; the Americans could still not accept that British reinforcements should be sent there in the first instance. Nevertheless, Tedder later described this compromise as an important concession by the Americans:

> as a result of [Tedder's] recent meeting with the United States [JCS] in Washington in early October, they agreed to put forces into the defence of the Rhine as opposed to their previous idea of going straight to a base in Morocco. ... They had therefore made a reasonable attempt to meet us ...[47]

'WHAT DO WE TELL THE FRENCH?'

The next step was the production by the JPS of a short-term strategic concept for Western Europe, to be used by the British planners in the North Atlantic Treaty Military Committee Standing Group.[48] The JPS argued once again that the answer to the short-term problem was to explain to the signatories of the North Atlantic Treaty the content of Britain's 'long range strategic concept'.[49] This plan would involve a bastion position in Scandinavia, 'and the Piave Line in addition to holding the Rhine'. The JPS felt that while this might be acceptable to the smaller countries, it would not satisfy French curiosity as to what the immediate strategy might be and the extent to which Britain and America might assist in the defence of France. However, given that the American emergency plan for war in 1950 was judged to be 'fatal to French morale', the problem was '"What do we tell the French?".' There were, as ever, three options: truth, dishonesty and dissemblance. The first option was to be frank and explain that Britain and America did not intend to reinforce France in the short term. The second was to tell a lie, that the Rhine would be reinforced. The third option was to 'give the French a concept which, even if not the best militarily, is yet just a possibility, and which we would carry out if, in fact, it proved feasible at the time.' This latter option would offer the most immediate reward (French morale), along with some long-term benefit (the possibility of expanding a sound defensive position) and with the least risk, and had been approved by Tedder and the JCS. But the JPS still saw a clear distinction between promises made for Cold War reasons concerning peace-time deployments of forces, and planning for a 'fighting' war. If the Rhine or a bridgehead in France were held, the JPS noted, then as British reinforcements became available, the case for sending them to the Middle East would be undermined. This was still not acceptable. The JPS gesture was thus a hollow one, reflecting their hope that Britain would not in the event be drawn into war in Europe.

Under continued pressure from Templer, the COS agreed in the same meeting to revise Britain's defence policy (DO (47) 44), in the light of recent developments such as the Washington and Brussels treaties and the 'strategy of the defence of the Rhine'. The revision was not intended, however, to challenge the existing three-pillared structure of defence policy:

> the campaign in Western Europe should not be regarded as a pillar of strategy itself but rather as a part of the defence of the United Kingdom.

What was more, the Americans still appeared reluctant to become committed to a European strategy. In a report on the 'ABC' meetings, the JPS had made known their scepticism regarding American long-term planning:

> The Long Range Strategical Planning Group also gave us a "presentation" of their ideas for bringing the war to a successful conclusion. This was less satisfactory as it included a campaign across Europe in the third year of the war by forces of the order of 150 Allied divisions, followed by an occupation of Russia after her surrender by a force of

> some 27 Allied divisions and 5 Allied Tactical air forces.[50]

The other main agenda item for the talks had been the short-term plan. Here, the JPS felt they had successfully challenged the American 'Center Strategy', and had managed to extract the 'simple logic' which lay behind the American plan; the defence, in order of priority, of Britain, North Africa and Spain, and the Middle East. The JPS were slightly surprised that the Americans had included the Middle East at all. In the end though, the inclusion was immaterial. Since the Allies had insufficient forces to meet the first and second tasks, the third did not merit serious consideration. With Britain's defence policy about to be revised and with doubts about American plans – at least in the long term – there was a need both for clarification from the Americans and for a JPS reappraisal of deployment and mobilisation plans. Once again, the WU would have to wait for a firm decision from Britain.

Britain's tentative commitment to the WU short-term plan nevertheless soon came into question. Templer felt that it would be wrong to agree to send forces to hold the Rhine when 'our overall strategy had not been finally settled'. The COS now 'agreed that we should not at this stage commit ourselves to a contribution on the Continent'. Subject to Alexander's approval, a short-term strategy paper[51] was to be forwarded to Britain's representative on the Standing Group. The paper appeared two days later,[52] providing a minimalist definition of short-term European defence:

> The plan allows for the deployment on the line of the Rhine of all Allied forces available on 1st January, 1949, assuming that Western Europe is to be defended no further west than the Rhine.

Following the American compromise of early October, however, a new short-term strategy now came into view.[53] The replacement for plan SPEEDWAY, plan GALLOPER, had now been produced.[54] But with so many revisions and re-assessments underway, the JPS felt that to issue the new plan 'would only lead to confusion'. The revisions then in progress should be completed before a new plan could be issued, in collaboration with the Americans. The COS accepted the JPS recommendation.

With the short-term planning agenda under review, a WO paper on the subject provides a timely illustration of the extent to which at least one sector of the British defence establishment – a sector from which an entirely different view might have been expected – was determined to maintain strict limitations on Britain's involvement in continental defence.[55] Procrastination, the WO maintained, was no longer possible. At the 19 July WUDC meeting Alexander had argued successfully that Britain should be allowed to delay its decision for a short time until American plans were known. These had now been revealed:

> Current American short-term plans are based on the assumption that their occupation forces in Europe will be written off. The [JCS] consider that no additional forces from the [US] could reach the Rhine for three months after the outbreak of war, though they would consider sending them there should the Rhine be holding.

British lack of commitment was becoming less excusable, especially since the Americans seemed also to 'consider that we ought ourselves to send reinforcements to Western Europe'. There seemed therefore to be compelling reasons for Britain to clarify its commitment and to end the equivocation which was having 'an increasing and cumulative ill-effect on French morale', ensuring that the WU was not yet on a sure footing, politically or militarily. The WO accordingly recommended a guarantee of a corps of two divisions and an armoured brigade for the reinforcement of BAOR in the event of war. But whatever the political or Cold War imperatives to which the WO was now responding, it was firm in one respect:

> This must not be taken to mean that the Chiefs of Staff are advising the adoption of a Continental strategy involving the build up of large scale land and air forces on the Continent of Europe; nor is it their opinion that the course recommended is sound from the military point of view.

Since the forces concerned would be territorial reservists, there was no chance that they could arrive in Western Europe before it had been overrun (the current assessment was that this would happen by D+90 days). The Middle East was still all-important; if the first corps to be mobilised were destined for the Middle East and the second for Europe, then the important 'gesture of guaranteeing reinforcements' would have been made and the second corps would, probably, find its way to the Middle East in any case. There would, furthermore, be no guarantee that the reinforcing corps would have any organic air support.

LIMITED LIABILITY

The WO paper was discussed two days later by the COS, when the debate moved forward somewhat.[56] For Slim, the priority was to prevent war.

The Cold War necessitated the build up of WU military capability to the point that Russia would be deterred and Germany would be attracted to the West. Slim agreed that a promise of two reinforcing divisions should be made. But, unlike the WO paper, he now saw such a promise in terms of its military as well as political utility, while noting that any 'commitment' would in any case be a singularly limited liability:

> The offer of two divisions would do much to build up the resistance of the land forces of the Western European countries: we would hope from it to gain a dividend of some 35 Divisions. ... It was not militarily unsound to promise to send another two divisions to the Continent. In the event of war the probable alternative situations were either that the Russians would over-run Western Europe within the first two months or, if the French army was built into an effective fighting force, that the Western Allies would succeed in holding the enemy on the Rhine. In the first eventuality there would not be time to send British reinforcements to the Continent so these forces would not be involved in the disaster; in the second case it would be to our military advantage to build up the Allied defences in Western Europe.

The COS accepted Slim's argument agreeing, for the first time, 'that on military grounds a strong case could be made for promising now to send additional land forces to the Continent'. Slim developed this point during a staff conference with Alexander the following day. Slim explained that there were strategic and political benefits to be gained from the reinforcement decision – with no additional expenditure. A promise of two divisions could yield substantial dividends with little risk since the forces concerned would be used for the defence of the United Kingdom if not sent to Europe. Thus, whereas previously the problem had been articulated as one of Europe versus Middle East as far as the four TA divisions were concerned, Slim now took an entirely different and more persuasive viewpoint:

> In fact, if Western Europe was overrun, it would be necessary to allot a substantial number of divisions to the defence of the United Kingdom; a successful defence of the Rhine was thus to our advantage from the point of view of home defence.[57]

It is instructive to consider for a moment precisely to what the COS had agreed. A war in the immediate future was not thought likely and if it did break out it was probable that Europe would be overrun within two to three months. In this case, there would be no time to send the forces to Europe and they would therefore not be lost. Slim's change of heart was therefore of doubtful value, since the promise clearly bore no great risk. As for the danger of war in the long-term, by this time the WU should have built itself up to the extent that it could offer serious opposition. In this instance the military risk – that is to say that the troops would actually have to fight – would be justified by the strategic advantage to be gained by supporting a more hopeful WU defence posture.

As the end of the year approached, however, there appeared to be more reasons to equivocate than to commit. The JPS report on long term strategic discussions with the Americans and Canadians was to be revised in the light of new intelligence (probably a response to the Soviet atomic test),[58] and Britain's own Overall (or long-term) Strategic Concept[59] was to be revised as soon as the review of the Future Defence Policy had been carried out and approved. The deliberations over Future Defence Policy reached their conclusion shortly before Christmas. Both the JPS paper,[60] and COS discussion of it[61] have now been released. The JPS paper was an 'update', incorporating no 'original thought'. The 'three pillars' were stressed, and it was accepted that 'as a buttress to the defence of the [UK], the holding of Western Europe is highly desirable.' Slim was not impressed with the report and called for a genuine review of the options, in the light of recent events such as the Brussels and Washington treaties and Russian atomic development. Slim felt that the requirements of Britain's security now meant that the loss of Europe could not be accepted as a planning assumption, and wondered whether 'a higher place in our strategy' should be given to 'the defence of Western Europe'. He demanded 'a complete review of our basic strategy', to be followed by a ministerial decision as to whether it was preferable to allow Europe or the Middle East to be overrun. But Tedder described the prospect of making a major land forces contribution as 'disastrous', and did not accept that the bases of British strategy were challenged. Whatever Britain could provide for a Cold War strategy should on no account prejudice preparations for a 'shooting war'. Creasy, the Vice Chief of the Naval Staff, agreed.

The same meeting also considered a paper by Slim concerning Britain's contribution to the defence of Western Europe.[62] Rehearsing many old arguments, this paper also demonstrates the tentative nature of the COS interest in Europe. The logic of a reinforcement promise was ever more compelling; French morale was deteriorating fast, and a promise of assistance by Britain could bolster the WU, the strength of which was vital in the Cold War and to deter Russian aggression. With America uncertain Slim felt that Britain should take the lead. The recommendation was for reinforcement by two infantry divisions and one armoured brigade. There was some risk that it might be lost. However, the corps would be made of reserve forces, requiring three months for preparation. By the time the corps would be fit for deployment, the Russians would either have overrun France or the WU would have held and, therefore, be worth reinforcing. As to the risk that Britain would be drawn into a large-scale 'continental strategy', involving land and air forces, 'when we might not desire it', Slim was dismissive:

> It must be remembered that the whole of B.A.O.R. including two Divisions will be already committed unavoidably to the Continent. Two more Divisions will have little effect in forcing us, if we do not wish to, into a great Continental build up. The new Corps would not be accompanied by tactical air force requirements for the simple reason that none would be available. Indeed, it is very unlikely that, in the opening stages, even B.A.F.O., the Tactical Air Force of B.A.O.R., would act in a direct tactical support role as every available aircraft from every source would be engaged in the battle for air supremacy over Western Europe.

So 1949 ended with a commitment which could hardly have been more tentative.

A CONTINENTAL STRATEGY AT LAST?

The themes which had emerged during 1949 also directed the debate on Britain's strategy for Europe in the first months of 1950. What appears most clearly is the basic tension between the strategically preferable and the politically necessary. So far, matters of strategy, of developing a workable combination of military, political and economic imperatives, had been seen by the COS to be the stuff of careful, long-term planning. Tension developed when short-term, militarily nonsensical political expedients such as making occupation troops battle-worthy and making hollow promises of reinforcement, proved unable to satisfy the demand from Britain's European allies and even threatened to undermine longer term planning processes where Britain considered its interests to be better served.

Britain's 'commitment' to Europe was still articulated in terms of building-up and preserving European (especially French) morale, and was less a policy for action than a symbol, or deterrent, which it was hoped would prevent war and thus avoid the risks and costs of military entanglement in

Europe. Even Slim who, among the COS, was moving closest to a European strategy, was clear both that the main task was to prevent war and that this might be achieved with a 'promise to send immediate reinforcements of the order of two or three divisions to help defend the Rhine if war came.'[63] Slim's European strategy only made sense if war did not break out in the near future. If it did, and there were no chance of defending Europe successfully, then Britain would be committed to an 'unsound strategic deployment of our forces'. Slim argued that the risk ought to be accepted, but in spite of his persuasive argument, there remained a good deal of inertia within the COS and the government against making a commitment or even a decision, and a good deal of scepticism regarding the purpose and quality of WU short-term planning.[64] The COS continued to hope that the possibility of a promise of reinforcement by the British might serve to galvanise the French and other European allies into making more of an effort for their own defence. This was the ideal course from the British point of view, especially since the JPS were now beginning to argue that although the defence of Europe was to be justified in terms of the UK's own defence,[65] any forces released to Europe would have to be surplus to the requirements of home defence of the UK.[66]

Yet, in spite of the inertia and the heavily qualified commitment to European defence, it was just a matter of weeks before the COS and Cabinet 'took the plunge and committed themselves to sending troops to the continent if Russia attacked'.[67] But what did the decision amount to? How did it come about given earlier reluctance and equivocation? The first suggestion that the deadlock over the reinforcement issue was about to be broken is contained in the minutes of a mid-March meeting.[68] The COS now accepted that procrastination over the size and timing of Britain's contribution to WU defence would no longer be tolerated by its allies. The JPS had accordingly been asked to review the matter, focusing especially on the 'beneficial effect that the promise of two extra British divisions *in the event of war* was likely to have' [emphasis added], while at the same time arguing 'the effect that a promise of this nature would have on our ability to defend the Middle East'.[69] In an annex to the terms of reference given to the JPS, the COS commented as usual that a strong France was essential to Allied strategy, both in the Cold War and in the event of war in Europe. The COS noted that, in the past, 'the defence of the [UK] had not been directly linked with that of Western Europe' and strategy had been drawn up on a Commonwealth rather than Allied basis. However, the JPS review of Allied Defence Policy and Strategy, then in progress, had noted that the Allies could no longer be complacent about the American atomic lead and that Britain's survival required that the

Russians be kept as far from the Channel coast as possible:

> When looked at from an Allied point of view in a war against Russia using modern weapons, the position is altered and we consider that the defence of the [UK] must be linked with that of Western Europe, in our future strategy.

The COS found the JPS work rather too forceful, and preferred to adapt a more moderate earlier paper on the subject.[70] The decision to reinforce BAOR with two divisions was taken in the Defence Committee on 23 March. No sooner had the decision been made, however, than the COS were attempting to qualify and moderate it.[71]

From the COS point of view, the essence of the decision was that the reinforcement would take place *in the event of war*. This meant, suggested Slim, that the reinforcing corps would be made available 'as soon as it could be mobilised'. Much would hang on this term, since the troops (TA) designated to form the corps 'could not land on the Continent and be ready for active operations in under three months'.[72] The agreement was, at least at first, to be communicated orally at the Hague Atlantic Pact meetings, and was to receive no publicity, in order not to alarm Commonwealth allies. But the clearest explanation of the COS understanding of the reinforcement decision can be found in the original COS paper on which the Defence Committee had based their decision.[73] The COS had noted that Britain could 'no longer postpone' a decision to invigorate the morale and physical defences of the WU. There were two options. In the first, Britain could admit that there was no faith in the possibility of European defence and would promise no more than the occupation forces. In the event of war, these forces would not be able to escape the Continent and should therefore join the fight. The second option was to name a 'definite contribution'. The paper referred to the COS suggestion of December 1948, made in revealing and self-contradictory language, for a 'firm and immediate promise of a token force'. The Cabinet had rejected the suggestion. The need to allay French fears and boost their morale was now more pressing since without the WU any war, hot or cold, would reach Britain. Defence of the UK was one of the three pillars of British defence policy and it was vital to do what was necessary to hold the enemy east of the Rhine.

With intelligence assessments now indicating that the threat to the Middle East would not materialise for six months after the outbreak of war, there was less of a conflict between the Middle East and Europe when allocating resources. There were risks in committing extra forces to the Continent, principally that they would be lost in a 'second Dunkirk'. However, given the type of troops of which the reinforcing corps would consist, and its mobilisation timetable, the risk that the troops would even be committed, let alone lost, was minimal. There was therefore a huge potential return on a relatively small, low-risk investment which would require, furthermore, no additional expenditure. The paper was conscious of the danger that Britain might be drawn into a commitment to build up a 'great Continental army', but was confident that such pressure could be resisted. There would be no possibility of increasing the tactical air support provided to Europe, even to accompany the two divisions, although some more flexible use of Bomber Command was considered a possibility. What was being proposed, therefore, was the familiar idea of defence of Britain on the Continent, rather than defence of the Continent *per se*, in which the risks taken and undertakings given would be kept to the minimum necessary to inspire the French and other Europeans to provide their own defence from and deterrence of the Russians.

However much the 23 March decision fell short of a full-scale 'continental strategy', in the sense of orienting British strategy around a plan to fight the Russians on the ground in Europe, it is clear that the COS and the JPS had come to an important point in their thinking about Europe. They now seemed prepared to accept that the defence of Europe made sense for Britain both in terms of Cold War deterrence and the maintenance of European morale, and in terms of military operations. Yet not only was British interest in the latter still indirect and not representative of real faith in a continental strategy, it is also clear that any change in British perceptions – however marginal – was a result of outside pressures. At about this time the initial attempts at strategic planning by the North Atlantic Regional Planning Groups were coming to fruition. Although the COS and JPS were somewhat stand-offish in their view of the Groups, believing that Britain's intimate involvement in four of the five Groups precluded exclusive membership of any one, they were nevertheless under pressure to declare a preference.[74] Slim noted that membership of the North Atlantic Ocean Group was unavoidable and that there was also a strong case for joining the Western European Group, a decision which would 'considerably boost the morale of the continental countries'. Although his colleagues disagreed, Slim's perception, along with the fact that the overall North Atlantic Medium Term Defence Plan would require Britain to make known those forces which were surplus to the defence of the UK, made it uncomfortably clear that Britain's equivocation over European defence was coming to the surface in another forum.[75]

Growth of interest in Britain's commitment to Europe was also a function of the erosion of confidence in the American atomic monopoly since the Soviet test in autumn 1949, and a subsequent new emphasis on a conventional strategy for Europe.[76] Although the COS were politely dismissive of the evolving North Atlantic MTDP, perceiving a serious mismatch between requirements (90 divisions) and available resources,[77] they were nevertheless aware of the pressing need to put flesh, in the form of divisions, on the plan to prevent its collapse: 'time was running out and we could no longer accept delays of two or three months'.[78]

As the Allies reviewed their plans for European defence, the question of German rearmament came very quickly into the debate. Following the establishment of the east German *Bereitschaften* paramilitary border police force, Allied High Commissioners in Germany had, since early December 1949, been aware of Adenauer's view that the Eastern Zone posed a growing threat, and of his calls for German rearmament.[79] Adenauer had also argued that the Allies were 'in duty bound to maintain the security of the Federal Republic' and that 'to speak of defence on the Rhine was a hollow phrase'.[80] That the COS were coming to view German rearmament as beneficial or necessary was not, however, entirely due to pressure from the new Federal German government. Demonstrating more flexibility in this area than the Foreign Office, the COS were now beginning to accept the military reality that 'Western Europe could not be defended without the help of German manpower.' Yet, revealing a traditional impulse to balance forces on the Continent, the COS also noted that it 'would not be practicable to create German armed forces until the French army had been built up.'[81] Thus, the most important issue in European force planning in late 1949/early 1950 seemed about to rehearse a familiar theme in that it required a British commitment to European defence, which would in turn boost the morale of the French and encourage them to rebuild their own forces.

DEFENCE POLICY AND GLOBAL STRATEGY REVIEW

External, Allied pressure for a more decisive view of the needs of European defence had greater influence on COS and JPS thinking by virtue of the revision of British defence policy and global strategy upon which the JPS had been working since late 1949. The next stage in the process was to turn policy into strategy, and it was this task upon which the JPS, in conjunction with the IDC, was engaged in early 1950.[82] The JPS revisions were to be accompanied by estimates of the forces which Britain could contribute to an agreed strategy. These estimates were to inform the British position during forthcoming Standing Group talks, thus linking the British revision process to the new European outlook and conventional force preferences of the North Atlantic Treaty forum.

The JPS produced their paper in early March. The JPS now decided in favour of a promise of a specific UK contribution of land forces, 'as an earnest to the continental powers of (Britain's) irrevocable and whole-hearted determination to co-operate in the defence of these territories.' The size of Britain's contribution was less important than the 'positive evidence of [the] full support' which it provided.[83] The COS found the paper 'too long and too discursive' and requested a condensed version dealing specifically with the need to boost the morale of the Europeans by promising two extra divisions in the event of war, while at the same time assessing the impact of such a promise on Britain's position in the Middle East.[84] JPS work on Allied strategy was now absorbed into the wider review of Britain's 'Global Strategy' which was to be completed in May and June.[85] The 'Defence Policy and Global Strategy' paper accepted that 'the defence of Western Europe, initially at least as far as East of the Rhine', was 'absolutely vital'. But Britain had only agreed to make a 'due contribution' to the land defence of Europe, and the COS insisted that 'the land and air defence of the Continent must in the main be the responsibility of the Continental Powers'. Furthermore, the COS were adamant that any reinforcement promise 'does not mean that we intend or shall be able to build up an army on a Continental scale.'[86] Thus, within weeks of the 'reinforcement promise', and in spite of the fact that the review contained 'slightly increased emphasis ... on the defence of Western Europe, at the expense of the Middle East',[87] the COS were still wary of making promises regarding European defence which would undermine Britain's Middle Eastern position, and were also wary of alienating members of the Commonwealth.

Any apparent change in the attitude of the British military to Europe was, in fact, a function less of a new strategic outlook on their part, than of the direction in which American strategic thinking was moving. Slim's comment on the review of global strategy illustrates the extent to which basic assumptions had now changed, and the dilemmas which the planners now faced:

> there was no fundamental alteration in the defence policy and strategy proposed in the present report but there was a most important change in the emphasis to be placed on the relative importance of Western Europe and the Middle East. In the past we had been prepared to contemplate the overrunning of Western Europe on the grounds that it would be possible for Britain and the United States to fight back from

> bases in the [UK] and elsewhere. The [COS] now considered that the defence of Western Europe must form part of the defence of the [UK]. The reason for this change in policy was that it was now considered that, if Europe was overwhelmed, the [UK] would be threatened as never before and might well not survive. Moreover, the effort required to liberate Europe once it had been overrun would be immense. A corollary to stepping up the importance of Western Europe was to lower somewhat the priority to be given to the defence of the Middle East. If we lost the Middle East we would still survive: if we lost Western Europe we might well be defeated. It would not, however, be possible to win the war unless we held on to the Middle East or regained it. [88]

The evolution of the new JIC assessment of the threat to the Middle East, upon which the new approach of the planners was based, is examined in detail in chapter one. Two reasons were suggested for this rather more sanguine view of the security of the Middle East. The first was that the JIC were now placing less emphasis on the need to retain control of Middle Eastern oilfields. However, this reassessment itself reflected a change in circumstances beyond Britain's control; a shift had taken place in American strategic thinking to which the British felt obliged to conform. The final part of this chapter will examine the American change of mind and the effect this had on British plans.

US STRATEGY

Tension between British and American strategies increased in the aftermath of the ABC planning talks in Washington in October 1949. In response to American pressure, the JPS had replaced plan SPEEDWAY with plan GALLOPER, which it was hoped would correlate more closely with the new American Emergency Plan.[89] The priority of the plan was the familiar one of a strategic air offensive against Russia, using atomic bombs. The UK was to be defended as an 'essential air base', with Western Europe listed among 'other essential areas'. The plan for the defence of the latter was clear:

> The operations of Allied forces in Western Europe will be conducted with the object of standing on the line of the Rhine, or failing this, of holding a substantial bridgehead in Western Europe,[sic] However, because of the large forces that the Soviets are able to bring to bear in the early days of the war and the meagre resources of the Allies, the

possibility of holding a bridgehead is problematical.

> Initially, Allied forces, other than the occupation forces in Austria and Trieste, will be withdrawn to the line of the Rhine in accordance with approved emergency war plans of the respective Commanders-in-Chief of the Occupation Forces.

Annex II to the plan listed 'Unresolved Differences of Opinion Between British and American Concepts.' These differences stemmed from one basic disagreement:

> The ABC Planners agreed that the defence of the [UK] should be the first priority task. As second priority, however, the [US] intend to build up a base in North West Africa with the object of keeping open the western end of the Mediterranean, supporting operations in the Iberian Peninsula and facilitating the earliest possible return to Western Europe. The British accord second priority to the defence of the Middle East and feel that this aim should not be jeopardized by considerations of subsequent operations in Europe. [90]

The final version of the plan has now been released to the PRO.[91] In it, the COS commented pessimistically that 'the possibility of holding even a bridgehead is problematical'. The American plan, known as OFFTACKLE, 'included, as a new objective, the "retardation" of Soviet advances in Western Europe'. OFFTACKLE planned for the outbreak of war in the two years following 1 July 1949, and reflected the overall American decision to combine a strategic offensive in Western Eurasia with a strategic defensive in the Far East. It called for the defence of Europe 'no farther to the West than on the Rhine', but noted that the number of Allied forces available would probably require either a withdrawal to a bridgehead in the Pyrenees or the complete abandonment of Europe and subsequent return. OFFTACKLE had been presented to the autumn 1949 ABC talks where, although a joint emergency plan could not be agreed, the American strategic concept was at least accepted as the basis for national plans.[92] The disagreement was explained more fully later in the Annex:

> The British planners consider that the defence of the Middle East and control of an LOC through the Mediterranean should be second in priority only to the defence of the [UK], in order to defend the strategic air base, to support Turkey and friendly countries in the Middle East, to arrest the spread of Communism in the Middle East, to give defence in

> depth to Africa, to deny this area to the enemy as a base for offensive operations westward against the Allies, and to maintain a position favourable for regaining at least a portion of the Middle East oil area. The [US] Planners do not consider maintenance of control of the Middle East to be vital to their strategy and feel that if [US] forces for this task were provided at the expense of the North West African area, the subsequent Allied re-entry into Europe would be delayed. The British planners are of the opinion that this consideration should not be an overriding factor.[93]

However much the JPS or JIC disagreed with the US view, there was pressure to conform to it. The JPS and JIC were thus faced with two uncomfortable realities. The first was that the Americans would be unable to contribute 'army or air forces to the defence of the Middle East in the first three months'. In earlier papers – especially the key Future Defence Policy paper of May 1947 – the COS had always been conscious that time would be of the essence in preparing a defence in the Middle East: 'The area in which Russian expansion would be easiest ... would be the Middle East ...'; 'There are greater possibilities than before of surprise attack ...'; '... in view of the speed with which we could be knocked out...'; 'The main problem of the defence of this area is the time factor ...'; 'The problem is primarily one of time, i.e., whether we can get the necessary forces into position before the Russians can attack in strength.'[94] By 1950 however, the JIC had evidently come to the conclusion that the threat to the Middle East, far from being immediate, would not materialise until six months after the beginning of the war; the three month unavailability of American forces may have pushed the JIC into making virtue out of necessity. The second reality was that the Americans would be unwilling to provide for the defence of Europe (and therefore, indirectly, of Britain) if this simply meant that Britain would then be able to release forces to carry out 'imperial' defence and policing tasks, ideologically unacceptable to the Americans. Faced with this situation, there was only one line for the JPS and JIC to take. This was to accept a strategy – and the threat assessment on which it would be based – in which British land and air forces were concentrated in Europe for the defence of Britain. This would not only find favour with the Americans but would also fall more easily within Britain's limited resources. At the same time, however, the need to defend the Middle East would have to be kept alive, if only in planning terms.

For all these reasons, British defence planning was increasingly focused on the defence of the UK rather than the Middle East; as this shift took place, the connection between the defence of Britain and that of the

Continent became closer. This was not, however, much of a departure from past thinking; the British military were familiar with the idea of a defensive glacis, which Germany and Europe might now afford. Nevertheless, the British military were, at last, beginning to accept that the defence of Europe was something with which the British could, and should, be militarily as well as politically involved.

SUMMARY

During the period covered by this chapter, British military thinking about Germany, and about European defence more widely, passed through three phases. The first, lasting until approximately the end of July 1949, began with the grudging agreement of the COS to the proposal to make just one division of the occupation troops already in Germany battleworthy by the end of the year. Gradually, however, the COS and JPS became more aware of the political dimension of the problem until, in June, something of a consensus had developed in that there was seen to be a political or Cold War requirement to prevent the collapse of the WU, to which a reinforcement promise might contribute. This did not, however, mean that the COS and JPS had in any way altered the underlying assumptions of strategic thinking in Britain. There were two such assumptions. The first was that the most appropriate way to deter and then fight and defeat the Russians was with a massive strategic air offensive using atomic weapons. The second was that the Middle East was vital to the survival in war of Britain and the Commonwealth. Defence of Europe was not entirely abandoned by this rationale; the strategic air offensive could be launched most effectively from the UK, and so it was essential that the UK be defended. If a defensive perimeter could be held in Europe, so much the better. However, both the British and Americans considered the chances of holding the Russians in Europe to be so slim that the likely loss of Europe had been accepted. Thus, from the British perspective, defence of Europe was qualified in two ways: first, it was not an objective in its own right, but derived from the need to maintain the UK strategic air base; second, it was a task to which Britain would be both unable and unwilling to allocate any military resources other than those which happened to be in Germany at the time; the under equipped and badly trained occupation forces. Out of this mix of political and military perspectives grew a series of suggestions regarding the formulation of a reinforcement promise. In each case, the aim was to stimulate European morale while constructing the offer in such a way that it would probably never come to anything.

The second phase lasted from early August 1949 to mid-March 1950. The basic assumptions of British strategic thinking were maintained. Thus, it was decided in advance that the review of defence policy and global strategy should not move in the direction of a continental strategy, and even the War Office argued vigorously against such a development. What characterised this second phase, however, was the challenge made to these assumptions by the new American 'Center Strategy' launched early in August. The defence of the UK as a base for the strategic air offensive remained the priority, but while the British gave second place to the defence of the Middle East, the Americans now stressed the need to defend Western Europe. The new American plan was at first just an extension of the existing plan to abandon Europe in the event of war; the novelty was merely that a bridgehead or lodgement would be held from which a major land counter-offensive would eventually be launched. In terms of the likelihood of a successful defence of Europe against the Russians, the Americans remained just as pessimistic as the British. The problem for the British, quite apart from the fact that the Americans had diverted a large proportion of their strategic air strength to tactical tasks in Europe, was that the reallocation of forces to the defence and expansion of the European lodgement would mean that the British would be left alone in the Middle East and incapable of mounting an effective defence. Eventually, the Americans were persuaded to adopt a more flexible posture and agreed to reinforce a defensive position on the Rhine in war, provided there were signs that it was being held. The main British goal in this was to deflect anticipated French demands for a more substantial British guarantee, ensuring that the Middle East would not be completely abandoned. Thus, when the British military seemed by the end of 1949 to have accepted a more direct military interest in European defence, this was more apparent than real, and in any case reflected external pressure rather than a change of heart on the part of the British. The result of this enforced reappraisal of strategic goals was the reinforcement decision of March 1950.

For the final phase, the three months before the beginning of the Korean War, British strategy for Europe was governed by the 23 March decision. Not only had the British been pushed in this direction, it is also clear that, by attaching so many limitations and qualifications to the reinforcement promise, the British still viewed European defence as defence of Britain by proxy, and had embraced neither a continental strategy for fighting the Russians, nor a serious British contribution to such a strategy. Thus, although the British military now saw both the political and military dimensions of European defence, their interest in the latter was at best only indirect. The movement was clearly in the direction of a more 'European' strategy but, as the Korean War broke out, there was still some distance to go.

Conclusion

> The primary problem that has to be solved is that of Western Europe's ability to withstand an *overland* invasion – and prevent the Continent being overrun before America could make her weight felt. In that respect, it is the forces on the scene which count, not a prospective reinforcement from overseas, however great this might ultimately become. The opening stage is crucial. For that reason a realistic examination must concentrate mainly on the land forces which are available, or could be made available.
>
> In Western Europe ... the counterbalance [to Russia] will be far from adequate so long as it depends mainly on the sparse British and American armies of occupation.
>
> Liddell Hart [1]

This book set out to account for the development of British military planning for the defence of Germany and Western Europe from the end of the war in Europe to the invasion of South Korea in June 1950. Planning was examined first thematically, in terms of threat perceptions and spending restrictions, and then chronologically.

In chapter one, the threat perceptions made by the Chiefs of Staff and their joint military planning staffs were discussed. In spite of the paucity of key primary sources, enough evidence is now available to show that 'worst-case analysis' may not be the most accurate description of the British military response to external threats and the requirements of strategic planning. Perceptions of the Soviet threat developed gradually, in many respects responsibly, and with some subtlety, over these years. With the final, pre-Korean War strategic review in 1950, influenced by a change of thinking in the US, the COS had finally come to accept that Britain's security interests were now closely related to the fate of Europe. In response, they recommended a combination of deterrence and defence. The former was to be achieved by air power and the atomic bomb, and the latter by ground defences provided mainly by Britain's European and American allies. Thus, although the British military had now openly accepted the need for military containment of the Soviet Union on European territory, Britain's contribution to the Allied posture was to be in the form of air power and extended deterrence rather than a territorial strategy requiring a large-scale British expeditionary force. Paradoxically, those British troops and tactical air forces already stationed in Germany, on occupation duties, were expected to contribute to a Western policy of political and ideological, rather than military and territorial, containment.

Chapter two examined the budgetary aspects of strategic decision-making, and showed how differences developed between Cabinet and COS, and among the COS themselves. Britain's presence in Germany as an occupying power was a peripheral matter. In this respect, the height of interest in Germany came with the Army's awareness that a political, rather than military or operational, commitment to 'fighting the Cold War' in Germany offered the best hope of securing an adequate share of the defence budget in the long term. Otherwise, the debate on long-term strategy was one in which the Army was reluctant to take part. The Korean War, however, finally gave the Army the opportunity to join that debate by establishing the need for a military or operational role for Britain in Europe as part of an overall, long-term strategy. The third chapter looked in detail at an issue which brought together both threat perceptions and pressures for retrenchment; the articulation and application of the 'five plus five, no war rule'. It was suggested that the rule was a reasonable response to the combination of budgetary and strategic pressures, rather than the outcome of competition between them. As far as planning for the defence of Germany was concerned, the rule had little direct effect and was something of a distraction. The rule did, however, fuel the deepening rivalry between the Chiefs of Staff over the allocation of scarce resources, and in that sense affected the way any commitment of troops to German and European defence was viewed.

Chapters four to six looked more closely at strategic planning and at the place of Germany in Britain's overall strategy. For the first two post-war years, the occupation of Germany was a low priority, and not really a strategic matter at all. The *Future Defence Policy* paper, DO (47) 44, of May 1947, defined strategic priorities in terms of 'three pillars': defence of the UK; a firm hold in the Middle East; and control of SLOC. The occupation of Germany was still not a serious strategic preference and was certain to be run down. In early 1948 interest was expressed in American planning for withdrawal from Europe in the event of war. However, increasingly aware of the need to make at least a political commitment to European defence, the COS saw that a withdrawal strategy would be practically difficult and politically disastrous. In chapter five, a cautious reassessment was offered regarding the image of Montgomery as the champion of a continental strategy for Britain. The debate was always uneven; the continental strategy was never a credible alternative to the air power orthodoxy. So Montgomery sought the most advantageous position for the Army within the strategic orthodoxy, rather than offering a serious challenge to it. By the end of 1948 a wide gap had developed between the growing political commitment to European defence, something the COS nevertheless understood, and the strategic preferences of Britain's military.

Gradually, during 1949, the COS came to accept that these political commitments to Western European cohesion and defence should be matched by a clearer signal of military support. However, such gestures as were made in this vein were tentative and minimalist: the offer, for example, to bring just one division of occupation troops up to battleworthiness. The fundamental convictions remained, that air power and atomic weapons offered the best means to deter, and then defeat, the Russians, and that the defence of the Middle East was vital to the security of Britain and the Commonwealth.

The launching of the US 'Center Strategy' in August 1949, with its new stress on fighting Russia in Western Europe, brought Britain's strategy for Europe – or lack of it – into question and led to the reinforcement decision of 23 March 1950. As an indication of the state of British strategic thinking, this decision should be viewed with some care. First, it was clearly driven by external pressures rather than by any domestic change of heart regarding European defence. Second, it was in sum merely another example of British tokenism, of the determination to limit Britain's liability for European defence. The object was to prevent the collapse of French and WUDO morale, thus improving the chances of holding a defensive position on the Rhine. If the Rhine could be held then it was more likely that the Americans might be persuaded to abandon their plan to evacuate to a lodgement area from which subsequent expansion could take place, in favour of a more straightforward agreement to reinforce a successful defensive position. American reinforcement would allow the British to concentrate their efforts on the Middle East and would put an end to uncomfortable calls from the French for a British *effort du sang*. Britain's reinforcement decision is therefore best seen as an exercise in damage limitation rather than a change of strategy. The British military certainly now accepted that Britain should be more involved in the military dimensions of European defence, but were more persuaded by the possibility of using European defence to improve Britain's own security, than by the requirements of European defence *per se*. They still could not accept the validity of a continental strategy for fighting the Russians nor, therefore, a serious British contribution to the battle for Europe.

This book confirms the view that the terms 'continental commitment' and 'continental strategy' are not synonymous,[2] and shows that it was possible to pursue the former – however reluctantly – without the latter. Much of the analysis of Britain's external relations after 1945 reflects a vigorous debate over the nature, suitability and consequences of Britain's 'self-image'; the tension between Britain as a 'world power' and Britain as a 'European power'. The British military clearly understood the complexities of Britain's relations with its European allies after the war, and to dismiss or caricature their view of Britain's place in Europe and the world could be to overlook the part played by an influential sector of the external and security policy-making establishment in Britain. Although not the most progressive or 'Europeanist' sector of the establishment, the British military were nevertheless fully aware that many basic assumptions were in need of review, that isolation from Europe was difficult, and that Britain's strategy for Europe had to be defined and discussed in both political and military terms. Military planning did not take place in a political vacuum, and the Chiefs of Staff fully accepted that what might have been militarily preferable (a complete withdrawal from Europe, either deliberately or in an emergency) would have been impossible politically. Equally, Britain's 'political commitment' to continental defence was always discussed in strategic terms, both in the sense of offering ideological resistance to Communist expansion into the depressed and war-damaged areas of Western Europe, resulting in the breakdown of civil society and a Russian victory by default, and in the sense of bolstering the morale of Britain's European allies such that they would be persuaded to mount their own, effective defence against the Russian threat. Militarily, however, the Chiefs of Staff remained deeply sceptical as to the wisdom of committing troops and air forces to a genuine continental strategy for the defence of Germany and Europe. Thus, to suggest that British strategy after 1945 in some way reflected growing interest and involvement in the political and economic development of Western Europe is to confuse the British military's receptiveness to the political dimensions of strategic policy-making with a willingness to contemplate a serious commitment of ground troops with supporting air forces to European defence.

'Defence of Germany' was always a heavily circumscribed notion. Long before German pressure for 'forward defence', up to the outbreak of the Korean War the Allies were only ever willing to countenance 'defending' Germany on the Rhine. When considering the various reinforcement promises discussed and made, it is also important to note the standard of the troops being offered; Territorial Army formations, requiring three to six months to prepare for war, would be of questionable value even if they arrived in time to make a contribution. The allocation of tactical air support to Army divisions is an important indicator of British interest and sincerity; without such support the life expectancy of Army divisions fighting in Europe would be limited, yet the COS were clearly aware that tactical air support would probably not be available. But a much more important consideration was the primacy of strategic air power. Faith in the deterrent and defensive potential of the atomic bomb did much to undermine interest in what were thought to be more peripheral areas of strategic thinking, including the conventional defence of Europe. The vigour with which the three services fought among themselves, and occasionally jointly against the Minister of Defence, over the allocation of resources also shaped the way strategy and European defence was discussed. Strategic planning was not an intellectual exercise quarantined from the normal run of policy-making, and was subject to the general and increasing scarcity of resources. It is, finally, essential to draw a careful distinction between 'occupation' on one hand, and 'commitment' and 'strategy' on the other. At first, Britain's role in post-war Germany as an occupying power was a matter solely of policing a defeated state and preventing revanchism. As time went on, Britain certainly became more committed, economically and politically, to Germany and Europe, and the occupation became more important from a political-strategic point of view. However, the occupation did not anticipate these shifts, and on the strategic level the occupation only became fashionable when it seemed to offer the Army a stronger position in the competition for resources. But even at this late stage, not even the Army's spokesmen could see in the occupation the kernel of a continental strategy. The metamorphosis of the occupation into a Cold War, peacetime political strategy more accurately represents the attempt by the Army to avoid the real strategic debate altogether.

There are some signs of convergence in early 1950, between the general political commitment to Europe and military thinking about German defence. Yet military plans were always heavily circumscribed and dominated by air power and the atomic bomb. It is thus difficult to find, in the minds of Britain's military chiefs, firm evidence of a reversal of Britain's traditional strategy of maritime flexibility and limited liability during these pre-Korean years. The British military were not even beginning to think, seriously, about a continental strategy for Britain; the notion that the Korean War confirmed existing trends towards such a strategy is therefore also debatable. The evidence suggests instead that before June 1950 Britain's strategic tradition was confirmed rather than challenged. Ironically, just as some contemporary commentators, such as Liddell Hart, were becoming less dogmatic regarding British involvement in the territorial defence of Europe, so the Chiefs of Staff were struggling to sustain a view of British strategy which corresponded to Liddell Hart's pre-war notion of 'limited liability'. Kennedy has argued that World War II broke the 'myth of the efficacy of the 'British way of warfare' against a power which straddled half a continent'.[3] This book argues that, at least until June 1950, that 'myth' was very much alive.

Appendix: Civil and Military Officials

ALANBROOKE, Viscount	CIGS, 1941-46
ALEXANDER, A.V.	Minister of Defence, 1946-50
ATTLEE, C.	Prime Minister, 1945-51
BEVIN, E.	Foreign Secretary, 1945-51
BRIDGES, E.	PUS, Treasury, 1945-56
CADOGAN, A.	PUS, Foreign Office, 1938-46
CREASY, G.	VCNS, 1949-51
CRIPPS, S.	Chancellor of the Exchequer, 1947-50
CUNNINGHAM, A.	FSL/CNS, 1943-46
CUNNINGHAM, J.	FSL/CNS, 1946-48
DALTON, H.	Chancellor of the Exchequer, 1945-47
DANIEL, C.	Commandant, IDC, 1949-51
DICKSON, W.	VCAS, 1946-47
EDELSTEN, J.	VCNS, 1947-49
ELLIOT, W.	Chief Staff Officer to Minister of Defence
EVILL, D.	VCAS, 1943-46
FRASER, Lord	FSL/CNS, 1948-51
GAITSKELL, H.	Chancellor of the Exchequer, 1950-51
HARWOOD, E.G.	Civilian Director, IDC, 1947
HYND, J.	Chancellor of the Duchy of Lancaster, 1945-47
KIRKPATRICK, I.	High Commissioner, Germany, 1950-53
McCREERY, R.	GOC-in-C BAOR 1946-48
MacFADYEN, D.	Director of Plans (RAF)
McGRIGOR, R.	VCNS, 1945-47
MONTGOMERY, Viscount	Military Governor/C-in-C Germany, 1945-46; CIGS, 1946-48; Chairman, WUCinC, 1948-51
NYE, A.	VCIGS, 1941-46
PAKENHAM, Lord	Chancellor of the Duchy of Lancaster, 1947-48
PARKER, H.	PUS, MoD, 1948-56
PORTAL, Viscount	CAS, 1940-45
REDMAN, H.	DMO, War Office, 1948-51

ROBB, J.	VCAS, 1947-48
ROBERTSON, B.	Military Governor/C-in-C Germany, 1947-49; High Commissioner, Germany, 1949-50
SANDERS, A.	AOC-in-C BAFO, 1947-48; VCAS, 1948-50
SARGENT, O.	PUS, Foreign Office, 1946-49
SHINWELL, E.	Minister of Defence, 1950-51
SHOLTO DOUGLAS, W.	AOC-in-C BAFO, 1945-46; Military Governor/C-in-C Germany, 1946-47
SIMPSON, F.	VCIGS, 1946-48
SLESSOR, J.	CAS, 1950-52
SLIM, Viscount	Commandant, IDC, 1946-7; CIGS, 1948-52
STRANG, W.	PUS, Foreign Office, 1949-53
SYFRET, N.	VCNS, 1943-45
TEDDER, Lord	CAS, 1945-49
TEMPLER, G.	Director of Military Intelligence, 1946-48
TIZARD, H.	Chairman, DRPC, 1946-52
WILSON SMITH, H.	PUS, MoD, 1947-48

Notes and References

Introduction

1. R.B. Brett, 2nd Viscount Esher: chairman, War Office Reconstruction Committee ('Esher Committee'), 1903-4, subsequently permanent member of the Committee of Imperial Defence. Quoted in M. Howard, *The Continental Commitment* (London: Temple Smith, 1972), p.49.
2. C. Barnett, *Britain and Her Army 1509-1970* (London: Allen Lane, 1970), p.492.
3. D. Greenwood, 'Defence and National Priorities Since 1945', in J. Baylis, *British Defence Policy: Striking the Right Balance* (London: Macmillan, 1989), p.187.
4. J. Corbett, *Some Principles of Maritime Strategy* (London: Brassey's, 1988), p.9.
5. *Ibid.*, p.16.
6. J. Gooch, 'Maritime Command: Mahan and Corbett', in C.S. Gray and R.W. Barnett, *Seapower and Strategy* (London: Tri-Service Press, 1989), p.37 (emphasis in original).
7. H.A. DeWeerd, 'Britain's Changing Military Policy', *Foreign Affairs* (34/1, 1955), p.103.
8. J.W. Young, *Britain, France and the Unity of Europe 1945-51* (Leicester University Press, 1984), p.6. For similar arguments see C. Barnett, *Britain and Her Army*, p.482; C. Coker, *A Nation in Retreat? Britain's Defence Commitment* (London: Brassey's, 1986), p.61; R. Holmes, *Nuclear Warriors* (London: Jonathan Cape, 1991), p.196; and Howard, *The Continental Commitment*, p.146.
9. M. Carver, 'Continental or Maritime Strategy? Past, Present and Future', *Journal of the Royal United Services Institute* (134/3, 1989), p.68. See also M. Dockrill, 'British Attitudes Towards France as a Military Ally', Diplomacy and Statecraft(1/1,1990), *passim;* R.J. Aldrich and J. Zametica, 'The Rise and Decline of a Strategic Concept: the Middle East, 1945-51', in R.J. Aldrich (ed.), *British Intelligence, Strategy and the Cold War, 1945-51* (London: Routledge, 1992), p.253; and J. Lewis, *Changing Direction; British Military Planning for Post-war Strategic Defence, 1942-1947* (London: Sherwood Press, 1988),pp.112ff.
10. See also P. Cornish, 'The British Military and European Security', in A. Deighton (ed.), *Building Postwar Europe: National Decision-makers and European Institutions, 1948-1963* (London: Macmillan, forthcoming 1995).
11. N.J. Wheeler, 'The Attlee Government's Nuclear Strategy, 1945-51', in A. Deighton (ed.), *Britain and the First Cold War* (London: Macmillan, 1990), p.142.
12. M. Evans, 'Rifkind tries to hold line on £22bn defence budget', *The Times*, 26 September 1994.

1 Threat Perceptions, 1945-50

1. On the Chiefs of Staff system, 16 November 1943. Quoted in M. Gilbert, *Churchill: A Life* (London: Heinemann/BCA, 1992), p.758.
2. S.P. Huntington, *The Soldier and the State: The Theory and Politics of Civil-Military Relations* (Harvard University Press, 1957), p.66.
3. M. Edmonds (ed.), *The Defence Equation – British Military Systems; Policy, Planning and Performance Since 1945* (London: Brassey's, 1986), p.6.
4. L. Freedman, *U.S. Intelligence and the Soviet Strategic Threat* (London: Macmillan, 1986), p.4.
5. Huntington, *The Soldier and the State*, p.66.
6. N.J. Wheeler, 'Perceptions of the Soviet Threat', in S. Croft (ed.), *British Security Policy: The Thatcher Years and the End of the Cold War* (London: Harper Collins,

1991), p.177.

7. D. Yergin, *Shattered Peace: the Origins of the Cold War and the National Security State* (London: Andre Deutsch, 1978), pp.14,112.
8. Lewis, *Changing Direction*, p.262.
9. See P.G. Boyle, 'The British Foreign Office and American Foreign Policy, 1947-1948', *Journal of American Studies* (16/3, 1982), p.384; S. Croft, 'British Policy Towards Western Europe, 1947-49: the Best of Possible Worlds?', *International Affairs* (Autumn 1988), p.80 (footnote 9); D.C. Watt, 'Britain, the United States, and the Opening of the Cold War', in R. Ovendale (ed.), *The Foreign Policy of the British Labour Governments, 1945-1951* (Leicester University Press, 1984), p.55 ff.; and D. Reynolds, ''The Big Three' and the Division of Europe, 1945-48: An Overview', *Diplomacy and Statecraft* (1/2, 1990), p.130.
10. S. Dockrill, *Britain's Policy for West German Rearmament, 1950-1955* (Cambridge University Press, 1991), p.7.
11. E.J.Grove and G. Till, 'Anglo-American Maritime Strategy in the Era of Massive Retaliation, 1945-60', in J.B. Hattendorf and R.S. Jordan (eds.), *Maritime Strategy and the Balance of Power: Britain and America in the Twentieth Century* (London: Macmillan, 1989), p.275.
12. T.A. Schwartz, *America's Germany: John J. McCloy and the Federal Republic of Germany* (Harvard University Press, 1991),p.37
13. COS (45) 97th Meeting, 13 April 1945, CAB 79/31, Public Record Office, Kew Gardens, Surrey (PRO).
14. COS (45) 11th Meeting, 10 January 1945, CAB 79/28, PRO.
15. COS (45) 252nd Meeting, 16 October 1945, CAB 79/40, PRO.
16. COS (46) 24th Meeting, 13 February 1946, CAB 79/44, PRO.
17. COS (46) 52nd Meeting, 1 April 1946, CAB 79/46, PRO.
18. COS (46) 78th Meeting, 16 May 1946, CAB 79/48, PRO.
19. COS (46) 128th, 131st, 135th Meetings, 22nd August, 27 August, 3 September 1946, CAB 79/51, PRO.
20. COS 1241/6 dated 9 October 1946 to FO, annexed to COS (46) 150th Meeting, 9 October 1946, CAB 79/52, PRO.
21. COS (46) 187th Meeting, 23 December 1946, CAB 79/53, PRO.
22. COS (46) 54th Meeting, 5April 1946, CAB 79/47, PRO. Lewis, *Changing Direction*, p.262, cites this COS meeting as evidence of the coming together in the spring of 1946 of Foreign Office doubts over Soviet intentions with COS concerns over Soviet capabilities. This may be to paint too clear a picture, certainly where the COS were concerned, who still saw the Soviet threat in fairly general terms. Furthermore, it is not certain that a synthesis between FO and COS views had developed by this point. The COS fears of Soviet intentions were to be passed on to the FO in the form of an amended JPS paper; COS (46) 105 (0).
23. COS (47) 34th Meeting, 28 February 1947; discussion of JP (47) 4 (Final), Military Control of Germany, 26 February 1947; DEFE 4/2, PRO.
24. COS (47) 57th Meeting, 23 April 1947, DEFE 4/3, PRO.
25. DO (47) 44, *Future Defence Policy*, 22 May 1947. This document is retained by the Cabinet Office but a copy of it is available in Lewis, *Changing Direction*, Appendix 7.
26. *Ibid.*
27. COS (47) 1st Meeting, 1 January 1947, DEFE 4/1, PRO.
28. J.L. Gaddis, *The Long Peace: Inquiries into the History of the Cold War* (New York: Oxford University Press, 1987), pp. 39-40. Kennan's article, entitled 'The Sources of Soviet Conduct', appeared in the July 1947 edition of *Foreign Affairs*.
29. *Ibid.*, p.43.
30. COS (47) 1st Meeting, 1 January 1947, DEFE 4/1, PRO.
31. Gaddis, *The Long Peace*, p.44.
32. COS (47) 1st Meeting, 1 January 1947, DEFE 4/1, PRO.
33. A. Deighton, *The Impossible Peace: Britain, the Division of Germany, and the Origins*

of the Cold War (Oxford: Clarendon Press, 1990), p.74.

34. *Ibid.*, p.225.
35. *Ibid.*, p.8.
36. *Ibid.*, p.58.
37. R. Badstübner, 'The Allied Four-power Administration and Sociopolitical Development in Germany', *German History* (7/1, 1989), p.25. See also R. Steininger, 'Germany after 1945: Divided and Integrated or United and Neutral?', *German History* (7/1, 1989), p.6.
38. COS (46) 54th Meeting, 5 April 1946, CAB 79/47, PRO.
39. See, for example, COS (46) 74th Meeting, 10 May 1946, CAB 79/48, PRO. The COS expected that, by late 1947, 'we should have largely reduced our occupation forces for Germany'.
40. COS (46) 102nd Meeting, 3 July 1946, CAB 79/50 PRO.
41. DO (47) 44, *Future Defence Policy*, 22 May 1947. Annex: National Policy, paragraph 3 (g). See Lewis, *Changing Direction*, p.386.
42. See also COS (47) 34th Meeting, 28 February 1947, DEFE 4/2, PRO.
43. COS (47) 34th Meeting, 28 February 1947, DEFE 4/12, PRO.
44. COS (47) 152nd Meeting, 8 December 1947 and 156th Meeting, 13 December 1947, DEFE 4/9, PRO.
45. COS (48) 16th Meeting, 2 February, DEFE 4/10, PRO.
46. COS (48) 30 (O), 7 February 1948, DEFE 5/10, PRO.
47. COS (48) 49 (O), 5 March 1948, DEFE 5/10, PRO.
48. COS (48) 59 (O), 18 March 1948, *International Security Arrangements*, DEFE 5/10, citing JIC (47) 76 (O), PRO. Further reference to this important JIC document can be found in COS (48)74 (O), 6 April 1948, DEFE 5/10, PRO. See also JP (48) 11 (Final), *Basic Assumptions for Planning – Joint Report by the [JPS] and [JIC]*, 8 April 1948, DEFE 4/12 [released October 1992], and JP (49) 124 (Final), *Future Defence Policy – Report by the [JPS]*, 16 December 1949, DEFE 6/10 [released October 1992].
49. Bevin to Alexander, C.3314/3314/G dated 27 April 1948. Copied at COS (48) 101 (O), 1 May 1948, DEFE 5/11, PRO.
50. Robertson to Bevin, MG/4103/C-in-C, 12 June 1948. COS (48) 142 (O) 25 June 1948, DEFE 5/11, PRO.
51. COS (48) 91st Meeting, 2 July, DEFE 4/14, PRO.
52. COS (48) 164th Meeting, 17 November 1948, DEFE 4/17, PRO. Discussion of JIC (48) 104 (Final), a report on Soviet intentions and capabilities in 1949 and in 1956/57, and JIC (48) 100 (Final), an agreed Anglo-American intelligence appreciation of Soviet intentions and capabilities for the same periods. The latter document was approved as a background paper for further planning and intelligence studies. Neither paper has been released in Britain.
53. On the subject of the Soviet Union's capacity to launch offensives in various theatres simultaneously, see JP (48) 11 [released October 1992] in which the planners were more sceptical of Soviet abilities, and JP (48) 64 (Final), *Defence of the Western Union – Report by the [JPS]*, 20 September 1948, DEFE 4/16 [released October 1992], where the JPS acknowledged a JIC assessment – JIC (48) 36 (O) – that the Soviets would be able to mount offensives of various sorts throughout Europe simultaneously. The final stage in this assessment process, wherein the Soviets were progressively held to be capable of bigger operations on more fronts, came with JP (49) 172 (Final), *Allied Defence Policy and Strategy – Report by the [JPS]*, 3 March 1950, DEFE 6/11 [released October 1992], PRO; the Soviets were now thought capable of simultaneous operations in Europe, the Middle East, the Far East, North America, at sea and through subversion generally, ' and still have enough to form an adequate reserve'.
54. The estimate of Soviet capabilities given in JP (48) 164 was rather more serious than that which the COS had accepted in COS (48) 30. By this latest count, the Russians would have some 83 divisions on the east bank of the Rhine by D+21 days.
55. This document was eventually to become the 'main assumption' behind the work of the

Harwood Working Party. See COS (48) 176th Meeting, 9 December 1948, DEFE 4/18, PRO.

56. COS (49) 8th Meeting, 15 January 1949, DEFE 4/19, PRO.
57. JIC (48) 121 (Final).
58. COS (49) 10th Meeting, 19 January 1949, DEFE 4/19, [released October 1992], PRO.
59. COS (49) 57th Meeting, 20 April 1949, DEFE 4/21, PRO.
60. COS (49) 14th Meeting, 28 January 1949; discussing JP (48) 117 (Final), DEFE 4/19, PRO.
61. COS (49) 10th Meeting, 19 January 1949, [released October 1992], PRO.
62. JP (49) 3 (Final), discussed at COS (49) 55th Meeting, 13 April 1949, DEFE 4/21, PRO. See also JP (48) 11 [released October 1992] for the list of operations open to the Soviet Union.
63. Two papers, *Soviet Intentions and Capabilities*, and *Appreciation of Russian Intentions*, both of which would appear to contain central information, are referred to in COS (50), 37th Meeting, 8 March 1950, DEFE 4/29 [Minute 2 – released October 1992], PRO. Although the papers are still retained by the Cabinet Office, they are now at least identifiable as JIC(UK) (49) 80 and JIC (49) 109 respectively. In commenting upon these papers, Fraser indicated that they had concentrated on the Soviet threat to Turkey. In his view, more stress should have been laid on 'the British view that the first aim of the Russians would be to knock this country out'.
64. COS (50) 8, 10 January 1950, DEFE 5/19, PRO.
65. COS (50) 9th Meeting, 13 January 1950, DEFE 4/28, PRO.
66. JP (49) 156 (Final), 15 March 1950. Discussed at, and appended to, COS (50) 52nd Meeting, 29 March 1950, DEFE 4/30, PRO.
67. JP (50) 46 (Final), *Use of German Resources for the Defence of Western Europe*, 21 April 1950. Discussed at COS (50) 70th Meeting, 2 May 1950, DEFE 4/31, PRO.
68. JP (50) 22 (Final), 10 March 1950, DEFE 4/29 and DEFE 6/12, PRO.
69. *Ibid.*, para 8. This conclusion appears to have been accepted in late 1949, as the following quotation from COS (48) 188th Meeting, 21 December 1949, DEFE 4/27 [Minute 11 – released October 1992], PRO, indicates: 'there was now an increasing realisation that the security of the United Kingdom was very closely bound up with the defence of Europe.'
70. JP (50) 4 (Final), *Joint Command for the Defence of the United Kingdom in War*, 8 February 1950. Discussed at COS (50) 42nd Meeting, 15 March 1950, DEFE 4/29, PRO. See also DEFE 6/12 for an additional copy of the JPS report.
71. JIC (49) 42 (Final Revise), date not known.
72. JP (49) 134 (Final), 1 March 1950, DEFE 4/29. This paper – Plan GALLOPER – was discussed at COS (50) 44th Meeting, 17 March 1950, PRO.
73. Newly released papers also make it clear that the *values* which the British military considered vulnerable to Soviet forces were Western forces and strategic assets rather than the territory of Britain's continental allies and neighbours: JP (48) 131 (Final), *Plan Speedway – Report by the [JPS]*, 18 November 1948, DEFE 6/7; JP (48) 140 (Final), *Digest of Plan Speedway – Report by the [JPS]*, 8 December 1948, DEFE 6/7: both released to PRO in October 1992.
74. COS (50) 39th Meeting, 13 March 1950, DEFE 4/29, PRO.
75. JP (49) 134 (Final), 1 March 1950, DEFE 4/29, PRO.
76. *Ibid.*, para 4(a).
77. *Ibid.*, paras 21-23.
78. *Ibid.*, para 103(b).
79. COS (47) 227 (O), *Review of World Strategic Situation*, 17 November 1947, para. 35, DEFE 5/6, PRO.
80. COS (50) 63rd Meeting, 24 April 1950, DEFE 4/30, PRO. Discussing JP (50) 40 (Final), *Strategic Implications of Re-allocating Certain Air Forces from the Middle East to Western Europe*, 20 April 1950.
81. The first and main version of the report – COS (50) 139, *Defence Policy and Global*

Strategy Report, 1 May 1950 – was described by the Ministry of Defence as 'still sensitive' in October 1992 and is therefore retained. As usual, several clues to the content of this paper can be gleaned from papers available in the PRO:JP (50) 22 (Final), 10 March 1950, DEFE 4/29 & DEFE 6/12;JP (49) 172 (Final), 10 March 1950, DEFE 4/29 [released October 1992]; and the instructions for the latter in COS (49) 188th Meeting. However, the clearest indication of COS thinking comes in the form of a slightly amended version of the report aimed at an American, Australian, Canadian and New Zealand readership which, on 7 June 1950, was circulated as DO (50)45. It is this version of the report to which R. Ovendale had access – *The English-speaking Alliance: Britain, the United States, the Dominions and the Cold War* (London: George Allen & Unwin, 1985), p.122ff. – and which Aldrich and Zametica described as representing a 'shift towards continental defence' by Britain – 'The rise and decline of a strategic concept', p.264. The amended report, DO (50) 45, is published in its entirety in *Documents on British Policy Overseas. Series II, Volume IV: Korea, June 1950-April 1951* (London: HMSO, 1991), appendix I, p.411.

82. DBPO II/IV, p.413; DO (50) 45, para. 11.
83. *Ibid.*, pp.422-3; paras. 31, 33.
84. *Ibid.*, p.415; para. 13(b).
85. *Ibid.*, p.417; para. 17.
86. *Ibid.*, p.414; para. 13(a).
87. See M. Howard, 'Liddell Hart', in M. Howard, *The Causes of Wars* (London:Temple Smith, 1983), p.203: describing Hart's analysis of British strategy in the 1930s.

2 The Defence Budget, 1945-50

1. M. Quinlan, 'British defence planning in a changing world', *The World Today* (48/89, 1992), p.160
2. Quoted in K.O. Morgan, *Labour in Power, 1945-51* (Oxford University Press, 1984), p.144.
3. American economic assistance has been seen as more than simply a 'backdrop' for strategic thinking in Britain: 'The core of Britain's strategy for Western Europe became inevitably one of securing American economic and military assistance ...': S. Dockrill, *Britain's Policy for West German Rearmament*, p.9.
4. The mismatch between aspirations and resources is addressed in C. Barnett, *The Audit of War* (London: Macmillan, 1986).
5. *Ibid.*, p.37.
6. *Ibid.*, p.237.
7. *Ibid.*, p.246.
8. A. Grosser, *The Western Alliance* (London: Macmillan, 1980), p.48.
9. H. Beach, 'British Forces in Germany, 1945-85', in Edmonds (ed.), *The Defence Equation*, p.157.
10. *Ibid.*, p.158.
11. Morgan, *Labour in Power*, p.284.
12. E. Barker, *Britain in a Divided Europe, 1945-1970* (London: Weidenfeld and Nicolson, 1971), p.146.
13. JP (44) 226 (Final), *Manpower One Year After the Defeat of Germany – Reduction of Service Requirements*, 3 January 1945, annexed to the minutes of COS (45) 12th Meeting, 11 January 1945, CAB 79/28, PRO.
14. COS (45) 197th Meeting, 13 August 1945, CAB 79/37, PRO.
15. See COS (44) 328th Meeting, 5 October 1944.
16. COS (45) 215th Meeting, 5 September 1945, CAB 79/38, PRO.
17. COS (45) 287th Meeting, 21 December 1945, CAB 79/42, PRO.
18. COS (46) 2nd, 7th, 12th and 15th Meetings, 4-29 January 1946, CAB 79/43-44, PRO.

19. COS (46) 176th Meeting, 3 December 1946, CAB 79/54, PRO.
20. *Ibid.*
21. COS (46) 23rd & 24th Meetings, 11 & 13 February 1946, CAB 79/44, PRO.
22. COS (46) 112th Meeting, 17 July 1946, CAB 79/50, PRO.
23. COS (46) 176th Meeting, 3 December 1946, CAB 79/54, PRO.
24. COS (46) 42nd Meeting, 18 March 1946, CAB 79/46, PRO.
25. COS (46) 74th Meeting,10 May 1946, CAB 79/48, PRO.
26. COS (46) 81st Meeting, 22 May 1946, CAB 79/48, PRO. A similar request was later made by Montgomery at the 112th Meeting, 17 July 1946, CAB 79/50, PRO.
27. COS (46) 131, *War Office Note on Netherlands Participation in the Occupation of Germany*, 22 May 1946, CAB 80/54, PRO.
28. COS (46) 176th Meeting, 3 December 1946, CAB 79/54, PRO.
29. COS (47) 31st Meeting, 24 February 1947, DEFE 4/2, PRO.
30. COS (47) 48th Meeting, 2 April 1947, and COS (47)52nd Meeting, 14 April 1947, DEFE 4/3, PRO.
31. COS (47) 33 (O), *Future Defence Policy*, 18 [?] February 1947, DEFE 5/2, PRO.
32. COS (47) 54th Meeting, 17 April 1947, DEFE 4/3, PRO.
33. COS (47) 57th Meeting, 23 April 1947, DEFE 4/3, PRO.
34. COS (47) 79th Meeting, 25 June 1947, DEFE 4/5, PRO.
35. DO (47) 4; see COS (47) 39, *Manpower – Strength of the Armed Forces at 31st March 1948*, 19 March 1947, DEFE 5/1, PRO.
36. Cmd. 7042, paragraph 14.
37. COS (47) 39, *Manpower – Strength of the Armed Forces at 31st March 1948*, 19 March 1947, DEFE 5/1, PRO.
38. *Ibid.*
39. COS (47) 91st Meeting, 21 July 1947, DEFE 4/5, PRO.
40. To add to the pressure on the COS, in another minute Alexander had asked that the COS examine the possibility of bringing forward the 1,087,000 target for 31 March 1948, as given in Cmd. 7042, to 31 December 1947, and setting a new target of 1,000,000 for 31 March 1948; COS (47) 132 (O), 23 June 1947, DEFE 5/4, PRO.
41. COS (47) 98th Meeting, 31 July 1947, DEFE 4/6, PRO.
42. COS (47) 99th Meeting, 1 August 1947, DEFE 4/6, PRO.
43. COS (47) 105th Meeting, 19 August 1947, DEFE 4/6, PRO.
44. COS (47) 179 (O), *Revised War Office Estimate*, 29 August 1947, DEFE 5/5, PRO.
45. COS (47) 112th Meeting, 30 August 1947, DEFE 4/6, PRO.
46. The National Service Bill of October 1946 recommended a period of service of 18 months. Following the 'backbench revolt' of April 1947, the period was reduced to 12 months, before the Act received Royal assent in July 1947. Pressure from the COS, and the reaction to the Berlin crisis, brought the figure back up to 18 months in September 1948. Finally, in September 1950, following the outbreak of the Korean War, the period rose again to 24 months. See D. Reynolds, *Britannia Overruled: British Policy & World Power in the 20th Century* (London: Longman, 1991), *passim*, and G. Whitely, 'The British Experience of Peacetime Conscription', *Army Quarterly and Defence Journal* (117/3, 1987).
47. COS (47) 185 (O), *Future Defence Policy; Size and Shape of the Armed Forces, Note by CIGS*, 1 September 1947, DEFE 5/5, PRO.
48. *Ibid.*
49. COS (47)114th Meeting, 2 September 1947, DEFE 4/7, PRO.
50. COS (47)115th Meeting, 3 September 1947, DEFE 4/7, PRO.
51. COS (47) 148th Meeting, 27 November 1947, DEFE 4/9, PRO.
52. Cmd. 7327, February 1948.
53. COS (47) 152nd Meeting, 8 December 1947, DEFE 4/9, PRO.
54. COS (47) 153rd Meeting, 10 December 1947, DEFE 4/9, PRO.
55. COS (47) 263 (O), discussed at COS (47) 156th Meeting, 13 December 1947, DEFE 4/9, PRO.

56. COS (47) 158th Meeting, 16 December 1947, DEFE 4/9, PRO.
57. McCreery to Sholto Douglas, BAOR/50854/9/AC, 11 June 1947. Quoted in COS (47) 136 (O), *Internal Security in the British Zone of Germany*, 28 June 1947, DEFE 5/5, PRO.
58. COS (47) 86th and 87th Meetings, 9 and 11 July 1947, DEFE 4/5, PRO.
59. COS (47) 97th Meeting, 30 July 1947, DEFE 4/6, PRO.
60. COS (47) 159 (O), *Germany – Internal Situation in the British Zone*, 8 August 1947, (copy of a letter from Sholto Douglas to COS dated 7 August 1947), DEFE 5/5, PRO.McCreery's paper, *The Future Organisation of BAOR*, is dated 31 July 1947.
61. COS (47) 177 (O) (Revise), *Germany – Internal Situation in the British Zone, Memorandum by CIGS*, 30 August 1947, DEFE 5/5, PRO.
62. COS (47) 158th Meeting, 16 December 1947, DEFE 4/9, PRO.
63. COS (48) 25, *Publication of Strengths of the Armed Forces*, 9 March 1948, DEFE 5/7, PRO.
64. COS (48) 35th Meeting, 9 March 1948, DEFE 4/11, PRO. Use of the expression 'continental strategy' is of interest here, as J. Kent and J.W. Young have pointed out that the 1948 white paper (Cmd. 7327) was drafted 'with no provision for a continental army': 'The 'Western Union' concept and British defence policy, 1947-8', in Aldrich (ed.), *British Intelligence*, p.172.
65. COS (48) 69 (O), *Memorandum by CIGS*, 1 April 1948, DEFE 5/10, PRO.
66. COS (48) 71 (O), 5 April 1948, DEFE 5/10, PRO.
67. COS (48) 78 (O), 7 April 1948, DEFE 5/10, PRO.
68. COS (48) 80 (O), 9 April 1948, DEFE 5/10, PRO.
69. JP (48) 11 (Final), *Basic Assumptions for Planning – Joint Report by the [JPS]*, 8 April 1948, DEFE 4/12, PRO [released October 1992].
70. COS (48) 63rd Meeting, 10 May 1948, DEFE 4/13, discussing Montgomery's memorandum, *Preparedness for War*, COS (48) 104 (O), 6 May 1948, DEFE 5/11, PRO.
71. Tedder cited COS (47) 74th Meeting, 11 June 1947, the minutes of which are retained by MOD.
72. COS (48) 82nd Meeting, 16 June 1948, DEFE 4/13, PRO.
73. COS (48) 131 (O), *Size and Shape of the Armed Forces; Inter-Service Preparation for War – Memorandum by CIGS*, 11 June 1948, DEFE 5/11, PRO.
74. COS (48) 136 (O), *Size and Shape of the Armed Forces – Note by CAS*, 16 June 1948, DEFE 5/11, PRO.
75. *Ibid.*
76. COS (48) 172 (O), *Role of the Army on the Outbreak of War and Plan for Long-Term Development of the Army to fulfil its Role – Note by CIGS*, 9 August 1948, DEFE 5/12, PRO.
77. COS (48) 112th Meeting, 11 August 1948, DEFE 4/15, PRO.
78. COS (48) 124th Meeting, 8 September 1948, DEFE 4/16, PRO. Montgomery's paper can be found at COS (48) 199 (O), *Manpower Requirements of the Army During 1949 – Note by CIGS*, 6 September 1948, DEFE 5/12, PRO. The paper, earlier drafts of it and subsequent comment on its reception by COS can all be found in WO 216/265, PRO.
79. COS (48) 127th Meeting, 10 September 1948, DEFE 4/16, PRO.
80. COS (48) 209 (O), *Size and Shape of the Armed Forces – Memorandum by Minister of Defence*, 16 September 1948, DEFE 5/12, PRO.
81. COS (48) 147th Meeting, 13 October 1948, DEFE 4/16, PRO. The COS discussed three papers: COS (48) 223 (O), a note by CIGS on the size and shape of the Army; COS (48) 226 (O), a memorandum by CAS; and COS (48) 227 (O), a note by the Secretary to the COS on the role of the three services, their strength and composition.
82. COS (48) 146th Meeting, 13 October 1948, DEFE 4/16, PRO.
83. COS (48) 159th Meeting, 9 November 1948, DEFE 4/17, PRO.
84. COS (48) 165th Meeting, 19 November 1948, DEFE 4/18, PRO.
85. COS (48) 166th Meeting, 22 November 1948, DEFE 4/18, PRO. For further informa-

tion on the terms of reference of the Harwood Working Party see COS (48) 176th Meeting, 9 December 1948, DEFE 4/18, PRO.
86. COS (48) 190, Cost of the Army in 1949/50, 4 December 1948, DEFE 5/9, PRO.
87. COS (48) 174th Meeting, 7 December 1948, DEFE 4/18, PRO.
88. COS (49) 48th Meeting, 28 March 1948, DEFE 4/20, PRO.
89. E.J. Grove has made the point that the working party was set up to illustrate the dangers of a £700m budget, rather than to show how this target could be achieved: *Vanguard to Trident: British Naval Policy Since World War II* (London: Bodley Head, 1987), p.47. Elsewhere, Grove has argued that the COS intended the Harwood Committee to produce 'horrific' recommendations with which they could strengthen their position against the Treasury: 'British naval policy 1945-57', in A. Gorst, L. Johnman and W. Scott Lucas (eds.), *Post-war Britain, 1945-64: Themes and Perspectives* (London: Pinter, 1989), p.157.
90. COS (49) 140, *Size and Shape of the Armed Forces – Report by CAS*, 22 April 1949; COS (49) 143, *Harwood Report – Memorandum by FSL*, 23 April 1949; and COS (49) 145, *Harwood Working Party Report – Memorandum by CIGS*, 23 April 1949. All in DEFE 5/14, PRO.
91. COS (49) 61st Meeting, 27 April 1949, DEFE 4/21, PRO.
92. COS (49) 68th Meeting, 10 May 1949, DEFE 4/21, PRO.
93. COS (49) 77th Meeting, 25 May 1949, DEFE 4/22, PRO.
94. COS (49) 83rd Meeting, 2 June 1949, DEFE 4/22, PRO.
95. COS (49) 89th Meeting, 16 June 1949, DEFE 4/22, PRO.
96. COS (49) 214, *Size and Shape of the Armed Forces 1950-52*, 6 June 1949, DEFE 5/14, PRO.
97. Grove, *Vanguard to Trident*, p.51.
98. For the Terms of Reference see COS (49) 251, *Inter-Departmental Committee on Defence Estimates, Note by Chairman*, 26 July 1949, DEFE 5/15, PRO.
99. COS (49) 110th Meeting, 28 July 1949, DEFE 4/23, PRO. See also Grove, *Vanguard to Trident*, p.51 for a brief explanation of the purpose of the Parker Working Party.
100. COS (49) 247, *The Future Shape and Size of the Army*, 21 July 1949, DEFE 5/15, PRO.
101. Alexander to COS, 18 August 1949, copied at COS (49) 268, *Defence Estimates*, 19 August 1949, DEFE 5/15, PRO.
102. COS (49) 251, *Inter-Departmental Committee on Defence Estimates – Note by Chairman*, 26 July 1949, DEFE 5/15, PRO.
103. COS (49)132nd Meeting, 9 September 1949, DEFE 4/24, PRO.
104. COS (49)136th Meeting, 15 September 1949, DEFE 4/24, PRO.
105. COS (49) 313 (Final), *The Size and Shape of the Armed Forces over the next Three Years – Report by COS*, 27 September 1949, DEFE 5/16, PRO.
106. COS (49)169th Meeting, 15 November 1949, DEFE 4/26, PRO.
107. COS (49) 178th Meeting, 30 November 1949, DEFE 4/27, PRO.
108. COS (50) 74th Meeting, 11 May 1950, DEFE 4/31, PRO.
109. *Ibid.*
110. *Ibid.*
111. COS (50) 77th Meeting, 17 May 1950, DEFE 4/31, PRO.
112. COS (49) 313 (Final), *The Size and Shape of the Armed Forces over the Next Three Years*, 27 September 1949, DEFE 5/6, PRO.
113. COS (50) 100th Meeting, 30 June 1950, DEFE 4/32, PRO.
114. A certain amount of rivalry was personal rather than professional, especially between Montgomery and Tedder & Cunningham; J. Gooch, 'The Chiefs of Staff and the Higher Organisation for Defence in Britain, 1904-1984', in Hattendorf and Jordan (eds.), *Maritime Strategy*, p.47.
115. A. Gorst, '"We Must Cut our Coat According to our Cloth"': the Making of British Defence Policy, 1945-8', in Aldrich (ed.), *British Intelligence*, p.163.

3 The 'No War Rule'

1. N. Bagnall, 'Keeping Up Our Guard Against the Unexpected', *Daily Telegraph*, 26 June 1990.
2. Quoted in S. Roskill, 'The Ten Year Rule – The Historical Facts', *Journal of the Royal United Services Institute* (March 1972), p.69.
3. C. Barnett, *The Collapse of British Power* (Gloucester: Alan Sutton, 1987), p.278.
4. Howard, *The Continental Commitment*, p.89.
5. Quinlan, 'British defence planning', p.161.
6. P. Silverman, 'The Ten Year Rule', *Journal of the Royal United Services Institute* (March 1971).
7. K. Booth, 'The Ten Year Rule; An Unfinished Debate', *Journal of the Royal United Services Institute* (September 1971).
8. Roskill, 'The Ten Year Rule'.
9. M. Edmonds, 'Planning Britain's Defence, 1945-85', in Edmonds (ed.), *The Defence Equation*, p.12.
10. R.M. Hathaway, *Ambiguous Partnership: Britain and America, 1944-1947* (New York: Columbia University Press, 1981), pp.253, 297. See also E. Barker, *The British Between the Superpowers, 1945-50* (Macmillan, 1983), p.100; M. Dockrill, *British Defence Since 1945* (Oxford: Basil Blackwell, 1988), pp.34-5; and Reynolds, *Britannia Overruled*, p.167.
11. W. Jackson and E. Bramall, *The Chiefs: The Story of the United Kingdom Chiefs of Staff* (London: Brassey's, 1992), pp.270-1.
12. E. Grove, 'The Post War "Ten Year Rule" – Myth and Reality', *Journal of the Royal United Services Institute* (129/4, 1984).
13. Silverman, 'The Ten Year Rule', p.42.
14. Lewis, *Changing Direction*, p.101.
15 *Ibid.*, ch.3.
16. PHP (44) 20, *The Air Defence of Great Britain During the Ten Years Following the Defeat of Germany*, 19 May 1944, CAB 81/42, PRO. G. Ross (ed.), *The Foreign Office and the Kremlin: British Documents on Anglo-Soviet Relations, 1941-45* (Cambridge University Press, 1984), p.148 also provides evidence, in the form of a Foreign Office paper on post-war Soviet policy of 29 April 1944, that the FO was thinking in terms of a five year rule in spring 1944.
17. PS (43) 2, *The Future of Germany*, 8 August 1943. Discussed at PS (43) 2nd Meeting, 11 August 1943, CAB 87/65, PRO.
18. Lewis, *Changing Direction*, p.262. Relevant papers are at COS (46) 54th Meeting, 5 April 1946. The COS discussed and amended JP (46) 65 (Final) which went to the Foreign Office as COS (46) 105 (O).
19. *Ibid.*
20. COS (46) 133rd Meeting, 30 August 1946. Annexed letter COS 1049/6 30 August 1946, Secretary COS to Foreign Office, CAB 79/51, PRO.
21. JP (46) 164. Grove, 'The Post War "Ten Year Rule"', p.49.
22. COS (47) 156th Meeting, 13 December 1947, DEFE 4/9, PRO. See also R. Smith and J. Zametica, 'The Cold Warrior: Clement Attlee Reconsidered, 1945-7', *International Affairs* (61/2, 1985), p.245, and J. Zametica, 'Three Letters to Bevin: Frank Roberts at the Moscow Embassy, 1945-46', in J. Zametica, (ed.), *British Officials and British Foreign Policy 1945-50* (Leicester University Press, 1990), p.82 for references to a five-year no war rule in JIC papers in February 1946. Grove has pointed out that the rule eventually covered a nine year period; *Vanguard to Trident*, pp. 40, 45.
23. COS (46) 187th Meeting, 23 December 1946, CAB 79/54, PRO.
24. A.J.P. Taylor, *English History 1914-1945* (Oxford University Press, 1965), p.460.
25. COS (46) 227, *The Army – Manpower Situation, Note by CIGS*, 5 October 1946, CAB 80/55, PRO.

26. *The British Army; Memorandum by CIGS*, 8 September 1947, WO 216/233, PRO.
27. COS (47) 1st Meeting, 1 January 1947, DEFE 4/1, PRO.
28. Howard, *The Continental Commitment*, p.80.
29. COS (46) 94th Meeting, 17 June 1946, CAB 79/49, PRO.
30. COS (46) 120th Meeting, 1st August 1946, CAB 79/50, PRO.
31. COS (45) 252nd Meeting, 16 October 1945, CAB 79/40, PRO.
32. M. Gowing, *Independence and Deterrence: Britain and Atomic Energy, 1945-1952. Volume I: Policy Making* (London: Macmillan, 1974), p.35.
33. *Ibid.*, p.169.
34. COS (46) 128th Meeting, 22 August 1946; 131st Meeting, 27 August 1946, CAB 79/51, PRO.
35. COS (45) 252nd Meeting, 16 October 1945, CAB 79/40, PRO.
36. COS (46) 176th Meeting, 3 December 1946, CAB 79/53, PRO.
37. *The Run-Down of the Army up to 1 April 1948*, 16 December 1947, WO 216/219, PRO.
38. Roskill, 'The Ten Year Rule', p.69.
39. COS (47) 79 (O) (Revise), 21 April 1947, DEFE 5/4 PRO. See also Grove, 'The Post war "Ten Year Rule"', p.49.
40. COS (47) 33 (O), 18[?] February 1947: a memorandum by Alexander circulated to COS.
41. COS (47) 106th Meeting, 20 August 1947, DEFE 4/6, PRO.
42. *Ibid.*
43. COS (47) 64th Meeting, 14 May 1947, DEFE 4/4, PRO. Discussion of JP (47) 55 (Final) [not yet released].
44. *Ibid.*
45. COS (47) 106th Meeting, 20 August 1947, DEFE 4/6, PRO.
46. COS (47) 107th Meeting, 21 August 1947, DEFE 4/6, PRO.
47. COS (47) 252 (O), *Balanced National Forces*, 3 December 1947, DEFE 5/6, PRO.
48. COS (48) 3rd Meeting, 7 January 1948, DEFE 4/10, PRO.
49. JP (48) 16 (Final), *Discussions on Policy for Western Europe*, 27 January 1948. Discussed at COS (48) 15th Meeting, 30 January 1948, DEFE 4/10, PRO.
50. COS (48) 34th Meeting, 9 March 1948, DEFE 4/11, PRO.
51. COS (48) 39th Meeting, 17 March 1948, DEFE 4/11, PRO: Discussing COS (48) 56 (O), 16 March 1948, DEFE 5/10, PRO.
52. COS (48) 104 (O), *Preparedness for War; Memorandum by CIGS*, 6 May 1948, DEFE 5/11, PRO.
53. COS (48) 106th Meeting, 28th July 1948, DEFE 4/15, PRO.
54. COS (48) 108th Meeting, 4 August 1948, DEFE 4/15, PRO.
55. COS (48) 171 (O), 4 August 1948, DEFE 5/12, PRO. If this is the point at which the Cabinet formally agreed to abandon the '5 plus 5' rule, then it is very slightly earlier than Grove's suggestion of 30 August; Grove, 'The Post War "Ten Year Rule"', p.51.
56. COS (48) 112th Meeting, 11 August 1948, DEFE 4/15, PRO.
57. COS (48) 159th Meeting, 9 November 1948, DEFE 4/17, PRO.

4 Fragile Logic: Strategic Plans, 1945-47

1. *The Memoirs of Field-Marshal the Viscount Montgomery of Alamein, K.G.* (London: Collins, 1958), p.345.
2. See F.S.V. Donnison, *Civil Affairs and Military Government North-West Europe 1944-1946* (London: HMSO, 1961), and F.S.V. Donnison, *Civil Affairs and Military Goverment Central Organization and Planning* (London: HMSO, 1966).
3. COS (45) 11th Meeting, 10 January 1945, CAB 79/28, PRO, discussing the PHPS paper PHP (44) 22 (O) (Final) of 3 January 1945.
4. COS (45) 62, 11 April 1945, CAB 80/47, PRO. This paper was revised the following

day and reference to "Stages" was dropped.
5. COS (45) 62, 11 April 1945, CAB 80/47, PRO. This document, a draft report by the VCOS, was entitled *Control Machinery in Germany*.
6. COS (45), 97th Meeting, 13 April 1945, CAB 79/31, PRO.
7. COS (45) 130th Meeting, 16 May 1945, CAB 79/32, PRO.
8. COS (45), 65th Meeting, 12 March 1945, CAB 79/30, PRO.
9. For some background to the idea of air control in British strategic thought see W.P. Snyder, *The Politics of British Defence Policy, 1945-1962* (Ohio State University Press, 1964), p.136, and D. Omissi, 'Technology and Repression: Air Control in Palestine 1922-36', *Journal of Strategic Studies* (13/4, 1990). The shortcomings of using strategic bombing aircraft in a tactical role during World War II are explained in I. Gooderson, 'Heavy and Medium Bombers: How Successful Were They in the Tactical Close Air Support Role During World War II?', *Journal of Strategic Studies* (15/3, 1992).
10. For comments on the place of the Strategic Reserve in strategic planning, see Barnett, *Britain and Her Army*, p.485; D.R. Devereux, 'Britain, the Commonwealth and the Defence of the Middle East , 1948-56', *Journal of Contempory History* (24/2, 1989), p.329; and Snyder, *The Politics of British Defence Policy*, pp. 11-18.
11. COS (45), 208th Meeting, 28 August 1945, CAB 79/38, PRO.
12. COS (45), 215th Meeting, 8 September 1945, CAB 79/38, PRO.
13. COS (45), 252nd Meeting, 16 October 1945, CAB 79/40, PRO.
14. COS (46), 42nd Meeting, 18 March 1946, CAB 79/46, PRO.
15. COS (46) 74th Meeting, 10 May 1946, CAB 79/48, PRO.
16. COS (46) 102nd Meeting, 3 July 1946, CAB 79/50, PRO. Montgomery's final report as C-in-C (*Notes on the German Situation*, 1 May 1946) can be found in WO 216/196, PRO.
17. COS (46) 52nd Meeting, 1 April 1946, CAB 79/46, PRO.
18. COS (46) 63rd Meeting, 18 April 1946, CAB 79/47, PRO.
19. COS (46) 74th Meeting, 10 May 1946, CAB 79/48, PRO.
20. COS (46) 187th Meeting, 23 December 1946, CAB 79/53, PRO.
21. COS (46) 39th Meeting, 13 March 1946, CAB 79/36, PRO.
22. COS (46) 51st Meeting, 29 March 1946, CAB 79/46, PRO.
23. COS (47) 7th Meeting, 8 January 1947, DEFE 4/1, PRO. The document in question is COS (47) 5 (O), *Future Defence Policy*, which was to become 'final' on 23 January 1947: DEFE 5/3, PRO.
24. COS (47) 9th Meeting, 13 January 1947, DEFE 4/1, PRO.
25. A. Bullock, *Earnest Bevin – Foreign Secretary 1945-1951* (London: Heinemann, 1983), p.354.
26. COS (47) 1st Meeting, 1 January 1947, *Imperial Defence College – General Policy*, DEFE 4/1, PRO.
27. COS (47) 34th Meeting, 28 February 1947, DEFE 4/2, PRO.
28. JP (46) 164, *Review of Defence Problems*. This document is not yet available for public scrutiny.
29. COS (47) 52nd Meeting, 14 April 1947, DEFE 4/3, PRO. The two additional papers, COS (47) 72 (O) and COS (47) 78 (O), were memoranda by CIGS and the First Sea Lord respectively, discussing aspects of the JPS report.
30. COS (47) 54th Meeting, 17 April 1947, DEFE 4/3, PRO.
31. COS (47) 57th Meeting, 23 April 1947, DEFE 4/3, PRO.
32. The terms of reference were eventually circulated as COS (47) 87 (O) (Limited Circulation).
33. COS (47) 79 (O) (Revise).
34. COS (47) 5 (O).
35. COS (47) 64th Meeting, 14 May 1947, DEFE 4/4, PRO.
36. COS (47) 66th Meeting, 21 May 1947, DEFE 4/4, PRO.
37. A version of DO (47) 44 is reproduced in Lewis, *Changing Direction*, appendix 7.

38. See Dockrill, *British Defence Since 1945*, p.28 and N. Hamilton, *Monty: The Field-Marshal 1944-1976* (London: Hamish Hamilton, 1986), pp.654, 700, 749.
39. W. Krieger, 'American Security Policy in Europe before NATO', in F.H. Heller and J.R. Gillingham (eds.), *NATO: The Founding of the Atlantic Alliance and the Integration of Europe* (London: Macmillan, 1992), p.102.
40. For a detailed explanation of the American background to the 1946 approach see J.F. Schnabel, *The History of the Joint Chiefs of Staff: The Joint Chiefs of Staff and National Policy. Volume I: 1945-1947* (Wilmington, Delaware: Michael Glazier, 1979), pp.136-160.
41. Hamilton, *Monty*, p.654.
42. Barker, *The British Between the Superpowers*, p.115ff.
43. COS (46) 24th Meeting, 13 February 1946, CAB 79/44, PRO.
44. COS (46) 54th Meeting, 5 April 1946, CAB 79/47, PRO.
45. COS (46) 74th Meeting, 10 May 1946, CAB 79/48, PRO.
46. COS (46) 128th Meeting, 22 August 1946, CAB 79/51, PRO.
47. COS (46) 131st Meeting, 27 August 1946, CAB 79/51, PRO.
48. COS(46) 135th Meeting, 3 September 1946, CAB 79/51, PRO.
49. COS (46) 187th Meeting, 23 December 1946, CAB 79/53, PRO.

5 Consolidation of the Cold War: Strategic Plans, 1947-48

1. Quoted in the minutes of COS (47) 158th Meeting, 16 December 1947, DEFE 4/9, PRO.
2. Aldrich and Zametica describe DO (47) 44 as the 'conceptual blueprint' for British strategy up to 1950, noting that the paper was opposed to strategic involvement on the Continent: 'The Rise and Decline of a Strategic Concept', p.249.
3. COS (47) 156th Meeting, 13 December 1947, DEFE 4/9. Discussion of COS (47) 263 (O), *Size and Shape of the Armed Forces*, DEFE 5/6, PRO.
4. COS (47) 158th Meeting, 16 December 1947, DEFE 4/9, PRO.
5. COS (47) 70th Meeting, 4 June 1947, DEFE 4/4, PRO. Discussing JP (47) 71 (Final), 2 June 1947.
6. Although the main source document – COS (47) 102 (O) – is not yet available for scrutiny, DO (47) 44, *Future Defence Policy*, of 22 May 1947, has now been released in CAB 21/1800, PRO: see Aldrich, 'Secret intelligence for a post-war world', p.41, note 3. As Aldrich acknowledges, this document had already been reproduced in Lewis, *Changing Direction*, pp.370-387, and it is to this reproduction of DO (47) 44 that reference is made here.
7. COS (47) 1st Meeting, 1 January 1947, DEFE 4/1, PRO.
8. COS (47) 57th Meeting, 23 April 1947, DEFE 4/3, PRO.
9. COS (47) 64th Meeting, 14 May 1947, DEFE 4/4, PRO.
10. COS (47) 105th Meeting, 19 August 1947, DEFE 4/6, PRO.
11. COS (47) 152nd Meeting, 8 December 1947, DEFE 4/9, PRO.
12. COS (47) 156th Meeting, 13 December 1947, DEFE 4/9, PRO.
13. Sargent to COS (Z 11127/25/G dated 1 January 1948), copied in COS (48) 2 (O), 2 January 1948, DEFE 5/10, PRO.
14. COS (48) 3rd Meeting, 7 January 1948, DEFE 4/10, PRO.
15. JP (48) 16 (Final), *Discussions on Policy for Western Europe*, 27 January 1948. Discussed at COS (48) 15th Meeting, 30 January 1948, DEFE 4/10, PRO.
16. Montgomery, *Memoirs*, p.500.
17. COS (48) 16th Meeting, 2 February 1948, DEFE 4/10, PRO.
18. R. Ovendale, *The English-Speaking Alliance* (London: George Allen & Unwin, 1985), pp.69ff.
19. '[Montgomery] thought discussions about the security of Western Europe were of

greater urgency and should be held first': COS (48) 7th Meeting, 14 January 1948, DEFE 4/10, PRO.

20. S. Dockrill, *Britain's Policy for West German Rearmament*, p.8; Hamilton, *Monty*, p.699; Kent and Young, 'The 'Western Union' Concept and British Defence Policy, 1947-8', in Aldrich (ed.), *British Intelligence*, pp.174-5.
21. COS (48) 26 (O), *The Problem of Future War and the Strategy of War with Russia*, DEFE 5/10, PRO. Discussed at COS (48) 16th Meeting, 2 February 1948, DEFE 4/10, PRO.
22. JP (48) 64 (Final), *Defence of the Western Union*, 20 September 1948, DEFE 4/16, PRO [released October 1992].
23. COS (48) 18th Meeting, 4 February 1948, DEFE 4/10, PRO.
24. Bullock, *Bevin*, ch. 13 especially pp.516, 523ff.
25. *Ibid.*, p.524-5.
26. J. Baylis, 'Britain, the Brussels Pact and the Continental Commitment', *International Affairs* (60/4, 1984), p.623. Baylis notes that the 'debate' in fact lasted even longer since it was not until 23 March 1950 that the vital agreement to send reinforcements to Europe in the event of a Russian attack was made. See also J. Baylis, *The Diplomacy of Pragmatism: Britain and the Formation of NATO, 1942-1949* (London: Macmillan, 1993), pp.85-90.
27. Montgomery, *Memoirs*, p.500.
28. *Ibid.*, p.501.
29. COS (48) 140, 28 October 1948, DEFE 5/8, PRO.
30. COS (48) 30 (O), *Future Strategy – Note by CIGS*, 7 February 1948, DEFE 5/10, PRO.
31. COS (48) 26 (O), 30 January 1948, DEFE 5/10, PRO.
32. COS (48) 39th Meeting, 17 March 1948, DEFE 4/11, PRO: discussing COS (48) 56 (O), 16 March 1948, DEFE 5/10, PRO.
33. COS (48) 59 (O), *International Security Arrangements*, 18 March 1948, DEFE 5/10, PRO.
34. COS (48) 58 (O), 17 March 1948, DEFE 5/10, PRO.
35. COS (48) 26 (O), *The Problem of Future War and the Strategy of Future War with Russia*, 30 January 1948, DEFE 5/10, PRO.
36. Grove and Till, 'Anglo-American Maritime Strategy in the Era of Massive Retaliation, 1945-60', in Hattendorf and Jordan (eds.), *Maritime Strategy*, p.276.
37. COS (48) 90 (O), 15 April 1948, DEFE 5/10, PRO.
38. Barker, *The British between the Superpowers*, p.118.
39. COS (48) 7th Meeting, 14 January 1948, DEFE 4/10, PRO. Discussion of JP (48) 4 (Final) (Limited Circulation), *Subjects for Discussion with the Americans*, 6 January 1948.
40. The idea, voiced in mid-1946, and later in 1947, was that the problems of evacuation from Europe should be studied as a precaution; Hamilton, *Monty*, p.698. The approach to Cunningham had been made by the US Navy.
41. COS (48) 62nd Meeting, 5 May 1948, DEFE 4/13, PRO. The relevant JPS reports were JP (48) 47 (Final) and JP (48) 50 (Final).
42. K.W. Condit, *The History of the Joint Chiefs of Staff. The Joint Chiefs of Staff and National Policy. Volume II – 1947-1949* (Wilmington, Delaware: Michael Glazier Inc.,1979), pp.283-292. See also Krieger, 'American Security Policy in Europe before NATO', in Heller and Gillingham (eds.), *NATO*. For the text of HALFMOON see T.H. Etzold and J.L. Gaddis, (eds.), *Containment: Documents on American Policy and Strategy, 1945-1950* (New York: Columbia University Press, 1978), pp.315-323.
43. COS (48) 110 (O), *Plan 'Doublequick' – Note by Secretary*, 18 May 1948, DEFE 5/11, PRO: released by the MOD in October 1992.
44. JP (48) 48 (Final), *'Doublequick'* – an outline British emergency plan in the event of war before July 1949: and JP (48) 52 (Final), *'Plan Doublequick' – Further Action* – an attempt to co-ordinate British and American plans 'to the greatest extent possible'.
45. COS (48) 64th Meeting, 10 May 1948, DEFE 4/13, PRO.

46. Baylis, 'Britain, the Brussels Pact', p.623 suggests that at this meeting Britain 'finally agreed to fight a campaign alongside its allies in Western Europe'. Similarily, Bullock states that this was the point at which 'the case for sending British troops to the continent at the outbreak of war' was 'finally accepted': Bevin, p.524.
47. Agreed at COS (48) 66th Meeting, 12 May 1948, DEFE 4/13, PRO.
48. COS (48) 68th Meeting, 19 May 1948, DEFE 4/13, PRO.
49. *Ibid.*
50. COS (48) 83rd Meeting, 18 June 1948, DEFE 4/13, PRO.
51. COS (48) 73rd Meeting, 28 May 1948, DEFE 4/13, PRO.
52. COS (48) 49th Meeting, 8 April 1948, DEFE 4/12, PRO.
53. COS (48) 110 (O) [released October 1992].
54. JP (48) 63 (Final), 11 June 1948, *Western Union Defence Policy*. Discussed at COS (48) 82nd Meeting, 16 June 1948, DEFE 4/13, PRO.
55. JP (48) 63 (Revised Final), *Western Union Defence Policy*, 26 June 1948, DEFE 4/14, PRO. Discussed at COS (48) 90th Meeting, 30 June 1948, DEFE 4/14, PRO.
56. COS (48) 145 (O), *Defence Policy of the Western Union*, 2 July 1948, DEFE 5/11, PRO.
57. COS (48) 95th Meeting, 9 July 1948, DEFE 4/14 PRO.
58. COS (48) 96th Meeting, 9 July 1948, DEFE 4/14, PRO. Chaired by Attlee, with Bevin and Alexander. Montgomery was represented by Templer.
59. COS (48) 97th Meeting, Item 1, 12 July 1948, DEFE 4/14, PRO, [minute 1 released in October 1992].
60. COS (48) 161 (O), 23 July 1948, DEFE 5/11, PRO.
61. COS (48) 168 (O), 30 July 1948, DEFE 5/11, PRO: covering Montgomery's memorandum, CIGS/BM/31/2524, 27 July 1948.
62. COS (48) 169 (O), 2 August 1948, DEFE 5/12, PRO.
63. COS (48) 118th Meeting, 25 August 1948, DEFE 4/15, PRO.
64. COS (48) 121st Meeting, 1 September 1948, DEFE 4/15, PRO. The JPS document under discussion was JP (48) 93 (Final).
65. JP (48) 91 (Final), *Short-Term Strategic Aims in Europe at the Outbreak of War*, 1 September 1948. Discussed at COS (48) 124th Meeting, 8 September 1948, DEFE 4/16, PRO.
66. COS (48) 209 (O), 16 September 1948, DEFE 5/12, PRO.
67. COS (48) 228 (O), 1 October 1948, DEFE 5/12, PRO.
68. COS (48) 153rd Meeting, 29 October 1948, DEFE 4/17, PRO.
69. COS (48) 160th Meeting, 10 November 1948, DEFE 4/17, PRO. Discussion of JP (48) 130 (Final), 4 November 1948 (Special Circulation).
70. DOUBLEQUICK had by now been renamed SPEEDWAY, and the American version of the plan – HALFMOON – had been renamed FLEETWOOD. The Canadian version was known as BULLMOOSE.
71. COS (48) 168th Meeting, 24 November 1948, DEFE 4/18, PRO. Plan SPEEDWAY was presented as JP (48) 131 (Final), 18 November 1948. This document was released by the MOD in October 1992.
72. JIC (48) 100 (Final). Access to this document was denied in October 1992.
73. JP (48) 131 (Final), 18 November 1948, DEFE 6/7, PRO [released in October 1992].
74. JP (48) 140 (Final), Digest of Plan Speedway – Report by the JPS, 8 December 1948, DEFE 6/7, PRO [released in October 1992]. The prognosis for the defence of Western Europe should be quoted in full:

    The Allies intend to fight on the line of the Rhine as long as possible. The forces available, i.e., British and US garrisons in Germany and those of the Western European countries, cannot exceed some 11 divisions and 500 aircraft in all. Some of the British and US garrisons in Austria, which total one division in all, may also join them. The assessed scale of enemy attack is some 50 divisions and 5,000-6,000 aircraft. Therefore, if the enemy presses his attack we cannot hold Western Europe.

75. COS (48) 171st Meeting, 2 December 1948, DEFE 4/18, PRO.

76. COS (48) 178th Meeting, 13 December 1948, DEFE 4/18, PRO.
77. Kent and Young, 'The 'Western Union' Concept and British Defence Policy, 1947-8', in Aldrich (ed.), *British Intelligence*, p.174.

6 Token Forces: Strategic Plans, 1949-50

1. COS (50) 93, *United Kingdom Contribution to the Defence of Western Europe*, 16 March 1950, DEFE 5/20, PRO.
2. COS (48) 178th Meeting, 13 December 1948, DEFE 4/18, PRO.
3. COS (49) 2nd Meeting, 5 January 1949, DEFE 4/19, PRO.
4. COS (48) 220, 22 December 1948, DEFE 5/9, PRO: copy of a minute from Montgomery to Hollis – W.E./H.Q./1/151/F.M. dated 17 December 1948.
5. See COS (48) 228 (O), 1 October 1948, DEFE 5/12, PRO. This paper listed the occupation forces in Germany as: 1 infantry division; 1 armoured brigade; 1 infantry brigade; 1 parachute brigade; 4 armoured car regiments; 4 infantry battalions , and commented that 'none of the forces in the BAOR are administratively complete for war'.
6. COS (49) 4th Meeting, 7 January 1949, DEFE 4/19, PRO. The agreed draft memorandum was circulated as DO (49) 3.
7. COS (49) 47, *Estimation of the Size of Forces Eventually Required for the Defence of Western Union*, 4 February 1949, DEFE 5/13, PRO.
8. COS (49) 21st Meeting, 9 February 1949, DEFE 4/19, PRO.
9. WE/HQ/1/147/ dated 27 January 1949 and circulated as COS (49) 50, *Outline Short-Term Plan for the Defence of Western Europe*, 8 February 1949, DEFE 5/13, PRO.
10. JP (49) 13 (Final) (Limited Circulation), attached to COS (49) 35th Meeting, 2 March 1949, DEFE 4/20, PRO. The JPS paper was a comment upon the outline plan contained in COS (49) 50.
11. COS (49) 36th Meeting, 3 March 1949, DEFE 4/20, PRO.
12. COS (48) 172 (O), *Role of the Army on the Outbreak of War and Plan for Long-Term Development of the Army to fulfil its Role – Note by CIGS*, 9 August 1948, DEFE 5/12, PRO.
13. COS (49) 42nd Meeting, 15 March 1949, DEFE 4/20, PRO.
14. COS (49) 52nd Meeting, 6 April 1949, DEFE 4/21, PRO.
15. COS (49) 57th Meeting, 20 April 1949, DEFE 4/21, PRO.
16. COS (49) 177, *UK Contribution to the Defence of Western Europe*, 16 May 1949, DEFE 5/14, PRO.
17. COS (49) 75th Meeting, 20 May 1949, DEFE 4/21, PRO.
18. COS (49) 79th Meeting, 30 May 1949, DEFE 4/22, PRO.
19. COS (49) 86th Meeting, 10 June 1949, DEFE 4/22, PRO.
20. COS (49) 177, 16 May 1949, DEFE 5/14, PRO.
21. COS (49) 203, *UK Contribution to the Defence of Western Europe*, 8 June 1949, DEFE 5/14, PRO.
22. COS (49) 177, 16 May 1949, DEFE 5/14, PRO.
23. COS (49) 88th Meeting, 16 June 1949, DEFE 4/22, PRO.
24. COS (49) 92nd Meeting, 22 June 1949, DEFE 4/22, PRO.
25. DO (49) 16th Meeting, 21 June 1949.
26. JP (48) 59 (Final – Second Revise), *Overall Strategic Concept for War in 1957*, 20 July 1949, DEFE 6/6, PRO [released October 1992]. This paper was a revision of JP (48) 59 (Revise) which had first been mentioned at COS (48) 134th Meeting, 22 September 1948, DEFE 4/16, PRO.
27. JIC (48) 100 [retained – Cabinet Office].
28. *Daily Telegraph* 1,2, and 10 February 1993.
29. See JP (48) 117, 19 January 1949 in COS (49) 14th Meeting, 28 January 1949, DEFE

4/19, PRO.

30. See JP (49) 3 (Final), 7 April 1949, COS (49) 55th Meeting, 13 April 1949, DEFE 4/21, PRO.
31. COS (49) 112th Meeting, 2 August 1949, DEFE 4/23, PRO, discussing JP (49) 73 (Final) *Anglo-American Strategy and Deployment of Forces in 1951*, 26 July 1949.
32. Plan SPEEDWAY: JP (48) 131/ABC 105. This document was released in October 1992.
33. COS (49) 113th Meeting, 3 August 1949, DEFE 4/23, PRO.
34. COS (49) 117th Meeting, 10 August 1949, DEFE 4/23, PRO.
35. DO (49) 16th Meeting, 21 June 1949: see COS (49) 92nd Meeting.
36. COS (49) 131st Meeting, 8 September 1949, discussing JP (49) 85 (Final), 5 September 1949, *Examination of the United States Strategic Concept for War in 1950/51*, and JP (49) 86 (Final), *Short-Term Strategy – A Campaign in Spain*, 7 September 1949.
37. US Directors of Plans to UK Directors of Plans, ABCM-5, dated 1 September 1949, attached at appendix D to JP (49) 85 (Final).
38. As one of the bases of their examination of the American concept, the JPS had themselves accepted that Western Europe up to the Pyrenees would probably be overrun by the Soviets by D+90 days.
39. These and other similar points were made by the JPS in a subsequent report on the defence of the Pyrenees and Spain: JP (49) 86 (Final), 7 September 1949, also attached to the minutes of COS (49) 131st Meeting, 8 September 1949, DEFE 4/24, PRO.
40. COS (49) 135th Meeting, 14 September 1949, DEFE 4/24, PRO.
41. JP (49) 106 (Final), *Report on the Brest-Brittany Bridgehead Proposal*, 15 September 1949, DEFE 6/10, PRO [released October 1992]. See also COS (49) 139th Meeting, 21 September 1949, DEFE 4/24, PRO.
42. COS (49) 136th Meeting, 15 September 1949, DEFE 4/24, PRO.
43. COS (49) 298, 12 September 1949, DEFE 5/16, PRO.
44. COS (49) 151st Meeting, 10 October 1949, DEFE 4/25, PRO.
45. COS (49) 154th Meeting, 19 October 1949, DEFE 4/25, PRO, discussing COS (49) 344, 13 October 1949, DEFE 5/17, PRO.
46. See also COS (49) 344, 13 October 1949, DEFE 5/17, PRO.
47. COS (49) 175th Meeting, 21 November 1949, DEFE 4/26, PRO, discussing JP (49) 149, 21 November 1949.
48. JP (49) 132 (Final), 15 October 1949, appended to COS (49) 154th Meeting, 19 October 1949, DEFE 4/25, PRO.
49. Referred to as JP (49) 130. This document has now been released: *Strategic Concept for the North Atlantic Treaty Powers – Report by the JPS*, 10 October 1949, DEFE 6/10, PRO.
50. JP (49) 133 (Final), *Visit of the United Kingdom Joint Planning Staff to Washington – September-October, 1949*, 14 October 1949, DEFE 4/25, PRO. This document, a report on the 'ABC' planning talks in Washington, 26 September to 4 October 1949, was attached to the minutes of the 154th meeting. The document also shows that the British and Americans had agreed to a review of Anglo-American short-term planning.
51. JP (49) 132 (Final), *Brief for United Kingdom Planners in the North Atlantic Treaty Military Committee Standing Group – Report by the JPS*, 15 October 1949, discussed at COS (49) 159th Meeting, 27 October 1949, DEFE 4/25, PRO.
52. COS (49) 363, *Short-Term Strategic Concept for Western Europe*, 29 October 1949, DEFE 5/18, PRO.
53. COS (49) 167th Meeting, 11 November 1949, DEFE 4/26, PRO. A review of short-term planning had been promised in the mid-October report on the ABC discussions; see JP (49) 133. The November discussion also provides a useful JPS summary of the progress of short-term Anglo-American planning to date: JP (49) 126 (Final), *Emergency Plans*, 3 November 1949.
54. JP (49) 134 (Draft).
55. COS (49) 387, *United Kingdom Contribution to the Defence of Western Europe*, 12

November 1949, DEFE 5/18, PRO.
56. COS (49) 168th Meeting, 14 November 1949, DEFE 4/26, PRO.
57. COS (49) 169th Meeting, 15 November 1949, DEFE 4/26, PRO.
58. COS (49) 171st Meeting, 16 November 1949, DEFE 4/26, PRO, considering JP (49) 136. This paper, promised earlier by the JPS in JP (49) 133, is retained by the MOD.
59. JP (48) 59 (Final – Second Revise), *Overall Strategic Concept for War in 1957*, 20 July 1957.
60. JP (49) 124 (Final), *Future Defence Policy – Report by the JPS*, 16 December 1949, DEFE 6/10, PRO [released in October 1992].
61. COS (49) 188th Meeting, 21 December 1949, DEFE 4/27, PRO [minute 11 released in October 1992].
62. COS (49) 413, 26 November 1949, DEFE 5/18, PRO.
63. COS (50) 20th Meeting, 2 February 1950, DEFE 4/28, PRO.
64. COS (50) 26th Meeting, 13 February 1950, DEFE 4/29, PRO.
65. COS (50) 37th Meeting, 8 March 1950, DEFE 4/29, PRO. The COS discussed JP (49) 72 (Final), a paper (retained by the MOD) dealing with Allied defence policy and strategy. Britain's survival would depend on keeping the Russians to the east of the Rhine and preventing their arrival at the Channel coast. The COS also noted, rather wistfully, that the loss of the Low Countries would mean that Britain would 'forego earlier warning of air attack'.
66. COS (50) 31st Meeting, 22 February 1950, DEFE 4/29, PRO. Discussion of JP (50) 17 (Final), *Inclusion of the United Kingdom Within the Area of Responsibility of a Regional Planning Group – Report by the [JPS]*, 14 February 1950.
67. Barker, *The British Between the Superpowers*, p.197. See also S. Dockrill, *Britain's Policy for West German Rearmament*, p.9 where the decision is described as 'a major shift in British defence priorities'.
68. COS (50) 39th Meeting, 13 March 1950, DEFE 4/29, PRO.
69. COS (50) 37th Meeting, 8 March 1950, DEFE 4/29, PRO. See also JP (50) 22 (S) (T of R), 9 March 1950, and JP (50) 22 (Final), *[UK] Contribution to the Defence of Western Europe*, 10 March 1950, DEFE 6/12 and DEFE 4/29, PRO.
70. COS (49) 413, *UK Contribution to the Defence of Western Europe – Note by CIGS*, 26 November 1949, DEFE 5/18, PRO. The adapted version of the report, designated COS (50) 93, received final amendments during the 43rd Meeting of 16 March, and was then forwarded to the Minister of Defence Committee as DO (50) 20; COS (50) 45th Meeting, 20 March 1950, DEFE 4/29. COS (50) 93 is located in DEFE 5/20, PRO.
71. COS (50) 48th Meeting, 23 March 1950, DEFE 4/30, PRO.
72. This comment is especially ironic since one of the reasons given earlier for Britain taking a more leading role in organising European defence had been that the Americans now considered that 'no additional [US] forces ... could reach the Rhine for three months after the outbreak of war ...'; JP (50) 22 (Final), 10 March 1950, DEFE 6/12, PRO.
73. COS (50) 93, *United Kingdom Contribution to the Defence of Western Europe*, 16 March 1950, DEFE 5/20, PRO.
74. COS (50) 19th Meeting, 1 February 1950, DEFE 4/28, PRO.
75. COS (50) 31st Meeting, 22 February 1950, DEFE 4/29, PRO.
76. Freedman, *The Evolution of Nuclear Strategy*, pp.72-5 provides an account of this important shift.
77. COS (50) 52nd Meeting, Minute 4 para. 2(b), 29 March 1950, DEFE 4/30, PRO.
78. COS (50) 53rd Meeting, 30 March 1950, DEFE 4/30, PRO. The MTDP called for 90 divisions, 8,800 aircraft and 1,000 combat ships: R.A. Wampler, 'Conventional Goals and Nuclear Promises: The Truman Administration and the Roots of the NATO New Look', in Heller and Gillingham (eds.), *NATO*.
79. See Barker, *Britain in a Divided Europe*, p.63 & ch.12; Young, *Britain, France and the Unity of Europe*, ch.18; Schwartz, *America's Germany*, ch.5; and S. Dockrill 'The Evolution of Britain's Policy Towards a European Army 1950-54', *Journal of Strategic*

Studies (12/1, 1989); *Britain's Policy for West German Rearmament*, especially ch.1; and 'Britain's strategy for Europe: must West Germany be rearmed? 1949-51', in Aldrich (ed.), *British Intelligence*.

80. COS (50) 8, *Western Germany – Defence*, 10 January 1950, DEFE 5/19, PRO.
81. COS (50) 52nd Meeting, 29 March 1950, DEFE 4/30, PRO.
82. COS (50) 19th Meeting, 1 February 1949, DEFE 4/28, PRO.
83. JP (49) 172 (Final), *Allied Defence Policy and Strategy – Report by the JPS*, 3 March 1950, DEFE 6/11, PRO [released in October 1992].
84. COS (50) 37th Meeting, 8 March 1950, DEFE 4/29, PRO. The summary version was produced as JP (50) 22 (Final), *United Kingdom Contribution to the Defence of Western Europe*, 10 March 1950, DEFE 4/29, PRO. The COS welcomed the latest JPS effort and now felt that the original work on 'Allied Defence Policy and Strategy' could be postponed: COS (50) 39th Meeting, 13 March 1950, DEFE 4/29, PRO.
85. COS (50) 62nd Meeting, 21 April 1950, DEFE 4/30, PRO. Redrafting of the Review of Global Strategy continued into April; COS (50) 63rd, 66th and 68th Meetings, 24, 26 and 28 April 1950, DEFE 4/30, PRO. At the latter meeting, final amendments were made and the paper was forwarded to the Minister of Defence/Defence Committee as COS (50) 139; this paper is withheld under a fifty year closure rule and, in October 1992, was described as 'still sensitive'. From COS (50) 74th Meeting, 11 May 1950, DEFE 4/31, PRO (a staff conference with Shinwell in the House of Commons), it appears that a review had two parts: 'Allied Defence Policy and Global Strategy'; and 'The British Commonwealth Contribution'. Having been seen by the Defence Committee, the review was then designated DO (50) 34, although in its final version, for wider distribution, it received the designation DO (50) 45. An amended version of the policy report is now available in *DBPO II/IV*, pp.411ff; DO (50) 45, *Defence Policy and Global Strategy – Report by the COS*, 7 June 1950.
86. DO (50) 45, *Defence Policy and Global Strategy – Report by the COS*, 7 June 1950; *DBPO II/IV*, pp.411ff, 418, 429. Aldrich and Zametica describe this paper as encapsulating 'Britain's shift towards continental defence', which seems a slight exaggeration: 'The rise and decline of a strategic concept', p.264.
87. COS (50) 66th Meeting Minute 1, 27 April 1950, DEFE 4/30, PRO; 'Foreign Office Views' presented to the COS by Sir William Strang.
88. COS (50) 74th Meeting, 11 May 1950, DEFE 4/31, PRO.
89. COS (50) 44th Meeting, 17 March 1950, DEFE 4/29, PRO.
90. JP (49) 134, *Plan Galloper – Report by the JPS*, 1 March 1950, DEFE 4/29 and DEFE 6/11, PRO, Annex II, para. 1.
91. COS (50) 100, 28 March 1950.
92. Condit, *The History of the [JCS]*, pp.294-301. A copy of OFFTACKLE can be found in Etzold & Gaddis, *Containment*, pp.324ff. For the gulf between the British and American plans caused by the American preference for a bridgehead in Europe, see Aldrich and Zametica, 'The Rise and Decline of a Strategic Concept', p.263.
93. JP (49) 134, para. 6.
94. Extracts from DO (47) 44; Lewis, *Changing Direction*, pp.374-382.

Conclusion

1. B.H. Liddell Hart, *Defence of the West: Some Riddles of War and Peace* (London: Cassell, 1950), p.115 [emphasis in original], p.148.
2. C. Barnett, 'From Past Glory to a more Limited Role Nearer Home', *Daily Telegraph*, 25 June 1990.
3. P. Kennedy, *Strategy and Diplomacy 1870-1945* (London: Fontana, 1984), p.80. See also B.H. Liddell Hart, *The British Way in Warfare* (London: Faber & Faber, 1932).

Bibliography

1. PRIMARY MATERIAL

A. Unpublished Papers: UK Public Record Office (PRO)

CAB 79/28-53	*COS: Minutes to 1946*
CAB 80/47-55	*COS: Memoranda to 1946*
CAB 81/40-46	*PHP: Minutes and Memoranda*
CAB 87/65	*Committee on the Post-War Settlement: Minutes and Memoranda*
CAB 87/66-69	*Armistice and Post-War Committee: Minutes and Memoranda*
CAB 87/83	*Ministerial Committee on Armistice Terms and Civil Administration: Minutes and Memoranda*
CAB 130/88	*Cabinet Committees GEN 240-241 ('Berlin Committee'): Minutes*
CAB 134/595	*Overseas Reconstruction Committee: Minutes and Memoranda*
DEFE 2/32-33	*Combined Operations Headquarters War Diary*
DEFE 4/1-32	*COS: Minutes 1947-50*
DEFE 5/1-24	*COS: Memoranda 1947-50*
DEFE 6	*JPS: Reports 1947-50*
FO 1030/353	*Targets in the Russian Zone of Germany*
FO 1038/1	*Organisation of Military Government in the British Zone after the Termination of the SHAEF Period*
FO 1038/2	*Occupation of Germany – Chain of Command*
FO 1038/3	*Control Commission, Military Sections: Charter and Establishment*
WO 216	*CIGS Papers*

B. PRO Papers Released in October 1992

Joint Planning Staff Papers

JP (48) 11 (Final), *Basic Assumptions for Planning*, 8 April 1948, DEFE 4/12.

JP (48) 38 (Final), *Western Union Defence Organisation*, 26 April 1948, DEFE 4/12.

JP (48) 59 (Final) (2nd Revise), *Overall Strategic Concept for War in 1957*, 20 July 1949, DEFE 6/6.

JP (48) 64 (Final), *Defence of the Western Union*, 20 September 1948, DEFE 4/16.

JP (48) 131 (Final), *Plan Speedway*, 18 November 1948, DEFE 6/7.

JP (48) 136 (Final), *Long Term Strategic Concept: Discussions with US Planners*, 6 November 1948, DEFE 6/7.

JP (48) 140 (Final), *Digest of Plan Speedway*, 8 December 1948, DEFE 6/7.

JP (49) 106 (Final), *Report on the Brest-Brittany Bridgehead Proposal*, 15 September 1949, DEFE 6/10.

JP (49) 124 (Final), *Future Defence Policy*, 16 December 1949, DEFE 6/10.

JP (49) 125 (Revised Final), *Deployment of [UK] and Commonwealth Forces in the Event of War in the Short Term*, 31 January 1950, DEFE 6/10.

JP (49) 130, *Strategic Concept for the North Atlantic Treaty Powers*, 10 October 1949, DEFE 6/10.

JP (49) 172 (Final), *Allied Defence Policy and Strategy*, 3 March 1950, DEFE 6/11.

JP (50) 39 (Final), *Implications of an Advance of the Possible Date of Outbreak of War*, 15 June 1950, DEFE 4/32.

Chiefs of Staff Memoranda

COS (48) 82 (O), *The Spread of Communism*, 12 April 1948, DEFE 5/10.

COS (48) 89 (O), *The Spread of Communism*, 15 April 1948, DEFE 5/10.

COS (48) 110 (O), *Plan Doublequick*, 18 May 1948, DEFE 5/10.

COS (50) 100, *Plan Galloper*, 28 March 1950, DEFE 5/20.

COS (50) 251, *North Atlantic Treaty Defence Plans – Western European Region*, 17 July 1950, DEFE 5/22.

Chiefs of Staff Minutes

COS (48) 52nd Meeting, 14 April 1948, *Basic Assumptions for Planning*, DEFE 4/12.

COS (48) 87th Meeting, 28 June 1948 (am), *Situation in Berlin*, DEFE 4/14.

COS (48) 88th Meeting, 28 June 1948 (pm), *Meeting with General*

Wedemeyer on the Subject of the European Command Organisation, DEFE 4/14.
COS (48) 91st Meeting, 2 July 1948, *Troop Reconnaissance in Germany*, DEFE 4/14.
COS (48) 97th Meeting, 12 July 1948, *Germany – Situation in Berlin*, DEFE 4/14.
COS (48) 100th Meeting, 15 July 1948, *European Situation – Command Organisation*, DEFE 4/14.
COS (48) 126th Meeting, 10 September 1948, *Scale and Nature of Initial Attack on the British Isles, 1957*, DEFE 4/16.
COS (49) 10th Meeting, 19 January 1949, *Possibility of War Before the End of 1956*, DEFE 4/19.
COS (49) 29th Meeting, 18 February 1949, *Staff Conference*, DEFE 4/20.
COS (49) 97th Meeting, 6 July 1949, *Overall Strategic Concept for War in 1957*, DEFE 4/22.
COS (49) 188th Meeting, 21 December 1949, *Strategy – Paper by Sir Henry Tizard*, and *Future Defence Policy*, DEFE 4/27.
COS (50) 37th Meeting, 8 March 1950, *Soviet Intentions and Capabilities*, and *Appreciation of Russian Intentions*, DEFE 4/29.

C. PRO Papers Not Released in October 1992

Retained by the Cabinet Office
All Joint Intelligence Committee papers and minutes, 1945-50.

Retained by the Ministry of Defence

Joint Planning Staff Papers
JP (48) 18 (Final) – [Western Union Stock-taking].

Chiefs of Staff Memoranda
COS (49) 122 – [West German State – Arrangements for Internal Security].
COS (49) 200 – [Plan SMARTWEED – Note by Secretary].
COS (49) 310, 19 September 1949 – [Plan SMARTWEED].
COS (49) 349 – [Establishment of Security Services in Germany].
COS (49) 385, 15 November 1949 – [Defence of River Lines].
COS (50) 112, 23 March 1950 – [Deployment of UK and Commonwealth forces in the event of war in the short term].
COS (50) 139, 1 May 1950 – [Defence Policy and Global Strategy Report].

Chiefs of Staff Minutes

COS (47) 74th Meeting, 11 June 1947.
COS (47) 111th Meeting, 27 August 1947 [Minute 2 in Confidential Annex].
COS (48) 21st Meeting, 11 February 1948 [Confidential Annex on Future Strategy].
COS (49) 113th Meeting, 3 August 1949 [Minute 3 in Confidential Annex].
COS (50) 74th Meeting, 11 May 1950 [Minute 3].

D. Published HMSO Command Papers (Cmd.)

6743	Statement Relating to Defence (February 1946)
6923	Central Organisation for Defence (October 1946)
7042	Statement Relating to Defence (February 1947)
7052	Army Estimates, 1947-48 (February 1947)
7087	Protocol of the Proceedings of the Berlin Conference (2 August 1945)
7327	Statement Relating to Defence, 1948 (February 1948)
7332	Army Estimates, 1948-49 (February 1948)
7631	Statement on Defence 1949 (February 1949)
7633	Army Estimates, 1949-50 (February 1949)

E. Published Documents

Bullen, R. and Pelly, M.E. (eds.), *Documents on British Policy Overseas. Series II, Volume II: The London Conferences, Anglo- American Relations and Cold War Strategy, January-June 1950* (London: HMSO, 1987). [*DBPO II/II*]

Etzold, T.H. and Gaddis, J.L. (eds.), *Containment: Documents on American Policy and Strategy, 1945-1950* (New York: Columbia University Press, 1978).

Grenville, J.A.S. (ed.), *The Major International Treaties 1914- 1973* (London: Methuen, 1974).

Ross, G. (ed.), *The Foreign Office and the Kremlin: British Documents on Anglo-Soviet Relations, 1941-45* (Cambridge University Press, 1984).

Ruhm von Oppen, B. (ed.), *Documents on Germany under Occupation 1945-1954* (Oxford University Press/RIIA, 1955). [*DGUO*]

Yasamee, H.J. and Hamilton, K.A. (eds.), *Documents on British Policy*

Overseas. Series II, Volume IV: Korea, June 1950-April 1951 (London: HMSO, 1991). [*DBPO II/IV*]

2. SECONDARY MATERIAL – ARTICLES, BOOKS AND THESES

Acland, A., 'The Relationship Between Foreign and Defence Policy', *Journal of the Royal United Services Institute* (128/2,1983).

Adamthwaite, A., 'Britain and the world, 1945-49; the view from the Foreign Office', *International Affairs* (61/2,1985).

Aldrich, R.J. (ed.), *British Intelligence, Strategy and the Cold War, 1945-51* (London: Routledge, 1992).

Aldrich, R.J., 'Secret Intelligence for a Post-war World: Reshaping the British Intelligence Community, 1944-51', in Aldrich (ed.), *British Intelligence.*

Aldrich, R.J. and Coleman, M., 'The Cold War, the JIC and British Signals Intelligence, 1948', *Intelligence & National Security* (4/3,1989).

Aldrich, R.J. and Zametica, J., 'The Rise and Decline of a Strategic Concept: the Middle East, 1945-51', in Aldrich (ed.), *British Intelligence.*

Ashton, S.R., *In Search of Detente: The Politics of East-West Relations Since 1945* (London: Macmillan, 1989).

Badstübner, R., 'The Allied Four-power Administration and Sociopolitical Development in Germany', *German History* (7/1,1989).

Ball, S.J., 'Bomber Bases and British Strategy in the Middle East, 1945-1949', *Journal of Strategic Studies* (14/4,1991).

Barker, E., *Britain in a Divided Europe 1945-1970* (London: Weidenfeld and Nicolson, 1971).

——, *The British Between the Superpowers, 1945-50* (London: Macmillan, 1983).

Barnett, C., *Britain and Her Army 1509-1970* (London: Allen Lane, 1970).

——, *The Collapse of British Power* (Gloucester: Alan Sutton, 1987).

——, *The Audit of War* (London: Macmillan, 1986).

——, 'From Past Glory to a more Limited Role Nearer Home', *Daily Telegraph*, 25 June 1990.

——, 'Total Strategy and the Collapse of British Power', *Journal of the Royal United Services Institute* (136/4,1991).

Barnett, R.W., 'Maritime and Continental Strategies: An Important Question of Emphasis', in Gray and Barnett (eds.), *Seapower and*

Strategy.
Bartlett, C.J., *The Long Retreat: A Short History of British Defence Policy, 1945-70* (London: Macmillan, 1972).
———, *British Foreign Policy in the Twentieth Century* (London: Macmillan, 1989).
Baylis, J. (ed.), *Alternative Approaches to British Defence Policy* (London: Macmillan, 1983).
Baylis, J., *Anglo-American Defence Relations 1939-84* (London: Macmillan, 1984).
———, 'Britain, the Brussels Pact and the Continental Commitment', *International Affairs* (60/4,1984).
———, '"Greenwoodery" and British defence policy', *International Affairs* (62/3,1986).
———, *British Defence Policy: Striking the Right Balance* (London: Macmillan, 1989).
———, *The Diplomacy of Pragmatism: Britain and the Formation of NATO, 1942-1949* (London: Macmillan, 1993).
Bellamy, C., *The Evolution of Modern Land Warfare: Theory and Practice* (London; Routledge, 1990).
Bitzinger, R.A., *Assessing the Conventional Balance in Europe, 1945-1975* (Santa Monica, California: RAND Corporation, May 1989).
Blake, R., *The Decline of Power 1915-1964* (London: Paladin, 1986).
———, 'Great Britain: The Crimean War to the First World War', in Howard (ed.), *Soldiers and Governments.*
Blaxland, G., *The Regiments Depart: A History of the British Army 1945-1970* (London: William Kimber, 1971).
Blunden, M. and Greene, O. (eds.), *Science and Mythology in the Making of Defence Policy* (London: Brassey's, 1989).
Bogue, A.G., 'Systematic Revisionism and a Generation of Ferment in American History' *Journal of Contemporary History* (21/2,1986).
Bond, B.,'Military Power in Modern British History', *Journal of the Royal United Services Institute* (631,1963).
———, Liddell Hart: *A Study of his Military Thought* (London: Cassell, 1977).
———, *War and Society in Europe 1870-1970* (London: Fontana, 1984).
Booth, K., 'The Ten-Year Rule; An Unfinished Debate', *Journal of the Royal United Services Institute* (September 1971).
Boyd, F., *British Politics in Transition: 1945-1963* (London: Pall Mall Press, 1964).
Boyle, P.G., 'The British Foreign Office View of Soviet-American Relations, 1945-46', *Diplomatic History* (3/3,1979).

——, 'The British Foreign Office and American Foreign Policy, 1947-1948', *Journal of American Studies* (16/3,1982).

——, 'Britain, America and the Transition from Economic Assistance', *Journal of Contemporary History* (22/3,1987).

——, *American-Soviet Relations: From the Russian Revolution to the fall of Communism* (London: Routledge, 1993).

Bramall, E., 'The Contributions of the Chiefs of Staff to UK Defence', *Journal of the Royal United Services Institute* (131/3,1986).

Broadbent, E., *The Military and Government from Macmillan to Heseltine* (London: Macmillan, 1988).

Bullock, A., *Ernest Bevin – Foreign Secretary 1945-1951* (London: Heinemann, 1983).

Burnham, P., 'Re-evaluating the Washington Loan Agreement: a revisionist view of the limits of post-war American power', *Review of International Studies* (18/3,1992).

Cairncross, A., *Years of Recovery: British Economic Policy 1945-51* (London: Methuen, 1987).

Carden, R.W., 'Britain's Economic Dilemma in Germany, 1945-46', *Journal of Contemporary History* (14/3,1979).

Carver, M., 'Continental or Maritime Strategy? Past, Present and Future', *Journal of the Royal United Services Institute* (134/3,1989).

——, *Out of Step; The Memoirs of FM Lord Carver* (London: Hutchinson, 1989).

——, *Tightrope Walking: British Defence Policy Since 1945* (London: Hutchinson, 1992).

Cave Brown, A., *Operation: World War III; The Secret American Plan 'Dropshot' for War with the Soviet Union, 1957* (London: Arms and Armour Press, 1978).

Clark, I., and Wheeler, N.J., *The British Origins of Nuclear Strategy, 1945-1955* (Oxford: Clarendon Press, 1989).

Coker, C., *A Nation in Retreat? Britain's Defence Commitment* (London: Brassey's, 1986).

Condit, K.W., *The History of the Joint Chiefs of Staff. The Joint Chiefs of Staff and National Policy. Volume II – 1947-1949* (Wilmington, Delaware: Michael Glazier Inc., 1979).

Connell, J., *The 'Office': A Study of British Foreign Policy and its Makers, 1919-1951* (London: Allan Wingate, 1958).

Corbett, J.S., *Some Principles of Maritime Strategy* (London: Brassey's, 1988 [1st edn. 1911]).

Cornish, P., 'The British Military and European Security', in A. Deighton (ed.), *Building Postwar Europe: National Decision-makers and*

European Institutions, 1948-1963 (London: Macmillan, 1995).
Creveld, M. van, *Technology and War: From 2000 B.C. to the Present* (London: Brassey's, 1991).
——, 'High Technology and the Transformation of War – Part 1', *Journal of the Royal United Services Institute* (137/5,1992).
Croft, S., 'British Policy towards Western Europe, 1947-49: the Best of Possible Worlds?', *International Affairs* (Autumn 1988).
——, (ed.), *British Security Policy: The Thatcher Years and the End of the Cold War* (London: Harper Collins, 1991).
Cromwell, W.C., 'The Marshall Plan, Britain and the Cold War', *Review of International Studies* (8/4,1982).
Danchev, A., 'In the Back Room: Anglo-American Defence Co-operation, 1945-51', in Aldrich (ed.), *British Intelligence*.
Deibel, T.L., 'Strategies Before Containment: Patterns for the Future', *International Security* (16/4,1992).
Deighton, A., 'The 'Frozen Front': the Labour Government, the Division of Germany and the Origins of the Cold War, 1945-7', *International Affairs* (63/3,1987).
——, (ed.), *Britain and the First Cold War* (London: Macmillan, 1990).
——, *The Impossible Peace: Britain, the Division of Germany, and the Origins of the Cold War* (Oxford: Clarendon Press, 1990).
——, 'Missing the Boat: Britain and Europe 1945-61', *Contemporary Record* (3/3,1990).
——, 'Arming the Key Battleground': German Rearmament, 1950-55', *Diplomacy and Statecraft* (3/2,1992).
Devereux, D.R., 'Britain, the Commonwealth and the Defence of the Middle East 1948-56', *Journal of Contemporary History* (24/2,1989).
DeWeerd, H.A., 'Britain's Changing Military Policy', *Foreign Affairs* (34/1, 1955).
Dilks, D. (ed.), *Retreat From Power. Volume 2: After 1939* (London: Macmillan, 1981).
Dockrill, M., 'The Foreign Office, Anglo-American relations and the Korean war', *International Affairs* (62/3,1986).
——, *The Cold War 1945-1963* (London: Macmillan, 1988).
——, *British Defence Since 1945* (Oxford: Basil Blackwell, 1988).
——, 'British Attitudes Towards France as a Military Ally', *Diplomacy and Statecraft* (1/1,1990).
Dockrill, M. and Young, J.W. (eds.), *British Foreign Policy, 1945-56* (London: Macmillan, 1989).
Dockrill, S., 'The Evolution of Britain's Policy Towards a European

Army 1950-54', *Journal of Strategic Studies* (12/1,1989).
——, *Britain's Policy for West German Rearmament, 1950- 1955* (Cambridge University Press, 1991).
Donnison, F.S.V., *Civil Affairs and Military Government North-West Europe 1944-1946* (London: HMSO, 1961).
——, *Civil Affairs and Military Government Central Organization and Planning* (London: HMSO, 1966).
Edmonds, J., *The Occupation of the Rhineland, 1918-1929* (London: HMSO, 1987).
Edmonds, M. (ed.), *Central Organizations of Defense* (London: Frances Pinter, 1985).
——, (ed.), *The Defence Equation – British Military Systems; Policy Planning and Performance Since 1945* (London: Brassey's, 1986).
——, *Armed Services and Society* (Leicester University Press, 1988).
Evangelista, M.A., 'Stalin's Postwar Army Reappraised', *International Security* (7/3,1982-83).
Finer, S.E., *The Man on Horseback: The Role of the Military in Politics* (London: Pinter, 1988).
Foschepoth, J., 'British Interest in the Division of Germany after the Second World War', *Journal of Contemporary History* (21/3,1986).
Frankel, J., *British Foreign Policy, 1945-1973* (Oxford University Press, 1975).
Frazier, R., 'Did Britain Start the Cold War? Bevin and the Truman Doctrine', *The Historical Journal* (27/3,1984).
Freedman, L., *The Evolution of Nuclear Strategy* (London: Macmillan, 1985).
——, *U.S. Intelligence and the Soviet Strategic Threat* (London: Macmillan, 1986 – 2nd Edition).
Fursdon, E., *The European Defence Community: A History* (London: Macmillan, 1980).
Gaddis. J.L., *Strategies of Containment: A Critical Appraisal of Postwar American National Security Policy* (Oxford University Press, 1982).
——, 'The Emerging Post-Revisionist Synthesis on the Origins of the Cold War', *Diplomatic History* (7/3,1983).
——, 'The United States and the Question of a Sphere of Influence in Europe, 1945-1949', in Riste (ed.), *Western Security*.
——, *The Long Peace: Inquiries into the History of the Cold War* (New York: Oxford University Press, 1987).
Gann, L.H. (ed.), *The Defense of Western Europe* (London: Croom Helm, 1987).
Garson, R.A., 'American Foreign Policy and the Limits of Power: Eastern

Europe 1946-50', *Journal of Contemporary History* (21/3,1986).
Garthoff, R.L., *Assessing the Adversary: Estimates by the Eisenhower Administration of Soviet Intentions and Capabilities* (Washington: The Brookings Institution, 1991).
——, 'Why Did the Cold War Arise, and Why Did it End?', *International Affairs* (Moscow: nos. 4-5,1992).
Gooderson, I., 'Heavy and Medium Bombers: How Successful Were They in the Tactical Close Air Support Role During World War II?', *Journal of Strategic Studies* (15/3,1992).
Gorst, A., Johnman, L. and Scott Lucas, W. (eds.), *Post-war Britain, 1945-64: Themes and Perspectives* (London: Pinter, 1989).
Gowing, M., *Independence and Deterrence: Britain and Atomic Energy, 1945-1952. Volume I: Policy Making* (London: Macmillan, 1974).
Gray, C.S. and Barnett, R.W. (eds.), *Seapower and Strategy* (London: Tri-Service Press, 1989).
Greenwood, D., 'Constraints and Choices in the Transformation of Britain's Defence Effort Since 1945', *British Journal of International Studies* (2/1,1976).
Greenwood, S., 'Return to Dunkirk: The Origins of the Anglo-French Treaty of March 1947', *Journal of Strategic Studies* (6/4,1983).
——, 'Ernest Bevin, France and 'Western Union': August 1945 – February 1946', *European History Quarterly* (Vol.14,1984).
Gregory, F., Imber, M. and Simpson, J. (eds.), *Perspectives upon British Defence Policy, 1945-70* (Southampton University, 1978).
Grosser, A., *The Western Alliance* (London: Macmillan, 1980).
Grove, E.J., 'The Post War "Ten Year Rule" – Myth and Reality', *Journal of the Royal United Services Institute* (129/4,1984).
——, *Vanguard to Trident: British Naval Policy Since World War II* (London: Bodley Head, 1987).
——, *The Future of Sea Power* (London: Routledge, 1990).
Hallion, R.P., *Air Power in Historical and Contemporary Perspective* (Massachusetts Institute of Technology: Defense and Arms Control Studies Program Seminar Series, 12 March 1991).
Hamer, W.S., *The British Army: Civil-Military Relations 1885-1905* (Oxford: Clarendon Press, 1970).
Hamilton, N., *Monty: The Field-Marshal 1944-1976* (London: Hamish Hamilton, 1986).
Harris, K., *Attlee* (London: Weidenfeld & Nicolson, 1982).
Hathaway, R.M., *Ambiguous Partnership: Britain and America, 1944-1947* (New York: Columbia University Press, 1981).
Hattendorf, J.B. and Jordan, R.S. (eds.), *Maritime Strategy and the*

Balance of Power: Britain and America in the Twentieth Century (London: Macmillan, 1989).
Heller, F.H. and Gillingham, J.R. (eds.), *NATO: The Founding of the Atlantic Alliance and the Integration of Europe* (London: Macmillan, 1992).
Hemsley, J., (ed.), *The Lost Empire: Perceptions of Soviet Policy Shifts in the 1990s* (London: Brassey's, 1991).
Henderson, N., *The Birth Of NATO* (London: Weidenfeld & Nicolson, 1982).
Hennessy, P., *Whitehall* (London: Secker & Warburg, 1989).
——, *Never Again: Britain 1945-51* (London: Jonathan Cape, 1992).
Hennessy, P. and Anstey, C., *Moneybags and Brains: The Anglo-American 'Special Relationship' Since 1945* (University of Strathclyde: Papers on Government and Politics No. 1, November 1990).
Heuser, B., *Western 'Containment' Policies in the Cold War: the Yugoslav Case, 1948-53* (London: Routledge, 1989).
——, 'NSC 68 and the Soviet Threat: a New Perspective on Western Threat Perception and Policy-making', *Review of International Studies* (17/1,1991).
Heuser, B. and O'Neill, R. (eds.), *Securing Peace in Europe, 1945-62: Thoughts for the post-Cold War Era* (London: Macmillan, 1992).
Hobkirk, M.D., *Land,Sea or Air? Military Priorities: Historical Choices* (London: Macmillan/RUSI, 1992).
Holmes, R., *Nuclear Warriors* (London: Jonathan Cape, 1991).
Hopkins, M.F., 'A British Cold War', *Intelligence & National Security* (7/4,1992).
Horner, D.M., 'The Continental School of Strategic Thought', *Defence Force Journal* (82,1990).
Howard, M. (ed.), *Soldiers and Governments: Nine Studies in Civil-Military Relations* (London: Eyre and Spottiswoode, 1957).
——, 'Civil-Military Relations in Great Britain and the United States, 1945-1958', *Political Science Quarterly* (75/1,1960).
——' (ed.), *The Theory and Practice of War* (London: Cassell, 1965).
——, *The Continental Commitment*, (London: Temple Smith, 1972).
——, 'The Strategic Approach to International Relations', *British Journal of International Studies* (2/1,1976).
——, *The Causes of Wars* (London: Temple Smith, 1983).
Huntington, S.P., *The Soldier and the State: The Theory and Politics of Civil-Military Relations* (Harvard University Press, 1957).
Jackson, W. and Bramall, E., *The Chiefs: The Story of the United*

Kingdom Chiefs of Staff (London: Brassey's, 1992).
Johnson, F.A., *Defence by Ministry* (London: Duckworth, 1980).
Jones, R.E., *The Changing Structure of British Foreign Policy* (London: Longman, 1974).
Jürgensen, K., 'British Occupation Policy after 1945 and the Problem of "Re-educating Germany"', *History* (68/223,1983).
Kaiser, R.G., *Cold Winter, Cold War* (London: Weidenfeld and Nicolson, 1974).
Keeble, C., *Britain and the Soviet Union, 1917-89* (London: Macmillan, 1990).
Kennedy, P., *The Realities Behind Diplomacy: Background Influences on British External Policy, 1865-1980* (London: Fontana, 1981).
——, 'The Continental Commitment and the Special Relationship in 20th Century British Foreign Policy, *Journal of the Royal United Services Institute* (128/3,1983).
——, *Strategy and Diplomacy 1870-1945* (London: Fontana, 1984).
——, *The Rise and Fall of the Great Powers: Economic Change and Military Conflict from 1500 to 2000* (London: Fontana, 1989).
Kettenacker, L., 'The Anglo-Soviet Alliance and the Problem of Germany, 1941-1945', *Journal of Contemporary History* (17,1982).
King, F., 'Allied Negotiations and the Dismemberment of Germany', *Journal of Contemporary History* (16/3,1981).
Kitchen, M., *British Policy Towards the Soviet Union During the Second World War* (London: Macmillan, 1986).
Knight, W., 'Labourite Britain: America's "Sure Friend"? The Anglo-Soviet Treaty Issue, 1947', *Diplomatic History* (7/4,1983).
Kozak, D.C. and Keagle, J.M. (eds.), *Bureaucratic Politics and National Security* (London: Lynne Rienner, 1988).
Krieger, W., 'Was General Clay a Revisionist? Strategic Aspects of the United States Occupation of Germany', *Journal of Contemporary History* (18,1983).
LaFeber, W., *America, Russia, and the Cold War 1945-1992* (New York: McGraw-Hill, 1992).
Laurendau, J., *The Politics of NATO Defense Policy: Lessons of the EDC Debate, 1950-1954* (Harvard: CSIA Working Papers No. 88-1, April 1988).
Leffler, M.P., 'From the Truman Doctrine to the Carter Doctrine: Lessons and Dilemmas of the Cold War', *Diplomatic History* (17/4,1983).
Lewis, J., *Changing Direction; British Military Planning for Post-war Strategic Defence, 1942-1947* (London: Sherwood Press, 1988).
Liddell Hart, B.H., *The British Way in Warfare* (London: Faber &

Faber, 1932).
——, *The Strategy of Indirect Approach* (London: Faber and Faber, 1941).
——, *Defence of the West: Some Riddles of War and Peace* (London: Cassell, 1950).
——, *Strategy: the Indirect Approach* (London: Faber and Faber, 1954).
Lider, J., *Essays on British Military Thought No.1. Facing the Change: 1945-1949* (Stockholm: Swedish Institute of International Affairs, Research Report No. 2, 1980).
——, *British Military Thought After World War II* (Aldershot: Gower, 1985).
Longmate, N., *Island Fortress: The Defence of Great Britain, 1603-1945* (London: Hutchinson, 1991).
Louis, W.R. and Bull, H., *The Special Relationship: Anglo-American Relations Since 1945* (Oxford: Clarendon Press, 1989).
Macmillan, A., *Britain and Atomic Weapons, 1945-1949: The Development of a Deterrence Frame of Mind* (Aberystwyth: International Politics Research Papers No. 9, 1991).
Mahan, A.T., *The Influence of Sea Power upon History, 1660-1783* (London: Methuen, 1965 [1st edition 1890]).
Marshall, B., 'The Democratisation of Local Politics in the British Zone of Germany: Hanover 1945-47', *Journal of Contemporary History* (21/3,1986).
Mayers, D., 'Soviet War Aims and the Grand Alliance: George Kennan's Views, 1944-1946', *Journal of Contemporary History* (21/1,1986).
Mearsheimer, J.J., *Liddell Hart and the Weight of History* (London: Brassey's, 1988).
Melissen, J. and Zeeman, B., 'Britain and Western Europe, 1945- 51: Opportunities Lost?', *International Affairs* (63/1,1986/7).
Merrick, R., 'The Russia Committee of the British Foreign Office and the Cold War, 1946-47', *Journal of Contemporary History* (20,1985).
The Memoirs of Field-Marshal the Viscount Montgomery of Alamein, K.G. (London: Collins, 1958).
Military Government Gazette/Control Commission Gazette, (British Zone), 1944-49.
Morgan, K.O., *Labour in Power, 1945-51* (Oxford University Press, 1984).
——, *The People's Peace: British History 1945-1989* (Oxford University Press, 1990).
Mulley, F.W., *The Politics of Western Defence* (London: Thames and Hudson, 1962).

Myers, F., 'Conscription and the Politics of Military Strategy in the Attlee Government', *Journal of Strategic Studies* (7/1,1984).
Nailor, P., Learning From Precedent in Whitehall (London: Institute of Contemporary British History, 1991).
Navias, M.S., 'Terminating Conscription? The British National Service Controversy 1955-56', *Journal of Contemporary History* (24/2,1989).
North Atlantic Treaty Organisation – Facts and Figures (Brussels: NATO Information Service, 1989).
Omissi, D., 'Technology and Repression: Air Control in Palestine 1922-36', *Journal of Strategic Studies* (13/4,1990).
Ovendale, R., 'Britain, the USA and the European Cold War, 1945-8', *History* (67/220,1982).
——, (ed.), *The Foreign Policy of the British Labour Governments, 1945-1951* (Leicester University Press, 1984).
——, *The English-speaking Alliance: Britain, the United States, the Dominions and the Cold War* (London: George Allen & Unwin, 1985).
Paret, P. (ed.), *Makers of Modern Strategy: from Machiavelli to the Nuclear Age* (Oxford: Clarendon Press, 1991).
Park, W., *Defending the West: A History of NATO* (Brighton: Wheatsheaf Books, 1986).
Peden, G.C., 'The Burden of Imperial Defence and the Continental Commitment Reconsidered', *The Historical Journal* (27/2,1984).
Pelling, H., *Britain and the Marshall Plan* (London: Macmillan, 1988).
Perlmutter, A., *The Military and Politics in Modern Times* (Yale University Press, 1977).
Perlmutter, A. and Bennett, V.P. (eds.), *The Political Influence of the Military – A Comparative Reader* (Yale University Press, 1980).
Quinlan, M., 'British Defence Planning in a Changing World', *The World Today* (48/8-9,1992).
Rees, W., 'The 1957 Defence White Paper: New Priorities in British Defence Policy?', *Journal of Strategic Studies* (June 1989).
——, 'Continuity and Change in British Threat Assessments 1945-1960', *Sandhurst Journal of Military Affairs* (1,1990).
Reid, B.H., *J.F.C. Fuller: Military Thinker* (London: Macmillan, 1987).
Reynolds, D., 'The United States and European Security from Wilson to Kennedy, 1913 – 1963: A Reappraisal of the "Isolationist" Tradition', *Journal of the Royal United Services Institute* (June 1983).
——, 'The Origins of the Cold War: The European Dimension 1944-

1951', *The Historical Journal* (28/2,1985).
——, 'A 'Special Relationship'? America, Britain and the International Order Since the Second World War', *International Affairs* (62/1,1985/6).
——, 'The 'Big Three' and the Division of Europe, 1945-48: An Overview', Diplomacy and Statecraft (1/2,1990).
——, *Britannia Overruled: British Policy & World Power in the 20th Century* (London: Longman, 1991).
Richardson, J.L., 'Cold War Revisionism: A Critique', *World Politics* (24/4,1972).
Riste, O. (ed.), *Western Security: The Formative Years.European and Atlantic Defence 1947-1953* (Norwegian University Press, 1985).
Robertson, B., 'A Miracle? Potsdam 1945 – Western Germany 1965', *International Affairs* (41/3,1965).
Roskill, S., 'The Ten Year Rule – The Historical Facts', *Journal of the Royal United Services Institute* (March 1972).
Ross, G., 'Foreign Office Attitudes to the Soviet Union 1941-45', *Journal of Contemporary History* (July 1981).
Rothwell, V., *Britain and the Cold War 1941-1947* (London: Jonathan Cape, 1982).
Rowe, P.J. and Whelan, C.J. (eds.), *Military Intervention in Democratic Societies* (London: Croom Helm, 1985).
Sanders, D., *Losing an Empire, Finding a Role: British Foreign Policy Since 1945* (London: Macmillan, 1990).
Schlesinger, A., Jr., 'Origins of the Cold War', *Foreign Affairs* (46/1,1967).
Schnabel, J.F., *The History of the Joint Chiefs of Staff: The Joint Chiefs of Staff and National Policy. Volume 1: 1945-1947* (Wilmington, Delaware: Michael Glazier, 1979).
Schnabel, J.F. and Watson, R.J., *The History of the Joint Chiefs of Staff: The Joint Chiefs of Staff and National Policy.Volume Three: The Korean War. Part 1* (Wilmington, Delaware: Michael Glazier, 1979).
Schulze, R., 'Growing Discontent: Relations between Native Rural Populations in a Rural District in Western Germany after the Second World War', *German History* (7/3,1989).
Schwartz, T.A., *America's Germany: John J. McCloy and the Federal Republic of Germany* (Harvard University Press, 1991).
Schweitzer, C. (ed.), *The Changing Western Analysis of the Soviet Threat* (London: Pinter, 1990).
Segrè, C.G., 'Giulio Douhet: Strategist, Theorist, Prophet?', *Journal of*

Strategic Studies (15/3,1992).
Sharp, T., *The Wartime Alliance and the Zonal Division of Germany* (Oxford: Clarendon Press, 1975).
Shlaim, A., 'Britain, the Berlin Blockade and the Cold War', *International Affairs* (60/1,1983/84).
——, 'The Partition of Germany and the Origins of the Cold War', *Review of International Studies* (11/2,1985).
Silverman, P., 'The Ten Year Rule', *Journal of the Royal United Services Institute* (March 1971).
Simpson, K., 'Frock Coats, Mandarins and Brass Hats; The Relationship between Politicians, Civil Servants and the Military', *Journal of the Royal United Services Institute* (137/1,1992).
Singh, A.A., 'Keeping India in the Commonwealth: British Political and Military Aims, 1947-49', *Journal of Contemporary History* (20,1985).
Smith, A.L., *Churchill's German Army: Wartime Strategy and Cold War Politics, 1943-1947* (London: Sage, 1977).
Smith, R. and Zametica, J., 'The Cold Warrior: Clement Attlee Reconsidered, 1945-7', *International Affairs* (61/2,1985).
Snyder, W.P., *The Politics of British Defence Policy, 1945-1962* (Ohio State University Press, 1964).
de Staercke, A. et al, *NATO's Anxious Birth: The Prophetic Vision of the 1940s* (London: C. Hurst & Co., 1985).
Steininger, R., 'Germany after 1945: Divided and Integrated or United and Neutral?', *German History* (7/1,1989).
Swain, R.M., 'B.H. Liddell Hart and the Creation of a Theory of War, 1919-1933', *Armed Forces and Society* (17/1,1990).
Taylor, T., *European Defence Cooperation* (London: Routledge & Kegan Paul/RIIA, 1984).
Thomas, A., 'British Signals Intelligence After the Second World War', *Intelligence & National Security* (3/4,1988).
Thomas, H., *Armed Truce: The Beginnings of the Cold War, 1945-46* (London: Sceptre, 1988).
Tiratsoo, N. (ed.), *The Attlee Years* (London: Pinter Publishers, 1991).
Tugwell, M., *Unquiet Peace: Stories from the Post-war Army* (London: Allan Wingate, 1957).
Turner, I.D., *British Occupation Policy and its Effects on the Town of Wolfsburg and the Volkswagenwerk 1945-49* (Unpublished Ph.D. thesis, University of Manchester Institute of Science and Technology, 1984).
Valki, L. (ed.), *Changing Threat Perceptions and Military Doctrines*

(London: Macmillan, 1992).
Verrier, A., *Through the Looking Glass: British Foreign Policy in an Age of Illusions* (London: Jonathan Cape, 1983).
Wagner, R.H., 'The Decision to Divide Germany and the Origins of the Cold War', *International Studies Quarterly* (24/2,1980).
Warner, G., 'The Division of Germany 1946-48', *International Affairs* (51/1,1975).
——, 'The Korean War', *International Affairs* (56/1,1980).
Watt, D.C., *Britain Looks to Germany: British Opinion and Policy Towards Germany Since 1945* (London: Oswald Wolff, 1965).
——, 'Rethinking the Cold War: A Letter to a British Historian', *Political Quarterly* (49/4,1978).
Welch, D., 'The Political Re-education of Germany after World War II; A need for a Reappraisal?', *German History* (No.4,1987).
Wheeler, N.J., 'British Nuclear Weapons and Anglo-American Relations 1945-54', *International Affairs* (62/1,1985/6).
Wheeler-Bennett, J.W. and Nicholls, A., *The Semblance of Peace: The Political Settlement After the Second World War* (New York: St Martin's Press/London: Macmillan, 1972).
Whiteley, G., 'The British Experience of Peacetime Conscription', *Army Quarterly and Defence Journal* (117/3,1987).
Wiebes, C. and Zeeman, B., 'The Pentagon Negotiations March 1948: the Launching of the North Atlantic Treaty', *International Affairs* (59/3,1983).
Woodhouse, C.M., *British Foreign Policy Since the Second World War* (London: Hutchinson, 1961).
Wylie, J.C., *Military Strategy: A General Theory of Power Control* (New Brunswick, New Jersey: Rutgers University Press, 1967).
Yergin, D., *Shattered Peace: the Origins of the Cold War and the National Security States* (London: Andre Deutsch, 1978).
Young, J.W., *Britain, France and the Unity of Europe 1945-51* (Leicester University Press, 1984).
Zametica, J. (ed.), *British Officials and British Foreign Policy 1945-50* (Leicester University Press, 1990).
Zeeman, B., 'Britain and the Cold War: An Alternative Approach. The Treaty of Dunkirk Example', *European History Quarterly* (16/3,1986).

Index